The Problem of American Realism

MICHAEL DAVITT BELL

The Problem of American Realism

STUDIES IN THE CULTURAL HISTORY OF A LITERARY IDEA

THE UNIVERSITY OF CHICAGO PRESS
CHICAGO AND LONDON

The University of Chicago Press, Chicago 60637
The University of Chicago Press, Ltd., London
© 1993 by The University of Chicago
All rights reserved. Published 1993
Paperback edition 1996
Printed in the United States of America

02 01 00 99 98 97 96   2 3 4 5 6

ISBN (cloth): 0-226-04201-4
ISBN (paper): 0-226-04202-2

Library of Congress Cataloging-in-Publication Data

Bell, Michael Davitt
   The problem of American realism : studies in the
cultural history of a literary idea / Michael Davitt Bell.
      p.   cm.
   Includes bibliographical references and index.
   1. American fiction—History and criticism.   2. Realism
in literature.   I. Title.
PS374.R37B39   1993
813.009′12—dc20   92-25231
                                                        CIP

♾ The paper used in this publication meets the minimum
requirements of the American National Standard for
Information Sciences—Permanence of Paper for Printed
Library Materials, ANSI Z39.48-1984.

Once again for Sophie and Cathleen:
Now it's your turn.

CONTENTS

Acknowledgments   ix

Introduction: American Realism   1

Part One: The First Generation
William Dean Howells, Mark Twain, Henry James   11

1   The Sin of Art: William Dean Howells   17
   The Problem of Howellsian Realism   18
   The Road to Realism   22
   A Portrait of the Artist as a "Real" Man   31
   The Problem of American Realism   35

2   Humor, Sentiment, Realism: Mark Twain   39
   Mark Twain as Critic   41
   Adventures of Huckleberry Finn   47
   A Connecticut Yankee in King Arthur's Court   58

3   Artist Fables: Henry James's Realist Phase   70
   A Different Road/A Different Realism   72
   Realism and Reform   84
   Naturalism, Impressionism, Revolution   92

Part Two: The Problem of Naturalism
Frank Norris, Stephen Crane, Theodore Dreiser   107

4   The Revolt against Style: Frank Norris   115
   The Road to Naturalism   116
   Naturalism and Style   121

5 Irony, Parody, and "Transcendental Realism":
   Stephen Crane 131

   The Language of the Street 134
   Words of War 142

6 Fine Styles of Sympathy: Theodore Dreiser's *Sister Carrie* 149

   Dreiser and American Naturalism 150
   Condescension and Identification 155

Part Three: A "Woman's Place" in American Realism
Sarah Orne Jewett 167

7 Local Color and Realism: Sarah Orne Jewett 175

   Jewett's Place in American Realism 176
   Maine Person and Boston Professional 179
   Realism, Feminism, and the World of Dunnet Landing 192

Notes 205

Index 239

ACKNOWLEDGMENTS

I am grateful, first of all, to the National Endowment for the Humanities and the John Simon Guggenheim Memorial Foundation: a fellowship from the former, in 1982–83, gave me the opportunity to begin work on this study in earnest, while a fellowship from the latter, in 1990–91, provided the time, at last, to finish it. These leaves were also supported by sabbaticals from Williams College. I have received generous assistance from the staffs of the Columbia University Library, the Williams College Center for Computing and, especially, the Williams College Library.

Most of the chapters of this book have been read, at one stage or another, by different friends and colleagues, including Richard Brodhead, Louis Budd, Cassandra Cleghorn, Robert Dalzell, Don Gifford, Lawrence Graver, June Howard, Jane Tompkins, and Christopher Wilson. I am grateful to them all for their support and their suggestions, and to any others whose names I inadvertently may have failed to mention. I am especially grateful to my friend and colleague, John Limon, who—during a year when I was on leave and he was not—rapidly read (and mercilessly critiqued) one revised chapter after another. A better book than I shall ever write was there in his criticisms had I only possessed the insight and cunning to transcribe it. Barbara Winn word-processed from typescript, and with her customary precision, drafts of chapters I had produced before my conversion to computing. I am also indebted to the generations of scholars who have labored to understand "American realism"—a debt I have done my best to acknowledge throughout the following pages. While I have disagreed with many of their conclusions, I have always done so with respect and appreciation.

Portions of this book have appeared in print in earlier forms. An earlier version of Chapter 1 and of some of the Introduction, entitled "The Sin of Art and the Problem of American Realism: William Dean Howells," appeared in *Prospects* 9 (1985), published by Cambridge University Press. An earlier version of part of Chapter 2, entitled "Mark Twain, 'Realism,' and *Huckleberry Finn*," was included in *New Essays on Huckleberry Finn* (1985), edited by Louis J. Budd and published by Cambridge University Press. An earlier version of Chapter 5, entitled "Frank Norris, Style, and the Problem of American Naturalism," appeared in *Studies in the Literary Imagination* 16, no. 2 (Fall 1983). And an earlier version of part of Chapter 7, entitled "*The Country of the Pointed Firs* and American Realism," was included in *New Essays on The Country of the Pointed Firs* (1993), edited by June Howard and published by Cambridge University Press. I am grateful to these publishers for permission to reprint revised versions of these essays here.

American Realism

What Vladimir Nabokov said of "reality" is equally true of its close cousin, "realism": it is one of those words "which mean nothing without quotes."[1] We use the term freely, nevertheless, to describe a supposed mode or kind of literature and, often in the same gesture, to organize or periodize our literary history. Warner Berthoff was simply expressing established critical consensus when he began *The Ferment of Realism*, his 1965 book on American literature from 1884 to 1919, by writing that "the great collective event in American letters during the 1880s and 1890s was the securing of 'realism' as the dominant standard of value."[2] This has long been, and still remains, the customary interpretation of the American literary generation that included William Dean Howells, Mark Twain, and Henry James. Ever since Howells declared his so-called Realism War in the 1880s, it has been a staple of literary history that the great development in American fiction after the Civil War was the rise of "realism"—or, in the generation following that of Howells, of "naturalism."[3]

Yet while it is certainly convenient to have labels for literary periods, in this American case generalizations about the rise of "realism" or "naturalism" present more than even the usual problems. It is hard to see Howells, Twain, and James—not to mention such successors as Sarah Orne Jewett, Frank Norris, Stephen Crane, and Theodore Dreiser—as constituting any single literary tradition or "school" of literature; the differences among their characteristic modes are far more striking than the similarities. It is also virtually impossible to extract from their novels and manifestos any consistent definition of "realism" (or of "naturalism") as a specific kind of literary representation. Only James, among the whole group, approached such defi-

1

nition with genuine rigor, and he was for this reason often at odds with, for instance, his friend Howells, the supposed leader of the war for realism.

Of course, Berthoff's generalization about "the securing of 'realism' as the dominant standard of value" frames its key term in skeptical, Nabokovian quotation marks, and Berthoff hastens to point out that if "realism" was the new standard it was, in American theory and practice, "peculiarly indefinite," being "concerned less with problems of artistic definition and discovery than with clearing a way to a more profitable exercise of individual ambition." In fact, he writes, American "realism"—as distinguished, for instance, from "realism" in nineteenth-century France—may have been little more than "a name, a borrowed label which happened to come so strongly into fashion (in an era not widely distinguished by searching critical discussion) that no one could avoid deferring to it." Hence "to attempt to define American 'realism' by classifying the particular books written in its name according to form and theme," he concludes, "is to sink into the mire of inconsequential distinctions and details."[4]

Why not, then, simply stop using the term "realism" altogether? Berthoff retains it because he believes it indicates "certain fundamental motives to expression" common to the literature of the period, arising from a sense of new "conditions of social and economic life" in America in the later nineteenth century; and this idea of American "realism"—what we might call the responsive or reflective model of the supposed movement—has been widespread in American literary history.[5] But it overcomes problems of generic definition ("realism" is not a mode or *genre* but a kind of generalized response to rapid social change) only to stir up other kinds of trouble. For one thing, the tactic inevitably makes literature secondary to the social or historical "reality" it is supposed to reflect; it denies the *literary* quality of literary works, and this denial has been central to realist thinking, and thinking about realism, in America.[6] The reflective model of American "realism" also raises a more basic problem. While there can, of course, be no doubt that American literature was deeply affected by the social developments that radically transformed the nation between the Civil War and World War I, it can be misleading or confusing to use a word meant to describe a mode of literary representation, a *kind* of literature, to describe instead a shift in *concern*—a new interest in industrialism, say, or in the growing dominance of a market economy, or in the emergence of an apparently permanent lower class. That American writers turned to new realities does not necessarily mean that they became, as literary artists, more "realistic."

In the years since Berthoff's *Ferment of Realism* in 1965, the responsive or reflective idea of American "realism" has retained much of its currency.[7] But it has also been challenged by some critics we might group, at the admitted risk of oversimplification, as "new historicists." Thus June Howard, in *Form and History in American Literary Naturalism* (1985), rejects "the notion that naturalism 'reflects' its historical period"; her own project, she explains, "is not to set literary texts against a 'history' or 'reality' whose own textuality is for that purpose repressed, but rather to trace how naturalism is shaped by and imaginatively reshapes a historical experience that, although it exists outside representation and narrative, we necessarily approach through texts." Walter Michaels, in *The Gold Standard and the Logic of Naturalism* (1987), disowns any wish "to identify a specific relation between literature and the real, or even a specific ideological function of literature in relation to the real"; he wants instead, he says, "to map out the reality in which a certain literature finds its place and to identify a set of interests and activities that might be said to have [a] . . . common denominator." Amy Kaplan, in *The Social Construction of American Realism* (1988), seeks "to recuperate realism's relation to social change not as a static background which novels either naively record or heroically evade, but as the foreground of the narrative structure of each novel."[8]

These critics characteristically implicate texts in discursive or cultural practices, in ideological formations; their distinctive move, however, is to insist that the texts are not *responses* to these practices or formations but *part* of them. This insistence provides an invaluable corrective to the traditional assumption that literary texts are secondary to "reality": for these new historicists a text is every bit as "real" (and also every bit as "unreal," every bit as fabricated) as so-called historical or cultural "reality." But even as one assents to this correction, one notes that it hardly helps us understand so-called "realist" texts as being distinctively "realistic," as being examples of something we can meaningfully call "realism." After all, the sorts of relation or implication these critics write about presumably hold for all texts in all periods, and to say that rapid social change in late nineteenth-century America shaped and was shaped by particular discursive practices, or even by particular generic conventions, is hardly to say that these practices and conventions are "realistic," or any more "realistic" than other practices and conventions. The new historicist argument, then, is not necessarily an argument for "realism," or even an argument *about* "realism" as such—and one hastens to add that it is clearly not meant to be. Kaplan combines formal analysis with historical criticism, but she mainly uses "realism" more as a period marker than as a generic label; and Howard and Michaels for the most part dispense with the term altogether, preferring the related but perhaps less controversial "naturalism."[9]

Nevertheless, in spite of all the problems their application to late nineteenth-century American fiction has engendered, I do not wish to dispense with either of these terms, most especially with "realism"; indeed these terms and their literary history are my principal subject. Let me try to avoid a confusion my holding on to these terms might produce. I do not mean to suggest that I intend to discover some *new* basis for describing American texts as "realistic"; nothing could be farther from what I have in mind. In fact, I do not believe that the works conventionally assembled under the umbrella of "American realism" (or "American naturalism") constitute in this sense a tradition of realism (or naturalism) or, for that matter, *any* coherent formal tradition. But the *terms* "realism" and "naturalism," and the ideas that have been explicitly and implicitly evoked by them, have nevertheless played a conspicuous and sometimes confusing role both in the production of American literature and in the construction of American literary history. The ideas of American realism and naturalism, as descriptions of the form taken by significant groupings of novels by American writers, may be little more than figments of our literary-historical imaginations. Still, like many such figments, they have been thoroughly functional—often most powerfully in ways that have had little or nothing to do with issues of mimetic accuracy. What I am concerned with in this book, to put it most simply, is the function of these ideas, the purposes they have served.

The terms "realism" and "naturalism" matter to me first of all, then, for the simple but important reason that they have been used by generations of American fiction writers, from the 1880s to the present, to describe what they thought they were doing—or at least what they wished others to think they were doing. Of course, to repeat a point I have already made, the fact that writers used the terms "realism" and "naturalism" does not make the texts they produced "realistic" or "naturalistic." But it does, as a cultural practice, suggest a way historians might usefully approach these texts. Moreover, the fact that these terms have been used imprecisely—that they often seem, in writers' comments on their intentions, almost devoid of any consistent meaning—is all the more reason to examine just how they have been used, to ask what purpose they have served and still serve, not only for nineteenth-century novelists but for twentieth-century critics and literary historians. This examination is my project in the present study. I do not propose to comb the novels of our so-called "realists" and "naturalists" in order to extract from them, one more time, some implicit common aesthetic which we can then, in tautological triumph, call "realism" or "naturalism"; Berthoff is surely correct in arguing that such a procedure leads into a "mire of inconsequential distinctions and details." I propose, rather, to look closely at what our so-called "realists" and "naturalists" have had to say about fiction, concerning myself less with what their statements *mean* (as I have said, I am not trying to find out what "realism" *is* or *was*) than with what they seem to be *meant for*. The labels "realist" and "naturalist" were embraced or resisted by writers who presumably felt some need to embrace or resist them. To understand the historical importance of these labels we must first seek to understand these needs.

Of course, it is probably impossible, in a study of so-called "American realism," even if one does not grant that a tradition of "realism" existed in the United States during the last two decades of the nineteenth century, to expunge all consideration of ways in which particular texts may or may not seem to be generically or formally "realistic"—and I will regularly be discussing qualities that have conventionally been associated with the supposed *genres* of literary "realism" or literary "naturalism." But I do wish to dismiss, or at least bracket, the nature of realism as a genre, as a *primary* question, and my motives for doing so are as much strategic or diagnostic as they are theoretical. Perhaps an analogy will help me explain them. When a component system—a stereo, say—develops a problem, you need to shut down or disconnect as many components as possible in order to isolate the problem, to figure out where it's coming from. It is in this sense that I want to shut down the question of the relation of "American realism" to the tradition of Continental realism or to some ideal model of realistic mimesis. One could certainly found a study of so-called "American realism," as a number of critics have done, on a prior consideration of seminal studies by such Continental writers as Auerbach, Lukács, and Gombrich,[10] and this procedure has much to recommend it. But it runs two risks I wish to avoid. First, it assumes that there *is* a *generic* tradition of "American realism," which may not be the case. And this assumption tends, in turn, to mask the true nature of what I have been calling realist thinking—by attributing to American theory (a phrase which is often, in the case of "realism," virtually an oxymoron) the sophistication of Continental theory and tradition. William Dean Howells was no Auerbach, no Lukács, and if we wish to understand Howells we must try to understand him on his own terms and in his own context.

Walter Michaels speaks for an important and valuable tendency in contemporary critical practice when he proclaims that "subverting the primacy of the subject in literary history" is, "from a certain standpoint, the whole point" of his analysis. The questions I am asking here demand, however, that the subject be kept rather steadily in view. I would certainly agree with Michaels that, as he has famously put it, "the only relation literature as such has to culture as such is that it is part of it."[11] But the same thing must be equally true of the relation between *writers* and culture, and I am inclined to historicize the former relation, at least at the outset, through what can be discovered (inevitably, of course, through other texts) about the latter.[12] In the following chapters I thus study, as I have said, the *function* of the terms "realism" and "naturalism" in American literary discourse from the mid-1880s, when Howells began calling for "realism" in American fiction, up to the beginning of the twentieth century. What, I ask, were the effects of these terms on writers who embraced them—what did these terms mean, and what did it mean to use them? And what, to raise an equally important question, were the effects of these terms on writers who resisted them?

In Part One I discuss the three writers usually considered to be the major figures of the first generation of American realists. I begin with Howells, in Chapter 1, focusing on the essays collected as *Criticism and Fiction* in 1891, which made him the most influential proponent of realism in America. Chapter 2 deals with Mark Twain's relationship to the rhetoric and ideology of American realism, and Chapter 3 turns to Henry James—who, because he openly dissected the confusions and evasions rampant in realist thinking, often found himself in conflict with self-proclaimed American realists. Part Two takes up the idea of American "naturalism" by exploring—in Chapters 4, 5, and 6—the theory and practice of Frank Norris, Stephen Crane, and Theodore Dreiser. All the writers named thus far were men, and this is no coincidence; as we will see, a prominent function of claiming to be a realist or a naturalist in this period was to provide assurance to one's society and oneself that one was a "real" man rather than an effeminate "artist." How, it seems reasonable to ask, might the emergence of such a stance, legitimized or disguised as literary "theory," have affected a contemporary American *woman* writer, particularly if she were inclined to think of *herself* as being in some sense a realist? I take this question up in Part Three, devoted to the case of Sarah Orne Jewett—a writer who has been part of the "realist" canon (albeit as a supposedly "minor" or marginal figure) ever since she began publishing in the 1880s. What, I ask, might Jewett's writing and career, and the place she has been accorded in the canon, tell us about changes and continuities in the ideas that have governed the construction of our literary history?

This book is in no sense intended as a survey of American fiction from Howells to Dreiser; for one thing, too much has been left out. I discuss only one novel by Dreiser, only two each by Twain and James—the major works these two writers published from the middle to the end of the 1880s. For reasons I set forth at the beginning of Part One, I discuss *no* fiction by Howells, confining myself instead to his critical writings and particularly those concerned with his campaign for literary realism. I do not discuss such possible precursors of the so-called realism of the 1880s and 1890s as the domestic best-sellers of the 1850s, such as Susan Warner's *The Wide, Wide World*—although in this case I could argue on behalf of my omission that, since I do not assume that there *was* a coherent tradition of "realistic" practice in America in the 1880s and 1890s, it would make little sense for me to talk about *influences* on such a tradition. And I have left out many late nineteenth- and early twentieth-century writers who might with good reason have been included, especially women writers: for instance, Mary Wilkins Freeman (whom I discuss only very briefly), Kate Chopin, Edith Wharton, Willa Cather. I do not mean by this omission to exclude these women from the "realist" canon; after all, to repeat again a point I have already perhaps excessively belabored, I am not arguing that there *is* a "realist" canon. But I actually confined my consideration of the relation of women writers and American realist thinking to Jewett for a more practical reason: I found her case particularly instructive and wanted time and space to consider the full trajectory of her career. I certainly hope my discussion of her (and my book taken as a whole) will provoke readers to think about other women writers of this period—such as Chopin, Wharton, and Cather—in some of my terms.

In any case, to repeat, this book is not meant to "cover" American fiction from the 1880s to the beginning of the twentieth century, or even all the writers in this period one might associate in some way with "realism" or "naturalism." It is intended, rather, as a study—or a series of related case studies—in what I have called in my subtitle the cultural history of a literary idea. The assumptions underlying proclamations of realist or naturalist conviction have had deep roots in the American culture these proclamations have often seemed to be defying. And while their overt message might at first appear to have been liberating to the writers who uttered them, their deepest effects were often, I argue, quite the reverse. To many of their American proponents, the ideas of realism and naturalism have mattered far less as theories of literature than as means for neutralizing anxieties about the writer's status in a culture still intensely suspicious or contemptuous of "art" and the "artistic." To proclaim oneself a realist or naturalist in this context was most fundamentally to claim for literature the status of a "real"—that is, socially normal—activity, to define literature not in its own terms but in the terms sanctioned by an abidingly anti-"literary" cultural orthodoxy.

I should frankly confess, by way of a final warning, that I have not emerged from this study with a great deal of sympathy for the ideas of "realism" and "naturalism" that passed current in the United States in the 1880s and 1890s. In a sense, of course, my want of sympathy places me in a critical tradition of longstanding: as I began this introduction by observing, it is pretty much a truism that late nineteenth-century discussions of "realism" and "naturalism" were far from rigorous and generally rather slipshod. What distinguishes my own approach is that having made this admission I do not then turn away from it, looking elsewhere for my understanding of American "realism." Instead, I make the very insufficiencies of realist thinking my focus or (to shift the metaphor) my gateway into the field I wish to explore. As a result, Howells and Norris, the two writers in my group for whom declarations of "realist" or "naturalist" ambition mattered the most, end up being exhibited in a light less flattering than some readers might wish. I mean these men no disrespect (and they are themselves, of course, beyond caring), but it has seemed to me important to be clear about what their literary ideas actually were—as distinguished from what we might perhaps prefer them to have been.

My sympathies have instead tended to align me with writers who resisted realist thinking, or remained immune to its assumptions, or who probed these assumptions deeply enough, whether intentionally or inadvertently, to tease out the contradictions and complexities underlying realist thinking. Luckily, this group includes, in my view, all the other writers in my book. If the book tells a story, it is a story not of uniformity but of variety, having to do not with linear progression but with something more like the turning of a globe—or a multi-faceted gemstone. My subject is not, finally, "American realism" but, as my title puts it, the *problem* of "American realism"; and to move from Howells through Twain and James—and then through Norris, Crane, Dreiser and Jewett—is not to move toward a solution to this problem, at least not in *my* telling of the story. It is rather to witness a series of individual engagements: accommodations, evasions, holding actions, even an occasional triumph. In the 1880s and 1890s, serious American fiction writers, whether or not they proclaimed themselves to be realists or naturalists, had to contend with a seriously problematic conception of literary realism. The true story of the transformation of American fiction after the Civil War, it seems to me, is less a triumphant saga of the rise of realism, less even a shift in cultural practices or ideological formations, than a history of this contention.

PART ONE

The First Generation

WILLIAM DEAN HOWELLS

MARK TWAIN

HENRY JAMES

It is pretty generally agreed, at least in standard literary histories, that the principal American realists of the first generation—the generation of American novelists born in the 1830s and 1840s, those who began their careers after the Civil War and came to first full maturity in the 1880s—are William Dean Howells, Mark Twain, and Henry James. But simply to name these writers in the same sentence is to indicate at the outset a significant dimension of the problem of using the idea of "American realism" to organize our literary history. If this is a group at all (and for the most part one is compelled to conclude that it is not), it is a famously and even scandalously odd one. While Twain and James were both friends of Howells, they would seem to have had little else in common; not only is it hard to imagine them as part of the same movement, it is sometimes a bit difficult to imagine them inhabiting the same planet. They were in fact acquaintances, having met as early as 1879, and they would seem to have had a certain amount of respect for each other as public figures.[1] But they had no *literary* connection—no connection, that is, as writers engaged in what either would have seen, regarding the other, as a common enterprise. Twain enjoyed abusing James, along with Jane Austen and George Eliot, in letters to his friend Howells; and while James was active as a book reviewer during the first two decades of his career, decades that saw the publication of much of Twain's best work, he never reviewed a work by Mark Twain.

There is another oddity, and probably a more important one, in the conventional grouping of Howells, Twain, and James as American realists. While Twain and James, for all their differences, are generally regarded as "major" writers, Howells is usually treated as important but "minor." But it is *Howells*, the "minor" writer, who functions as the central figure of the supposed "Age of Realism."[2] There are perfectly good reasons for Howells's having been assigned this central role: he is, after all, the one who campaigned openly for literary realism, and he was closer than either Twain or James to the institutional centers of high-cultural literary practice in postbellum America. But the result of the central role he has been assigned in our literary history, now that at least some critics think they have sorted the "minor" writers out from the "major" (and few of those now challenging the canon are doing so on behalf of Howells), is a curious imbalance or disproportion—as if, say, an army of generals were being led by a colonel.

I call attention to this imbalance because it accounts for what might seem an oddity in my own treatment of Howells: in Chapter 1, I discuss only Howells's critical writings, particularly the essays collected in 1891 as *Criticism and Fiction*, and not his novels. I do not mean by this tactic to dismiss Howells's fiction, nor do I wish to deny the influence of his novels on Twain or on James. I am, for instance, completely willing to accept Richard Brodhead's assertion that Howells's novels were "always more important to James than Jamesians will allow."[3] But whatever the influence of his fictional practice, Howells's centrality to the category "American realism" is not based on his fiction but on his public campaign for literary realism, and it has seemed to me advisable to focus as tightly as possible on the meaning and function of this campaign. The influence of Howells's fiction—and the ways in which his fiction might seem, more generally, to resemble the fiction of James or even, at a stretch, Twain—must be distinguished carefully from the issue of the influence (or the prevalence) of his conception of literary realism. While it is his novels that now make him seem "minor," it is his critical essays that have for so long made him seem central. In Chapter 1, I thus explore the meaning and apparent function of the idea of realism that Howells expounds *in his critical writing*. Chapters 2 and 3 then proceed to ask how relevant Howellsian realism was to the fictional theory and practice of Mark Twain and Henry James. My answer, briefly put, is that it was not very relevant at all, at least not in any direct sense. While Howells, Twain, and James may have had more in common, as novelists, than we might at first suppose, there is little reason to think that what they had in common was a commitment to the assumptions underlying Howellsian realism. And when Twain and James do seem to come under the influence of Howells's ideas, of what I call realist thinking, the result is for the most part a warping of their most characteristic talents and inclinations.

1

The Sin of Art

WILLIAM DEAN HOWELLS

"People . . . require of a novelist whom they respect unquestionable proof of his seriousness. . . . He can no longer expect to be received on the ground of entertainment only; he assumes a higher function, something like that of a physician or a priest."

William Dean Howells, *Criticism and Fiction* (1891)

"I find . . . you are a little given to the sin of authorship, which I renounce."

Buckthorne to Geoffrey Crayon, in Washington Irving, *Tales of a Traveller* (1824)

To understand what "realism" meant to William Dean Howells, we first need to understand how he came to be a proponent of the idea; we need to place his advocacy of realism in the context of his full literary career. Born in Ohio in 1837, Howells turned early to literature. In 1860, on the strength of having placed four poems in Boston's *Atlantic Monthly*, he traveled east for his now famous meeting with the lions of New England literary society; here Oliver Wendell Holmes, at a dinner in Howells's honor, leaned toward James Russell Lowell to remark: "Well, James, this is something like the apostolic succession; this is the laying on of hands."[1] A campaign biography of Lincoln, published the same year, earned Howells the American consulate in Venice, where he served from 1861 to 1865, thus avoiding the Civil War. He then returned briefly to Ohio, but in 1866 Holmes's "apostolic succession" prophecy bore fruit: Howells was appointed assistant editor of the *Atlantic*, and he became chief editor in 1871. Ten years later he resigned this influential position to devote more time to the writing of fiction, and two of his best novels appeared in the early

1880s: *A Modern Instance* in 1882, and *The Rise of Silas Lapham* in 1885. In the latter year Howells moved from Boston to New York, to take on the "Editor's Study" column in *Harper's* magazine. It was with the "Editor's Study" essays, beginning in 1886 and selectively reissued as *Criticism and Fiction* in 1891, that Howells emerged as the primary definer and defender of realism in America.[2]

The Problem of Howellsian Realism

Most discussion of *Criticism and Fiction*, since the first "Editor's Study" essays began appearing in 1886, has concentrated on Howells's idea of "reality"—not in terms of philosophical definition but with respect to the subjects he saw as being open (and closed) to the novelist. Contemporary opponents—usually dismissed now as belated "romantics" or "idealists"—attacked his permissiveness, his opening the floodgates to vulgarity, mediocrity, or scandal.[3] More recent critics have tended to complain, on the other hand, that Howells did not open the gates far enough, and they have found especially troubling his infamous contention that our novelists "concern themselves with the more smiling aspects of life" not in evasion but because these aspects are "the more American."[4] Probably the best-known complaint of this sort is Sinclair Lewis's denunciation of "Victorian and Howellsian timidity and gentility" in his 1930 Nobel Prize Acceptance Speech.[5] It is important to recognize that Howells and his opponents, both "romantic" and "realistic," share a basic assumption: that realism, whether for good or for ill, depends upon the "reality" of the writer's subject matter. As we will see, this assumption is the bedrock of realist thinking in America, connecting Howells, for instance, to the so-called "naturalism" propounded by Frank Norris. A few contemporary reviewers, however, objected to this assumption, arguing against the "Editor's Study" essays that even realism has to be seen as a mode of representation, a species of literary *art*. As Horace Scudder wrote in the *Atlantic:* "There is . . . in Mr. Howells's creed an assumption that literary art is of necessity false; that art is a foe to the best fiction. It is true that he understands by art something that is derivative and not in itself original, but there is throughout his book a latent distrust of any art of fiction." Or as Brander Matthews put it in *Cosmopolitan:* "In his fight for nature, even if it be raw, perhaps Mr. Howells is unduly negligent of form"; he forgets that "the masterpieces of literature are not mere fragments of human experience seized at haphazard" but are "composed as a picture is composed."[6]

Scudder and Matthews were not simply fighting a "romantic" holding action against the new realism; they were pointing to an important tendency in Howells's critical thought, a tendency that still matters because it has figured so prominently in the thinking of many American writers and critics. To be sure, Howells was no crude philistine; he often, if fleetingly, acknowledges the requirements of art even in realistic fiction. For instance, in *Literary Friends and Acquaintance* (1900) he objects to the great New England writers—in terms faintly echoing Poe's attack on "the heresy of *The Didactic*," lodged against these same writers—that "sometimes they sacrificed the song for the sermon." He writes of Zola, in a 1902 essay, that "he supposed that he was recording and classifying"; but, Howells adds, "he was creating and vivifying." Or there is the declaration in *Criticism and Fiction* that "when realism becomes false to itself, when it heaps up facts merely, and maps life instead of picturing it, realism will perish."[7] This last even sounds a bit like Matthews's observation that works of literature are composed "as a picture is composed."

Nevertheless, Scudder and Matthews seem largely correct in their understanding of Howells. There is surely something vague and perfunctory in the isolated use of words like "song," "creating," and "vivifying" to describe the *art* of realism, and it is never clear just what, for Howells, distinguishes a picture from a map. Howells was so notoriously and confessedly insensitive to pictorial art that one wonders what "picture" meant to him;[8] and the context of the "map"/"picture" passage in *Criticism and Fiction* offers more confusion than clarification. After insisting that realism must picture life, and not merely map it, Howells adds that "every realist instinctively knows this, and it is perhaps the reason why he is careful of every fact, and feels himself bound to express its meaning at the risk of over-moralizing."[9] Art, here, is a matter not of craft but of instinct, and what apparently distinguishes a picture from a map, astonishingly enough, is not consciousness of form, of pictorial composition, but attention to "fact" and "meaning"!

"Where Tolstoy becomes impatient of his office of artist, and prefers to be directly a teacher," Howells writes in the final chapter of *My Literary Passions* (1895), "he robs himself of more than half his strength." Yet Howells's conception of the artist's distinctive "office" remains, at best, extremely cloudy; indeed, within two pages we are told, in the closing sentence of the chapter, that "the supreme art in literature had its highest effect in making me set art forever below humanity." The latter sentence is the more characteristically Howellsian. "Nothing in a story," he wrote to his publisher in 1884, "can be better than life." He sums up the essential character of his closest literary friend, in *My Mark Twain* (1910), by saying that "of all the literary men I have known he was the most unliterary in his make and manner"—which is evidently meant as a compliment. The same tendency appears in Howells's account of his early development as a reader, in *My Literary Passions:* "I . . . was coming to read more with a sense of the author, and less with a sense of his characters as real persons; that is, I was growing more literary, and less human." The "literary," this is to say, is to be suppressed in the interest of the "real" and "human"; this distinction is absolute, and it lies at the heart of the discussion of realism in *Criticism and Fiction*. The burden of being "literary" is even shifted from writers to critics. "That which criticism seems most certainly to have done," Howells insists, "is to put a literary consciousness into books unfelt in the early masterpieces." Even now, he adds, the best writing is that which remains—to use the word he applies to Grant's *Memoirs*, apparently without irony—"unconscious"; in these *Memoirs*, we are told, "there is no thought of style, and so the style is good as it is in the Book of Chronicles, as it is in the Pilgrim's Progress, with a peculiar, almost plebeian, plainness at times."[10]

It is important to recognize that Howells's insistence on the radical opposition of interest in "style" and concern for "truth" is by no means an inevitable component of literary realism as such. In France, after all, Flaubert and others had demonstrated that the cult of style was perfectly compatible with the pursuit of even the most sordid "reality," and Sarah Orne Jewett, for example, pinned to the writing desk in her Maine study Flaubert's dictum: "*Écrire la vie ordinaire comme on écrit l'histoire.*"[11] For Howells, however, the truest realists were not writers like Flaubert but writers like Tolstoy (as Howells understood him) or like Ulysses Grant, writers who suppress the "literary" for the sake of the "human." As early as 1886 Henry James, whose own idea of "realism" owed far more to the French school than to Howellsian precept, saw this tendency in his friend's critical thought and strongly objected to it. Central to the "Editor's Study" essays, James noted, is the idea "that the style of a work of fiction is a thing that matters less and less all the while," but to James this idea is nonsense. "The style of a novel," he protests, "is part of the execution of a work of art; the execution of a work of art is part of its very essence, and that, it seems to me, must have mattered in all ages in exactly the same degree, and be destined always to do so."[12] This is not an aesthete rebuking a realist but a serious writer reminding his friend that even realistic literature neither can nor should seek to evade the "literary"—that realism involves not a rejection of style (if such a thing were even possible) but a particular *use* of style. Of course, as Harry Levin puts it, "to convince us of his essential veracity, the novelist must always be disclaiming the fictitious and breaking through the encrustations of the literary."[13] Howells, however, surely takes such disclaiming to an extreme, so much so that it ends up constituting, in effect, the central theoretical underpinning of his version of realism.

Faced with this fundamental weakness in Howellsian realism—with the absence, in Howells's critical writings, of a theory of fictional *representation*—we may wish to smile, to make allowances, to acknowledge with Warner Berthoff that American realism first emerged, after all, "in an era not widely distinguished by searching critical discussion,"[14] but we follow this course at our peril. For one thing, Howells's bias against "art" and "style" is no personal idiosyncrasy; it has been shared by many other self-proclaimed American "realists," even by those who have thought they were turning against Howells. Sinclair Lewis, accepting the Nobel Prize in 1930, may have rejected "Victorian and Howellsian timidity and gentility," and he may have denounced Howells's "fantastic vision of life, which he innocently conceived to be realistic," but in one respect at least he is perfectly Howellsian. Objections have been made, he notes, to Dreiser's "style." "I am not exactly sure," he replies, "what this mystic quality 'style' may be, but I find the word so often in the writings of minor critics that I suppose it must exist."[15] Here we have both Howells's characteristic depreciation of "style" and his habit of tracing the "literary" not to literature but to criticism. Howells's denigration of "style" in the interest of "truth" is only one of a number of possible versions of literary "realism," one with which writers like James, for instance, consistently took issue. But it is Howells's version, not James's, that is most representative of what has tended to pass for "realism" in most American critical discourse.

There is yet another reason for caution about attributing Howells's bias against the "artistic" to personal naiveté or to the lack of theoretical sophistication in his literary contemporaries, always excepting James. If someone keeps saying something to us, over and over, we should be prepared at least to entertain the possibility that he means it. Is it possible, then, that the apparent *problem* of Howellsian realism—its persistent denigration of the "literary"—is in fact one of its principal *tenets*? In my Introduction I noted that when people make claims, perhaps especially when they make claims that do not quite seem to make sense, they presumably do so because they need to do so. Howells's discussions of realism are permeated with attacks on "art" and the "artistic." Might we not reasonably infer from this that Howells *needed* to dissociate his identity as a writer from its "artistic" implications and that this dissociation was an important, perhaps a crucial component of the realism to which he turned in the 1880s? Such an approach might help us understand why so naive a notion of realism appealed to a man as intelligent as Howells—a man, moreover, with a friend as intelligent, and as intelligently critical of Howellsian realism, as Henry James. It also might help us understand why this sort of realism has appealed to so many others, both American writers and American critics.

In this light let us return to the contention, in *Criticism and Fiction*, that critics have brought into books a "literary consciousness . . . unfelt in the early masterpieces." Such consciousness, Howells claims, is "unfelt now only in the books of men whose lives have been passed in activities, who have been used to employing language as they would have employed any implement, to effect an object, who have regarded a thing to be said as in no wise different from a thing to be done"; and in such books "there is not a moment wasted in preening and prettifying, after the fashion of literary men."[16] Here, clearly, the most significant distinction is not between modes of literary expression or representation but between kinds of men. On the one side is the artist, overwhelmed and enervated by "literary consciousness," metaphorically feminized by his concern with "preening and prettifying," with "fashion." On the other side are "real" men, "men whose lives have been passed in activities," men who handle language as a burly carpenter hefts his tools. Howells's entire literary career was an effort to reconcile these divergent images of his potential identity as a writer, an effort undertaken long before he turned to the open advocacy of realism in the 1880s. And realism itself mattered to Howells, first of all, not as an aesthetic theory but as one more in a continuing series of attempts at reconciliation—attempts to portray the "artist" as a "real" man by obscuring the distinction between "a thing . . . said" and "a thing . . . done." The problem, for Howells as for many of his contemporaries and successors, was that the "artist" was by accepted definition *not* a "real" man.

The Road to Realism

Howells grew up, in the 1840s and 1850s, in a series of small Ohio towns; his family was always on the move, but always within this Western province of a still provincial nation. Neither the setting nor the circumstances of such an upbringing would seem ideal, in retrospect, for fostering a sense of literary vocation. Nevertheless, according to Lionel Trilling, when "Howells determined on a life of literature . . . his community respected his enterprise and encouraged him in it." Trilling's image of community support for artistic endeavor is appealing; it is also, in some respects, accurate. As Henry James, Howells's junior by six years, would report the situation in 1879, the American writer "is not looked at askance . . . ; literature and the arts have always been held in extreme honour in the American world," where the successful writer is in fact "an object of . . . admiration." Even in mid-century Ohio literary fame was not unimaginable, and in mid-century Ohio it may have seemed especially desirable. As the artist Westover, in Howells's *The Landlord at Lion's Head* (1896), explains the effect of his own Western upbringing: "I lived in the woods there till I began to paint my way out." There was a darker side to the picture, however, that is suggested by James's comments immediately preceding those quoted above:

It is not too much to say that even to the present day it is a considerable discomfort in the United States not to be "in business." The young man who attempts to launch himself in a career that does not belong to the so-called practical order; the young man who has not, in a word, an office in the business-quarter of town, with his name painted on the door, has but a limited place in the social system, finds no particular bough to perch upon.

Indeed, James continues, the very excess of the "exaggerated homage rendered to authorship" in America mainly reinforced the writer's sense of marginality, of being "a solitary worker."[17]

"It is worth observing," Trilling writes of Howells, "that . . . he devoted himself to a literary career not so much out of disinterested love for literature as out of the sense that literature was an institutional activity by which he might make something out of himself in the worldly way." This is certainly an accurate report of the outcome or effect of Howells's literary career; his most important influence may have been his demonstration, first in Boston and then in New York, that literature in America could be an "institutional activity," a profession. But it is far less clear that this goal figured prominently in his initial ambition to become a man of letters; on the contrary, there is a good deal of evidence that something very like "love for literature" (whether "disinterested" or not) first inclined the young Westerner toward authorship. For instance in 1865, returned home from Venice and deciding between Ohio and Boston as stages for his future career, Howells faced a clear choice, and it was quite obvious which would most likely allow him, in Trilling's words, to "make something out of himself in the worldly way." As Edwin Cady has put it, "he knew he could succeed [as a journalist] in Columbus. What that success pointed toward, in the dawning Ohio period, was political power, perhaps high public office." Ohio men were soon to dominate national politics, and Howells—who in 1876 would add a campaign biography of his cousin by marriage, Rutherford B. Hayes, to his earlier book on Lincoln—could count on most of them. "But what Howells wanted," Cady continues, "was to be a man of letters."[18] He chose something like the isolation of the "solitary worker" over the "worldly" satisfactions of being "in business" or in politics—which, in the Ohio period, were much the same thing. Howells went to Boston.

That Howells chose Boston as the scene of his literary activity made his decision somewhat less stark than the preceding account might indicate, and I will return to this matter presently. Nevertheless, the choice of literature was important, and its sources extended back to Howells's Ohio youth. They led back to a young man who had always felt himself to be socially marginal, and to a culture which still, in the 1840s and 1850s, saw writers in strikingly similar terms. In 1813 Washington Irving, one of Howells's early literary enthusiasms, described the situation of the imaginative American writer in ways that anticipate what James would say on this subject in 1879: "Unfitted for business, in a nation where every one is busy; devoted to literature, where literary leisure is confounded with idleness; the man of letters is almost an insulated being, with few to understand, less to value, and scarcely any to encourage his pursuits." The situation was no doubt less acute during Howells's early years, although one might note Nathaniel Hawthorne's fantasy, in the "Custom-House" introduction to *The Scarlet Letter*, of his ancestors' likely reaction to his literary vocation: "'What is he? . . . A writer of story-books! What kind of a business in life,—what mode of glorifying God, or being serviceable to mankind in his day and generation,—may that be? Why, the degenerate fellow might as well have been a fiddler!'"[19] When Hawthorne published *The Scarlet Letter* in 1850, Will Howells was thirteen; Hawthorne was one of the New England literary lions he would visit during his 1860 pilgrimage. But even the golden apple contained this bitter core, this testimony to the American writer's abidingly "insulated" or irrelevant social status.

I have speculated elsewhere that to become a fiction writer in pre-Civil War America was in a sense to enter a deviant career, that the deviant status of being a writer very likely appealed (at least at first) to some of those who chose so to identify themselves, and that many of these writers' careers can be fruitfully understood in terms of the writers' subsequent attempts to manage or neutralize the more subversive implications of their original choices of vocation.[20] I will not rehearse this argument here; what matters is that it would appear to be as relevant to Howells as to fiction writers of the prewar generation. The ambivalence of earlier writers toward their marginal social status is suggested by the story "Buckthorne," in Washington Irving's *Tales of a Traveller* (1824), from which I have drawn the second of this chapter's epigraphs. Buckthorne tells Irving's *persona*, Geoffrey Crayon, that he turned early to literature, encouraged by his mother; his father was as outraged by this choice as Hawthorne would later imagine his ancestors being at his own literary vocation. "Indeed," Buckthorne says of his father, "I believe he would have pardoned anything in me more readily than poetry, which he called a cursed, sneaking, puling, house-keeping employment, the bane of all fine manhood." First disinherited on account of his inclinations, Buckthorne becomes a literary success in London. But when he comes into the family fortune after all, he simply abandons literature for a more "real" prosperity. "I find," he declares to the literary Geoffrey Crayon at the close, "you are a little given to the sin of authorship, which I renounce."[21]

Irving's sense of his situation seems clear enough: "authorship," in a social sense, is a kind of "sin," an abandonment of responsibility and "manhood." But Irving's response to this situation is rather ambiguous. Should one cultivate the marginality of a literary career, perhaps as a means of covert rebellion against responsibility and masculinity, or at least as an alternative means of self-definition? Or should one instead renounce "the sin of authorship," the sin of "art"? While "Buckthorne" is a rather silly story, it nevertheless suggests the sort of social climate Howells still had to face, in however modified a form, as he was deciding to become a writer. Howells, too, and from a relatively early age, was torn between the sin of art and the socially sanctioned imperatives of worldly, "masculine" success. Moreover, Buckthorne's movement from "artistic" isolation to a more "real" status might serve nicely as a kind of paradigm for the shape of Howells's own career.

Howells described his childhood in a small Ohio village in *A Boy's Town* (1890)—the first of a loose series of autobiographies and literary reminiscences that would come to include, most notably, *My Literary Passions* (1895), *Literary Friends and Acquaintance* (1900), and *Years of my Youth* (1916). *A Boy's Town* portrays a strangely nervous and morbid child, feebler than his companions, subject to nightmares, severe homesickness, and fears of early death. As Kenneth Lynn summarizes this portrait: "While Will Howells joyfully shared in the wild sports and savage usages of the other boys, he also lived apart from them in an imaginative world of his own. . . . He played and fought with them, on 'intimate' terms, and he was a 'good comrade' with any boy who wanted to go in swimming or out hunting. But with none of his schoolmates did he feel complete sympathy." "The only boy in town with whom Will became intimately friendly," Lynn notes, "was an outcast from the group." Gail Parker summarizes *A Boy's Town* in even more suggestive terms. "Howells," she writes, "remembered growing up in a kind of limbo, allowed to be the bookish one while his [older] brother was forced to be a little man. Clearly he had mixed feelings about his exempted status." *A Boy's Town*, she continues, "is full of descriptions of what real boys were like—as opposed to girl-boys. Although he insisted that 'there were mighty few girl-boys' in the neighborhood, he made his definitions in such a way that it is hard to imagine just where he thought he fit in."[22]

These gender anxieties matter because they crop up, again and again, in Howells's writings—especially in his worryings about his own status as a writer and about the general standing of authorship in America. In 1824 the father of Irving's Buckthorne denounced literature as a "housekeeping employment, the bane of all fine manhood." "I like to see a man *act* like a man," the title character of Howells's *The Rise of Silas Lapham* declares to his future son-in-law; "I don't like to see him taken care of like a young lady." In Howells's *Letters Home* (1903), Otis Birning characterizes his reception by a businessman in similar terms: "He early decided that I was intellectual, I think, and with the admirable frankness of his class, he conceived of me . . . as a kind of mental and moral woman."[23] Or we might recall the association of "literary consciousness," in the discussion of Grant's *Memoirs* in *Criticism and Fiction*, with "preening and prettifying."

There can be little question that the Will Howells who turned to literature in the 1850s was troubled by his ambiguous social and sexual identity. Moreover, he clearly embraced literature, first of all, not (to use Trilling's terms) as a "worldly" or "institutional" activity but as an *alternative* to such activities. By 1850, he recalls in *My Literary Passions*, "the love of literature, and the hope of doing something in it, had become my life to the exclusion of all other interests"—these interests including, he continues, the growing political crisis over slavery. Later in the same volume he describes his love of books in curiously sensual terms, writing that "the look of the type took me more than the glance of a girl, and I had a fever of longing to know the heart of a book, which was like a lover's passion." Nor did Howells turn to literature, at first, to gain social acceptance; on the contrary, as he later recalled in *My*

Literary Passions, "my reading gave me no standing among the boys, and I did not expect it to rank me with boys who were more valiant in fight or in play; and I have since found that literature gives one no more certain station in the world of men's activities, either idle or useful. We literary folk try to believe that it does, but that is all nonsense." To turn to literature, apparently, was not to embrace but to *forsake* "the world of men's activities." Howells's first literary efforts, finally, were hardly in the mode of even an incipient "realism"; they were attempts, rather, "to write in the style of Edgar A. Poe, as I knew it from his tales of the Grotesque and Arabesque."[24]

My point here is not to psychoanalyze Howells but simply to note that he chose to be a writer in full awareness of the marginal or sexually ambiguous implications of such a choice in mid-century America, and these implications may even have provided, for the already somewhat marginal young man, part of the first attraction of literary vocation. What matters most, however, is that he soon set out to alter or bury these initial implications of his "love of literature." In 1857 he turned down a job as city editor of the Cincinnati *Gazette.* "I did not know then," he later wrote in *My Literary Passions,* "that life was supremely interesting and important. I fancied that literature, that poetry was so; and it was humiliation and anguish indescribable to think of myself torn from my high ideals by labors like those of a reporter." Another foray into journalism, early in 1858, ended in a characteristic breakdown, but in November of the same year Howells was back at work— in Columbus, as city editor of the *Ohio State Journal*—and this time he was able to sustain his commitment to "the world of men's activities." Not that he gave up literature; he would never go that far, and by 1860 he had placed poems in New York's *Saturday Press* and, to his passionate delight, in Boston's *Atlantic.* Still, he had worked out a compromise: he was now a "poet" *and* a "man." In the offices of the *Journal* and in his Columbus boardinghouse he had finally joined, as Edwin Cady puts it, "the kind of ambitious but lighthearted masculine society [he] badly needed."[25] It was in the spirit of this compromise between the allure of "poetry" and the imperatives of "men's activities" that he traveled to Boston in 1860 and chose to work there in 1866. That he chose Boston should not surprise us, and not just because it boasted a pride of literary lions; for as Howells clearly recognized, these lions had already worked out a compromise very like his own, and they had made it famous.

"All that day," Howells writes of his 1860 visit to Boston in *Literary Friends and Acquaintance,* "I believed authorship the noblest calling in the world, and I should still be at a loss to name any nobler. The great authors I had met were to me the sum of greatness."[26] This greatness had been quite deliberately achieved. The late William Charvat, in a brilliant though never finished essay, has detailed the steps by which Henry Wadsworth Longfellow managed to become the first American to find "security in society as a poet." Longfellow set out to identify the "poet" not with "art" but with the concerns of his audience, to portray the poet as a *"useful* citizen" and to neutralize the "feminine" associations of writing poetry. Thus Paul Flemming, poet-hero of the novel *Hyperion* (1839), is no tremulous, visionary Geoffrey Crayon; he is described, instead, "in aggressively masculine terms." In the late 1830s and early 1840s, according to Charvat, Longfellow experienced a kind of "professional schizophrenia," alternately cultivating the image of *"useful* poet" and that of the "artist type," but by the time of *Evangeline* (1847) he had perfected his "campaign to make the Poet socially as respectable with the practical citizen as Poetry"—achieving this respectability by abandoning the image of the "artist type," by identifying the poet's concerns with those of "the many." Longfellow's readers ultimately "exempted him from the common suspiciousness of the Poet," Charvat writes, "because of the persistent reassurance in his verse that the Poet is not a creature set apart from other men but a working citizen subject to the same responsibilities as everyone else."[27] Neutralize the "artist" image and identify the writer with the working citizen, with what Howells called "the world of men's activities": thus could one be a writer without ceasing to be (or to appear to be) a man. If this was Longfellow's formula of success these are also the terms, we should recognize, in which Howells would portray the ideal writer, the "realist," in *Criticism and Fiction.*

And Howells fully appreciated what Longfellow and his Boston contemporaries had accomplished. The author of *Evangeline*, we are told in *Literary Friends and Acquaintance* (in rather suggestive terms), "was . . . gentle beyond all mere gentlemanliness. But it would have been a great mistake to mistake his mildness for softness. It was most manly and firm." Howells writes similarly of Holmes that he was "kind to any sensitiveness, for he was as sensitive as he was manly"; yet "he had not much patience with the unmanly craving for sympathy in others, and chiefly in our literary craft, which is somewhat ignobly given to it. . . . He used to say . . . that unless a man could show a good reason for writing verse, it was rather against him, and a proof of weakness." This surely sounds like a portrait of the artist as the artist's hostile father; Holmes apparently disarmed the opposition by siding with it! "Of morbidness," adds Howells, himself alarmingly morbid as a child, "Holmes was often very tender; he knew it to be disease." Lowell seems to have been somewhat less successful than the others at sustaining the masculine performance, which may help explain why Howells got closer to him than he did to the other lions. In relation to money, Howells writes, there was in Lowell "something unworldly . . . something almost womanlike"; in the face of criticism "he would try to hide his hurt, and he would not let you speak of it, as though your sympathy unmanned him, but you could see that he suffered."[28] Still, Lowell knew at least to try to hide his hurt; if he was unmanned he did not talk about it.

The New England lions had indeed learned how to be, or seem to be, "men" and "writers" at the same time. In Boston, apparently, art was no longer a sin, authorship no longer (as the father of Irving's Buckthorne puts it) "the bane of all fine manhood"; the writer was no longer a social outcast or curiosity. "Elsewhere," Howells writes in *Literary Friends and Acquaintance*, "we literary folk are apt to be such a common lot, with tendencies here and there to be a shabby lot . . .; but at Boston we were of ascertained and noted origin. . . . We were good society from the beginning."[29] The "we" here is crucial; Howells could describe *himself* as part of this perfect literary community. Its reigning journal, the *Atlantic*, had accepted his poems, and then accepted their author as assistant editor. By 1871, when Howells became chief editor, Holmes's "apostolic succession" prophecy would surely seem to have been fulfilled.

But was it in fact fulfilled? Fourteen years later, after all, Howells left Boston for New York.[30] We are bound to ask why he did so—to wonder what, for him, went wrong with the Boston compromise, or what, perhaps, was wrong with it from the beginning. Kenneth Lynn sees the move as a result of Howells's awareness that Boston was no longer relevant, in the 1880s, that "the writer in post–Civil War America was no longer considered 'a type of greatness,' as he had been in Longfellow's day." According to Lewis P. Simpson, "Howells could never reconcile his ideal of being a writer in America with the realities—the contingencies—of being one"; if Boston "worked" it did so only by ignoring the new social developments of the 1880s, the growing congestion and inequality of urban life.[31] It was to these developments that Howells turned in New York, most notably in another of his best novels, *A Hazard of New Fortunes* (1890), in which a transplanted New Englander who bears a striking resemblance to the author confronts the chaotic social reality of the national metropolis.

It should also be recognized, though, that while the Boston compromise may have worked for those who had fashioned it, these men had never been clearly disposed to let it work for Howells—or so, at least, it seemed. The Westerner could feed the animals, even guide tours of their haunts, but he could never quite be a lion in his own right, and *Literary Friends and Acquaintance* is laced with stories of the young Westerner being put down by his seniors. There is the story of Holmes, for instance, interrupting a rare remark by Howells to observe, curtly, "Yes, . . . I have spoken of that," and then proceeding to tell him "just where." Or there is the wonderful story of Longfellow, in what became one of the central social activities of literary Boston, reading proofs of his Dante translation to a select and admiring audience, rejecting Howells's only suggested revision, and then staring down the presumptuous interloper who felt, so he writes, that he was "growing smaller and smaller, like something through a reversed opera-glass." Lowell was more generous, but even with Lowell there was a crucial distance: "He was only too ready to hand down his laurels," Howells writes, "but he wished to do it himself."[32] If complete manhood required some rite of passage, these mentors were not prepared to acknowledge the challenge—or Howells, perhaps, was not prepared to force it, at least not in Boston. After all, he had come East for the support of these fathers, for the support of what they stood for. If he should challenge their authority, and win, might he not simply be left with nothing?

In any case, it seems likely that Howells moved to New York above all because he had, finally, to work out his own compromise—his own reconciliation of the "man" and the "artist"—and he had to do it in a different setting. It is extremely significant, in this connection, that his move to New York exactly coincided with his decision to become an outspoken advocate of realism; for realism was precisely the new compromise he needed, and the central emphases of this realism were not even all that new. Howells's advocacy of realism has often been seen as a defiance of Boston, a repudiation of its literary principles, and Howells's views did offend such Boston literary spokesmen as the *Atlantic*'s Horace Scudder.[33] It is crucial, however, that we recognize the *continuities* between the compromise worked out by the New England writers in the 1840s and 1850s and the realism elaborated by Howells in the 1880s and after. Many of the hallmarks of the Longfellow formula reappear in *Criticism and Fiction*, and if Howells's abiding contribution to American letters was, as Lionel Trilling puts it, "the sense that literature [is] an institutional activity by which [one] might make something out of himself in the worldly way,"[34] was this not the guiding principle of Boston's literary society well before Howells ever arrived there? I have already observed what critics since Henry James have in any case long recognized, that *Criticism and Fiction* makes little sense as a theoretical definition, a poetics if you will, of "realistic" fiction. But it makes a good deal of sense, to paraphrase William Charvat, as an effort on Howells's part to find security in society as a fiction writer, to include literature in what Howells himself called "the world of men's activities."[35]

A Portrait of the Artist as a "Real" Man

One of *Criticism and Fiction*'s most overt strategies is its effort to ally realism with the concerns of "ordinary"—that is, non-"artistic"—people. "Let fiction cease to lie about life," Howells proclaims in a well-known passage, "let it portray men and women as they are, actuated by the motives and the passions in the measure we all know; . . . let it speak the dialect, the language, that most Americans know—the language of unaffected people everywhere." It is not just that ordinary people, "men and women as they are," constitute the proper *subject* of realistic fiction, nor that their language constitutes its most appropriate *expression;* what is most important is that their judgment, what "we all" or "most Americans" know, is the underlying *standard* of realism. "'The true standard of the arts,'" Howells quotes approvingly from Burke, "'is in every man's power.'" Thus the realist, bearing the banner of "most Americans" or of "unaffected people everywhere," struggles on their behalf and with their support against "the vested interests of criticism." Howells's language suggests that the significance of the realist campaign is for him ultimately political, an attack on "vested interests," and this sort of language is characteristic, at least as metaphor. "The art which . . . disdains the office of teacher," Howells writes in the final paragraph of *Criticism and Fiction,*

is one of the last refuges of the aristocratic spirit which is disappearing from politics and society, and is now seeking to shelter itself in aesthetics. The pride of caste is becoming the pride of taste; but as before, it is averse to the mass of men. . . . It seeks to withdraw itself, to stand aloof. . . . Democracy in literature is the reverse of all this. It wishes to know and to tell the truth.

Phrases like "aristocratic spirit," "pride of taste," and "stand aloof" sound like covert attacks on Boston and have often been so interpreted; but Longfellow, we recall, had himself secured a place for poetry among "men's activities" by rejecting the pose of artistic exclusiveness, by identifying the poet not with the aesthetic but with "the many." Nor could it be said of any of the great Boston writers that he had "disdained the office of teacher"; on the contrary, as Howells himself would note in *Literary Friends and Acquaintance*, they more typically "sacrificed the song for the sermon."[36]

The idea that realism or naturalism can be legitimized by being conceived of as part of a popular political struggle has appeared again and again—most notably, in America, in the 1930s—but it had as little basis in political and social actuality in the 1880s as it has had since.[37] Howells's equation of realism with "democracy" reflects no very accurate assessment of the public taste; one thinks, for instance, of the vogue during the Great Depression of movies about debutantes and other elegantly fantasized socialites. Howells recognized intermittently that his political rationale was built on sand—on a wishful, metaphorical equation of art with aristocracy and of realism with popular democracy. In 1902, for instance, he wrote that "it was the error of the realists whom Zola led, to suppose that people like truth in fiction better than falsehood; they do not; they like falsehood best." Was this not equally true of the realists whom *Howells* led? Nevertheless, Howells's assertion that realism was "democracy in literature" makes perfect sense as a kind of public relations gesture, in the manner of Whitman's assertion at the end of his preface to the first edition of *Leaves of Grass* that "the proof of a poet is that his country absorbs him as affectionately as he has absorbed it."[38] A market consisting of "most Americans," the writer's whole "country," or—perhaps best of all—"unaffected people everywhere" would certainly relieve the writer from financial anxiety. Even more important for both Howells and Whitman, clearly, were the psychological benefits of the pose of "democratic" writer: as against the conventional notion of the irrelevance of literary activity, this pose gave the writer a sense of "real" social significance; it provided, to use James's phrase, the largest possible "bough to perch upon." And most important, to associate the writer with what was most normal or ordinary in his audience was to dissociate him from the socially marginal and sexually ambiguous implications of the "literary" and "artistic."

Criticism and Fiction takes pains, therefore, to present the writer—at least the realist—as anything *but* an "artist." The "true realist," Howells writes, "cannot look upon human life and declare this thing or that thing unworthy of notice, any more than the scientist can declare a fact of the material world beneath the dignity of his inquiry." The ideal critic is described in nearly identical terms: he will "understand," Howells writes, "that it is really his business to classify and analyze the fruits of the human mind very much as the naturalist classifies the objects of his study."[39] Of course, such comparisons are meant to clarify Howells's notion of objectivity in fiction and criticism, but one suspects that on a deeper level they function (as do naturalist appeals to the prestige of science) to associate realism, once again, with "real" pursuits, "men's activities." If the writer was a scientist, he was *not* an "artist."

Howells reveals the impulses at the heart of his thinking about realism nowhere more clearly than in his discussion, in *Criticism and Fiction*, of the circumstances under which the American realist might appropriately describe usually forbidden phases "of the physical or of the emotional nature." It is from this discussion that I have drawn this chapter's first epigraph:

People . . . require of a novelist whom they respect unquestionable proof of his seriousness, if he proposes to deal with certain phases of life; they require a sort of scientific decorum. He can no longer expect to be received on the ground of entertainment only; he assumes a higher function, something like that of a physician or a priest, and they expect him to be bound by laws as sacred as those of such professions; they hold him solemnly pledged not to betray them or abuse their confidence.[40]

This passage is less interesting for its specific account of the conditions under which "certain phases of life" might be dealt with than for its more general vision of the writer's relationship to his society, and in this respect it is very interesting indeed. The "conditions" of authorship, first of all, are set not by the "producer" but by consumers, by the "people." This concession might be explained as simple pragmatism, and Howells certainly had an acute understanding of the American market for fiction, but there is in fact an air of personal and social insecurity from the beginning to the end of the passage. There is the need for the "confidence" and "respect" of others, the anxiety not about whether the writer's work will be *read* but about whether the writer himself will be "received." And how is this insecurity overcome? Most simply, by transforming the "writer" into something else, something "higher": "a physician or a priest," a member of one of the "professions." Here again, *Criticism and Fiction* takes pains to present the writer as anything *but* an "artist."

This is why Howellsian realism cannot acknowledge and must indeed strive to deny the importance of "form" and "style." This is why Howells cannot present realism as a species of fictional *representation*. It is not that Howells and his contemporaries were theoretically unsophisticated, that they would have done better had they only known how. Rather, to admit the importance of "form" and "style" would have been to proclaim openly what Howellsian realism seems to have been fashioned to obscure: that one was indeed an artist and therefore, by implication, irrelevant to "the world of men's activities." I have already quoted Howells's apparently laudatory statement, in *My Mark Twain*, that "of all the literary men I have known [Clemens] was the most unliterary in his make and manner." Even more suggestive is the praise, a few pages earlier, of Twain's "unsophisticated use of words, of the diction which forms the manly backbone of his style." Should it surprise us that Howells also writes of Twain, again in apparent admiration, that "he did not care much for fiction"? Howells ends *My Literary Passions* with the essay on Tolstoy to which I referred some time ago. The great Russian novelist, he writes, was the "noblest" of his literary "enthusiasms" because "I can never again see life the way I saw it before I knew him"—and we should note here, once again, the transformation of the solitary act of reading into a form of social intercourse: "before I *knew* him." "Tolstoy," Howells writes, "awakens in his reader the will to be a man; not effectively, not spectacularly, but simply, really. He leads you back to the only true ideal, away from the false standard of the gentleman, to the Man who sought not to be distinguished from other men, but identified with them." Even Christ, whose claim of divinity would certainly seem to involve some sort of distinction, becomes for Howells a kind of pro-torealist, seeking "not to be distinguished from other men, but identified with them." "The supreme art in literature," Howells writes of Tolstoy at the end of the essay, "had its highest effect in making me set art forever below humanity."[41]

Criticism and Fiction, for all its shots at "romantic" literary idols and however much hostility it aroused in its time, was no revolutionary manifesto. On the contrary, in its persistent denigration of "art," "style," and the "literary" in the interest of "reality," "humanity," and the "natural" it in fact hearkens all the way back to the conservative ideology, derived from Common Sense "realism," against which American fiction writers had been struggling since the end of the eighteenth century. Thomas Jefferson, in an 1818 denunciation of what he called "the inordinate passion prevalent for novels," nicely exemplified the main tendencies of this rational orthodoxy:

When this poison infects the mind, it destroys its tone and revolts it against wholesome reading. Reason and fact, plain and unadorned, are rejected. Nothing can engage attention unless dressed in all the figments of fancy, and nothing so bedecked comes amiss. The result is a bloated imagination, sickly judgment, and disgust towards all the real businesses of life.[42]

To understand just how conservative Howellsian realism is we need only recognize that Howells, while he might have made some minor changes in Jefferson's expression, would have completely endorsed his meaning. *Criticism and Fiction* apparently mattered far less to its author as an aesthetic manifesto than as an attempt to work out his own status as a writer, to reconcile the culturally divergent identities of "artist" and "man" by presenting authorship as one of what Jefferson called "the real businesses of life." In realism, this is to say, Howells found the laurel Boston had seemed to offer but had never quite handed over; indeed, this new laurel was cut, it would seem, from the same shrub. Moreover, this new laurel was Howells's own; small wonder that he cherished it. Yet he paid a considerable price for it all the same, and this price is still being exacted, however unconsciously, by a good deal of what passes for "realist" thinking in America.

The Problem of American Realism

In *The Problem of Boston* (1966), Martin Green explores the paradox that in the one major city in nineteenth-century America where "culture" was wholly respectable, where "writing was taken seriously, as a major form of human activity," the "literary product" was so notably "undistinguished." In what would seem to have been the most favorable of climates, he writes, "writers' talents were being not fostered but deformed." The problem, Green decides, was the very respectability of literature: in Boston "the literary life was centrally a matter of clubs and sociability; there was no need for gestures of radical independence; indeed there was no room for them, because the only useful and truthful gestures were those which expressed social participation and co-operation." Thus literary Boston cut itself off from the creative introspection, alienation, and protest of true Romanticism. This is a convincing analysis, and my only quarrel with it would be that such limitation seems to have been very much the point, and not just an unfortunate result, of what I have been calling the Boston compromise.[43] The campaign to make literature socially respectable, to transform the "artist" into a "man," succeeded by paying an obvious price. By identifying himself as a man like other men, the writer lost touch with what it had meant to him, in the first place, to want to be an "artist."[44] But paying this price had always, apparently, been the *point* of the Boston compromise; evading what it still saw as the sin of art in order to secure genteel cultural respectability, literary Boston denied its writers only what these writers apparently wished to shun: that marginal status which alone, so even they believed, gave access to the full power, the full engagement, available to the true "artist."

It would be nice to see Howellsian realism as a repudiation of this evasion, and it has been so seen by a great many literary historians. Yet it would seem that the body of ideas about realism Howells expressed in *Criticism and Fiction* and elsewhere was in fact a perpetuation of the Boston compromise in new, and not always new, terms. Howells's reasons for going to New York in 1885 were finally the same as his reasons for having come to Boston in 1866: he was seeking a place where he could be a "man" and a "writer" at the same time. If he wrote too much, spent too much time protecting his position and defining the conditions of his relationship to "men's activities," so be it; he got only what he went for. What matters is that when Howells moved from New England to New York, what Green calls "the problem of Boston" became the problem of American realism.

But it is hardly my purpose to belittle Howells, or to attack his influence as having been somehow uniquely pernicious, however vigorously he may have insisted on the distinction between "life" and "literature." He produced, as a novelist, an interesting and important body of work, at the very least a perceptive portrait of the manners of his time. He showed considerable courage when he publicly protested, in 1887, the unjust conviction of anarchists in the aftermath of the Haymarket riots in Chicago. He was not without humor. What is at issue here, though, is not Howells's personal character or his achievement as a fiction writer but the nature and importance of his ideas about fiction, and it is worth noting that Howells himself thought he had sacrificed artistic dedication and success, in some measure, to the advocacy of realism. In 1900, for instance, he lamented to Thomas Bailey Aldrich: "If I could have held out fifteen years ago in my refusal of the Study, when Alden tempted me, I might have gone on and beat *Silas Lapham*. Now I can only dream of some leisure day doing better." Even more poignant is a 1908 letter to James. "You have imagined your fiction," Howells generously acknowledges, "and better fulfilled a conscious intention in it than any of your contemporaries." "I am, as usual," Howells sadly continues, "in the midst of a book which as usual, I did not distinctly mean to write."[45] During their lifetimes Howells was far more successful, in a worldly or professional sense, than James, and James was no pure, disinterested artist; he, too, courted wide popularity and influence and generally failed to win them. James, however, dedicated himself to a body of work which would and has come to be regarded, in most quarters, as "major." Howells did not, and he knew it.

As for the perhaps pernicious influence of Howellsian realism, we could easily exaggerate it. I have dealt with his critical ideas at such length not because they "caused" the problem of American realism but because Howells's career and critical writings provide an especially vivid example both of the problem and of its sources in the cultural circumstances of American literary vocation. Howells's specific influence was not only mainly beneficent but often notably generous (although, as we will see in some of our discussions of later writers, this generosity was occasionally rather coercive). Howells helped find a public, after all, for many younger writers, most of whom we still value; and who else at the time could have fervently admired and championed both Henry James and Mark Twain? Even the fact that some of Howells's most distressing ideas keep recurring in definitions of realism framed by American literary historians, critics, and novelists is by no means entirely his fault, since these ideas were around long before he was, and they will keep sprouting up as long as received American wisdom assumes that art, however shocking or amusing, cannot be "real" on its own terms. *Criticism and Fiction* is important less because it was influential than because it is so nearly perfectly characteristic of an enduring body of American ideas about literature.

It is surely no coincidence that Howells came to associate realism with "masculine" normalcy, and to distinguish it from concern for "art," at a time when modern stereotypes of male sexual identity—rigidly differentiating "effeminate" homosexuality from "virile" heterosexuality—were being solidified into what sociologists call master status traits.[46] It was only ten years after Howells moved to New York to take on the "Editor's Study" that Oscar Wilde, the most notorious aesthete in the Anglo-American literary world, was imprisoned for homosexuality. Some of the younger American writers who followed in Howells's footsteps, notably Frank Norris and Jack London, would turn masculine realism into something like a parody, albeit an unwitting one, of the cult of virility, and it requires no great leap to get from Howells and his Boston mentors to a writer like Ernest Hemingway, with his compulsion to conceal "artistic" sensitivity and true concern for style under a near-burlesque exterior of aggressive masculinity. One might note, too, the tendency of those twentieth-century attacks on Howells that accuse him of having been *insufficiently* realistic to present *him* in "feminine" terms—for example, Sinclair Lewis's declaration, in his 1930 Nobel Prize address, that Howells "had the code of a pious old maid whose greatest delight was to have tea at the vicarage."[47] But to be a "realist" in Lewis's sense was finally not essentially different from being a "realist" in Howells's sense. To claim to be a "realist," in late nineteenth- and early twentieth-century America, was among other things to suppress worries about one's sexuality and sexual status and to proclaim oneself a man; no wonder Howells portrayed a military hero, General Ulysses S. Grant, as a literary (or, to speak more precisely, anti-"literary") exemplar.

But this version of literary "realism," while it surely gained much of its intensity from such things as the increasingly brutal regulation of "homosexual" identity in the later nineteenth century, was not itself particularly new; in one form or another these ideas about literature, style, and gender had been current, in American literary discourse, for a long time. Thus in his preface to *Psalterium Americanum* (1718), his blank verse translation of the Psalms, Cotton Mather insists that "tho' the *Hymns* have not the Trifle of *Rhime*, as a Lace to set them off, yet they are *all Glorious within*, which is the thing that *Manly Christianity* has its eye most upon." The main elements of the Boston compromise, and of the Hemingway "code" for that matter, have a considerable ancestry. Ultimately, of course, the anti-"artistic" bias of American realism could be traced back to St. Augustine and Plato, but, confining ourselves to this side of the Atlantic, we can find this bias in the first book issued in the American colonies, *The Bay Psalm Book* (1640). "Gods Altar," proclaims Cotton Mather's grandfather, John Cotton, in his preface to these translations, "needs not our pollishings"—which is why, he explains, attention has been paid in the translation of the Psalms to "fidelity rather then poetry."[48] We keep finding substitutes for "Gods Altar" in Cotton's famous formulation: Jefferson's "real businesses of life," Howells's "world of men's activities"—always, in one form or another, "reality." But as long as art is equated with Cotton Mather's "Lace," or with his grandfather's "pollishing," we are likely to have a realism rather similar to that elaborated by Howells in *Criticism and Fiction*. As long as art seems a sin not only to the writer's audience but to the writer, American realism will continue to be a problem.

Humor, Sentiment, Realism

MARK TWAIN

"Tolstoy awakens in his reader the will to be a man; not effectively, not spectacularly, but simply, really."
William Dean Howells, *My Literary Passions* (1895)

"A king is a mere artificiality, and so a king's feelings . . . are mere artificialities; but as a man, he is a reality, and his feelings, as a man, are real, not phantoms. . . .
"The fact is, the king was a good deal more than a king, he was a man; and when a man is a man, you can't knock it out of him."
Mark Twain, *A Connecticut Yankee in King Arthur's Court* (1889)

"He was getting up his last 'effect,' but he never finished it."
A Connecticut Yankee in King Arthur's Court

Mark Twain is one of the half-dozen or dozen "major" American writers: on this much there is almost universal agreement. But attempt to go farther and consensus rapidly breaks down. Given the near u-nanimity about Twain's stature, there is surprisingly little agreement about the nature of his achievement, about the characteristic qualities in his work that *make* him major. The terms of disagreement crystal-lized early in the history of Twain criticism—in Van Wyck Brooks's *The Ordeal of Mark Twain* (1920) and Bernard DeVoto's *Mark Twain's America* (1932). According to Brooks, Twain was essentially a "serious" writer, a "born, predestined artist" who was unfortunately seduced into humor by social pressure and a desire for fame. Twain's "impulse," Brooks writes, "was not that of the 'humorist'; it was that of the satirist," and "the making of the humorist was the undoing of the artist." For DeVoto, by contrast, Twain's essential gift was precisely that of the "humorist." "Clemens's earliest impulses," he writes, "led to the production of humor and nothing whatever suggests any literary impulse or desire of any other kind." Brooks's and DeVoto's positions have been considerably modified by subsequent critics, but these critics still divide between proponents of the serious Twain—the satirist, social critic, and moralist—and proponents of Twain the humorist. Moreover, from Brooks and DeVoto to the present, critics who have promoted one facet of Twain's genius as essential have mostly blamed the opposite facet for impeding or subverting his development. Thus while champions of the serious Twain tend, like Brooks, to deplore any humor that cannot be explained in terms of satirical purpose, champions of the humorist generally see impulses to *seriousness* as regrettable lapses.[1]

On one matter, however, these opposed critical camps seem to be in agreement: Mark Twain, readers of both persuasions assure us, was a "realist."[2] His closest literary friend, after all, was William Dean Howells, and Howells's ideas, at least at first glance, would seem to be quite pertinent to Twain's fiction. Think, for instance, of Howells's famous rallying cry in *Criticism and Fiction*:

Let fiction cease to lie about life; let it portray men and women as they are, actuated by the motives and the passions in the measure we all know; let it leave off painting dolls and working them by springs and wires; let it show the different interests in their true proportions; let it forbear to preach pride and revenge, folly and insanity, egotism and prejudice, but frankly own these for what they are, in whatever figures and occasions they appear; let it not put on fine literary airs; let it speak the dialect, the language, that most Americans know—the language of unaffected people everywhere—and there can be no doubt of an unlimited future, not only of delightfulness but of usefulness, for it.[3]

Like Howells, we have been assured, Mark Twain turned from the artifice of "springs and wires" to the portrayal of "men and women as they are." Does not the Grangerford episode in *Huckleberry Finn* show the horror of "pride and revenge"? Do not Huck's growing love and respect for Jim reveal the horror of "prejudice"? And there is Twain's justly celebrated development of vernacular, especially in *Huckleberry Finn;* what other post–Civil War American writer managed better to "speak the dialect"?

As I have said, Mark Twain's supposed realism is about the only quality in his work on which the schools of Brooks and DeVoto can agree. According to DeVoto, for example, the tradition of newspaper humor to which Twain turned at the beginning of his career "was the first vigorous realism in American literature," and "Twain's books are the culmination not only of the literature's humor but of its realism as well." According to readers of Brooks's persuasion, on the other hand, it is Twain's satirical *seriousness* that is fundamentally realistic, so that an innate inclination to realism is, in their view, what Twain's cultivation of humor unfortunately *suppressed*. "In addition to, and in spite of, his humorous bent," Theodore Dreiser wrote in 1935, Twain "was a realist at heart"; "in his soberer moods [he] was always the realist."[4] Of course, the main reason DeVoto and Dreiser can agree about Twain's "realism" is that they mean quite different things by the term, and in this respect they are quite typical of those who have stressed Twain's connection to the supposed tradition of American realism. For the most part, the adjective "realistic" has simply been attached to whatever qualities, serious or humorous, a particular reader happens to find in Twain's fiction.[5] We also have been assured, however, that Mark Twain *thought* of himself as a realist, that he was a realist not only in practice but in principle. Twain's pronouncements on literature—his insistence on clear writing, his attacks on "romantic" sloppiness—have thus generally been seen as the pronouncements of a realist opponent of "fine literary airs." Given the vagueness of "realism" as a descriptive term, at least as it has been applied to Twain, we might do well to begin our consideration of Twain's classification as a realist with his critical writings. Just what are the ideas that emerge from these writings? And what relationship do these ideas bear to the assumptions of American realist thinking—especially as that thinking was expressed by Twain's close friend Howells?

Mark Twain as Critic

It must be admitted at the outset that Mark Twain's ideas about literature are more than a little difficult to fix with any certainty. His pronouncements on these matters, as on so many others, are generally so laced with irony and humor as to leave his actual opinions in considerable doubt; and unlike his contemporaries, Howells and Henry James, Twain wrote little formal criticism, certainly no declaration of literary principles on the order of James's "The Art of Fiction" or Howells's *Criticism and Fiction*. Instead, Twain produced a few occasional essays, pieces like "How to Tell a Story" (1894), "What Paul Bourget Thinks of Us" (1895), "Fenimore Cooper's Literary

Offenses" (1895), or—to cite a rare instance of literary *appreciation*—
"William Dean Howells" (1906).[6] Mostly, Twain's literary opinions
must be sifted out of his letters, his notebooks, or the much-discussed
passages in his travel books and fiction burlesquing or satirizing romance and the Old Masters. The first notable fact about this body of
criticism is its fragmentary, incomplete, and occasional nature. Unlike
Howells and James, Twain apparently did not need or want to write
sustained manifestos about the nature and purpose of the art of fiction,
and for this reason, if for no other, he would stand apart from the
so-called realists who rose to prominence in the 1880s.

Twain's literary opinions have been tied to realism because they
seem to be based on an ingrained hostility toward romantic literature,
toward art or writing derived from outworn tradition and cliché rather
than from observation and experience. He complained to Howells in
1892, for instance, that Bret Harte "is as blind as a bat. He never sees
anything correctly, except California scenery." Twain's favorite targets
for such abuse were Sir Walter Scott and James Fenimore Cooper.
"Can you read [Scott] and keep your respect for him?" he asked Brander Matthews in a 1902 letter. "Of course a person could in *his* day—an
era of sentimentality & sloppy romantics—but land! can a body do it
to-day?"[7] And Cooper's "literary offenses," according to Twain, included above all violations of probability and failures of observation.
With such overt statements in mind, critics have read much of Twain's
burlesque humor—the attacks on the Old Masters in *The Innocents
Abroad*, the vapid sentimentality of Emmeline Grangerford's verses
and crayon drawings in *Huckleberry Finn*, the burlesques of Malory and
others in *A Connecticut Yankee in King Arthur's Court*—as involving, at
bottom, a declaration of realist principle. Such critics also point to the
qualities Twain singles out for praise in works he admires. Especially
notable, as an index of his preferences, are the terms in which he expressed his career-long admiration for Howells. "It is all such truth,"
he wrote to his friend in 1879, praising his most recent novel, "—truth
to the life; everywhere your pen falls it leaves a photograph"; and this
metaphor keeps recurring. Of a character in another Howells novel
Twain wrote in 1883: "You have photographed him accurately." Of one
of Howells's autobiographical volumes he wrote in 1890: it "is perfect—perfect as the perfectest photograph the sun ever made."[8] The
realistic photograph was apparently the proper alternative to the dis-
tortions of the Old Masters, to "sentimentality & sloppy romantics."

Yet does all this, as we have so often been assured, in fact add up to
even an implicit theory of, or manifesto for, literary realism? We
should recognize, for one thing, that most of Twain's overt literary

criticism is devoted not to a discrimination of literary kinds or modes (the novel, say, as opposed to the romance) but to a more simple distinction between good and bad writing, of whatever kind or mode; most of what he says about fiction suggests less the manifesto than the advice manual for fledgling authors. For instance, most of the eighteen "rules governing literary art" listed in "Fenimore Cooper's Literary Offenses" involve strictures of this technical variety—particularly the last seven, requiring that the author shall

12. *Say* what he is proposing to say, not merely come near it.
13. Use the right word, not its second cousin.
14. Eschew surplusage.
15. Not omit necessary details.
16. Avoid slovenliness of form.
17. Use good grammar.
18. Employ a simple and straightforward style.

Even the first eleven rules—calling for believable and interesting action and character, and for dialogue resembling human speech and consistently appropriate to the characters who speak it—hardly depart from the genre of the practical literary handbook.[9] All of this, of course, may be good advice, but that it is good advice hardly means that it therefore constitutes an implicit theory of literary realism, or any sort of theory at all.

Twain's taste in fiction is revealed nowhere more clearly than in a well-known letter to Howells, written in 1885, celebrated for its opening praise of the recipient ("You are really my only author") and for its closing, picturesque dismissal of Henry James's *The Bostonians* ("I would rather be damned to John Bunyan's heaven than read that"). What makes this letter interesting, as a kind of touchstone of Twain's critical principles, is the way it gets from the praise of Howells to the dismissal of James:

> You are really my only author; I am restricted to you; I wouldn't give a damn for the rest. I bored through Middlemarch during the past week, with its labored & tedious analyses of feelings & motives, & its paltry & tiresome people, its unexciting & uninteresting story, & its frequent blinding flashes of single-sentence poetry, philosophy, wit, & what-not, & nearly died from the over-work. . . .
> Well, you have done it [that is, recreated experience—the reference being to Howells's most recent novel] with marvelous facility—& you make all the motives & feelings perfectly clear without analyzing the guts out of them, the way George Eliot does. I can't stand George Eliot, & Hawthorne & those people; I see what they are at, a hundred years before they get to it, & they just

tire me death. And as for the Bostonians, I would rather be damned to John
Bunyan's heaven than read that.[10]

Except for the fact that there is less fun in it, this attack on Eliot,
Hawthorne, and James has a good deal in common with the attack on
Cooper published ten years later: Twain considers all of these writers,
ultimately, "labored & tedious." This letter, however, is hardly a condemnation of romance by a realist; Eliot and James, after all, were
among Howells's *favorite* realists. Moreover, what bothers Twain about
Eliot, Hawthorne, and James (and his sense of their common ground
is in fact quite perceptive) is not that they indulge in "sentimentality &
sloppy romantics" but that they engage in extended psychological
analysis—which is surely a property of a good deal of fiction that has
been described as "realistic." The reason Twain admires Howells, by
contrast, is that Howells *avoids* such analysis; this is the essence of his
economy, his "marvelous facility."[11] Finally, and perhaps most important, Twain detests analysis not because it is unrealistic but because it
is—to use a word dear to modern undergraduates—*boring:* "labored &
tedious," "unexciting & uninteresting"; "they just tire me to death."
We may or may not agree with Twain's taste, but we had better in any
case recognize it for what it is; and if we simply invert his terms of
condemnation we can see clearly just what he values: "facility," economy as a relief from tedium, surprise as opposed to the elaboration of
the expected, clarity as opposed to complexity, characters who are
"interesting" rather than "paltry & tiresome"—above all, "excitement." If these are the values of a realist the author of the present
study is the father of the late Dauphin. If anything, and always keeping
in mind the crudeness of the celebrated distinction between the (realistic) novel and the romance, these are the values of a writer who
always preferred romance—provided, of course, that it generate "interest" and "excitement" while obeying the "rules governing literary
art in the realm of romantic fiction."[12]

I am not concerned here with the question of whether Mark
Twain's fiction is or is not realistic. For the moment I am concerned
instead with the quite different question of whether the position set
forth in his scattered critical writings is, as has so often been supposed,
that of a realist, in any meaningful sense of that term. And my answer
would be, simply: No, it is not. We also ought to note that in his
occasional criticism Twain never, in fact, uses the word "realism," not
even in his letters to Howells, and not even after Howells began, in
1886, to publicize the term. For instance, in an 1889 letter to Howells, Twain is full of praise for the "Editor's Study" essays in which the

campaign for realism was being conducted. "I am waiting," he writes, "to see your Study set a fashion in criticism. When that happens—as please God it must—consider that if you lived three centuries you couldn't do a more valuable work for this country, or a humaner." Here, if anywhere, one expects some comment about Howells's *ideas*, his ideas about the need for literary realism. Instead, Twain proceeds to praise not the substance of Howells's dissent but his manner of presenting it, his "courteously reasoning" rather than "lecturing."[13] Nor, finally, does the term "realism" appear in the appreciation of Howells's achievement Twain wrote for *Harper's* in 1906. The absence of this term from Twain's critical vocabulary, even at a time when his closest literary friend was making it the rallying cry of the American literary vanguard, ultimately has the force of a deliberate avoidance, and it seems likely that Twain avoided the term because he knew that whatever a "realist" was, he was not one. Howells, after all, consistently praised Eliot and James, and especially Jane Austen, as realists; Twain, whether he understood the term or not, just as consistently abused these very writers.[14] Perhaps, then, we ought to take him at his word—or, to speak more precisely, at his refusal to use Howells's word. Henry James, I noted in the previous chapter, subjected Howellsian realism to penetrating criticism. Mark Twain—perhaps out of personal loyalty, maybe because he just didn't like literary theory—never took issue with his friend's ideas, but he no more embraced these ideas than James did; he merely, it would seem, ignored them. Thus it simply will not do to imagine that Twain's scattered critical writings reveal a realist in principle. The case for his connection to the tradition of American realism, if it is to rest anywhere, must rest somewhere else than on his overt literary opinions.

We can only speculate about why Mark Twain, unlike Howells, might not have *needed* the label "realist." They were both fiction writers, after all, as well as contemporaries and close friends, and the circumstances of Samuel Clemens's early years were in many respects strikingly similar to the circumstances in which young Will Howells grew up.[15] Clemens was born in 1835, two years before Howells, just after his family's move from Tennessee to Florida, Missouri; the move to Hannibal would take place when Sam was four. The Clemenses, like the Howellses, moved frequently within the Western provinces, in quest of that elusive prosperity which, like Gatsby's green light, receded year by year before them. In its main outlines, the culture of small-town Missouri was not all that different from the culture of small-town Ohio, and like Will Howells, Sam Clemens was apparently as a child something of an outsider. Born prematurely, he was for four years delicate and sickly, again recalling Howells, and he suffered from somnambulism and from strong feelings of irrational guilt. It is all too easy to exaggerate or romanticize Clemens's early alienation, and nothing about his life is murkier than the record of his childhood, especially his early childhood, but it is nevertheless clear that he did not, at first, "fit in"; at least he did not think he did, and this worried him. The obsessive symptom of this concern was, and remained, an extraordinary propensity for guilty self-accusation. Samuel Clemens would come to blame himself, among other things, for his father's death in 1847 (which led to the most famous episode of somnambulism), for the death of his brother Henry in 1858 (in a steamboat accident), for the death of his infant son Langdon in 1872 (Clemens took him out in cold weather), for his favorite daughter Susy's death in 1896 (he was on a worldwide lecture tour, trying to make a comeback from his bankruptcy), and—over many years, and with rather better reason—for the erosion of his wife's religious faith. As Albert Bigelow Paine writes, "Remorse was always Samuel Clemens's surest punishment."[16]

But what, one wonders, was it punishment *for*? "Why," as Van Wyck Brooks asks, "those continual fits of remorse, those fantastic self-accusations?"[17] There can be no certain answer to this question, but Clemens's extravagant fantasies of guilt would seem to suggest an equally extravagant sense of alienation and aggression; he was capable of feeling responsible when *anybody* died.[18] Behind the guilt, one suspects, lurked a profound and quite broadly directed sense of hostility, established (for whatever reason) quite early. Clemens would soon learn to channel this hostility into humor, and he would eventually rationalize (or at any rate publicize) it by labeling all of humankind the "damned human race." But what matters for the moment is that young Sam Clemens apparently felt at least as alienated from society as did his near contemporary, Will Howells. He would later even remember, incorrectly, that when his family moved from Florida to Hannibal, in his fourth year, they left him behind.[19] But while Will Howells turned early to literature as a refuge from "the world of men's activities," Sam Clemens never did anything of the sort. He did not turn to literature to confirm his marginality, and in fact he did not turn to literature at all. He overcame his sense of marginality, rather, in the manner prescribed by the norms of his culture: he did not retreat into the refuge of "literature" but instead entered "the world of men's activities"—or, first of all, the world of boys' activities. By 1844, Paine writes, "he had acquired health, with a sturdy ability to look out for himself"; the formerly "delicate little lad," by the time he was nine, "could swim better than any boy in town his own age."[20] However alienated Sam Clemens may have felt as a child, his early alienation did not lead him in his early years to a sense of "artistic" or "literary" identity; he became, instead, one of the boys.

By the time he had mastered the craft of the Mississippi riverboat pilot, in the later 1850s, Samuel Clemens had clearly become one of the men. Van Wyck Brooks argues that Clemens was a "born, pre-destined artist," that "the life of a Mississippi pilot had, in some special way, satisfied the instinct of the artist in him,"[21] but one wonders about a psychological system based on "artistic" instincts and "pre-destined artists," and there is in any case simply no evidence that the Samuel Clemens of 1860 thought of himself as anything like what his culture called an "artist."[22] In 1865, we recall, William Dean Howells, newly returned from Italy, chose a literary career over a future in journalism. Clemens, by contrast, came to writing *through* journalism. Is it any wonder, then, that Mark Twain felt no need for the identity of "realist" and that, whether through disinclination or through incomprehension, he kept his distance from Howells's campaign for literary realism?

But there are still other ways in which we might pursue our consideration of Mark Twain's supposed relationship to Howellsian realism. If he was not a Howellsian realist in overt principle—as he most surely was not, and as he apparently had no personal need to be—might we not argue that he was a realist *in practice*? I do not mean by this that his fiction might be described as realistic; it certainly might be, but as I have already noted, the term is so flexible as to deprive such a description of any precise meaning, and it has mainly allowed critics to describe as "realistic" just about any quality they happen to admire in Twain. What I mean, rather, is that we might look in Twain's fiction for some sort of *implicit* declaration of realist principles, of affinities with what I have been calling realist thinking. While it is true that in his occasional criticism Twain mainly abuses or ignores the preferences and principles of his friend Howells, it is still possible that the values at work in his novels are the values of a realist and that *this* is what might establish his connection to the tradition of Howellsian realism.

Adventures of Huckleberry Finn

Howellsian realism, we have seen, is less a theoretical idea than an ideological construct. At its center stand two fundamental, and fundamentally related, ideas. First of all, the task of literature is defined almost wholly in moral terms; the proper role of the writer (which is

what, most basically, Howellsian realism is about) is understood almost entirely in terms of his *responsibility* to society. "The art which . .
. disdains the office of teacher," Howells writes in the final paragraph
of *Criticism and Fiction*, "is one of the last refuges of the aristocratic
spirit which is disappearing from politics and society, and is now
seeking to shelter itself in aesthetics. . . . Democracy in literature is the
reverse of all this."[23] The second essential component of Howellsian
realism grows directly out of the first: the realist exercises social
responsibility, first of all, by discrediting what is *irresponsible*—the
"romantic," the "literary," the "artificial," the merely "artistic."

How relevant is all this to *Huckleberry Finn*? Deferring for the
moment Howells's primary definition of the realist in terms of social
responsibility, his emphasis on the need to discredit the artificial and
literary would seem to have an obvious and important relevance to
Huckleberry Finn—which, like so many of Twain's novels and travel
books, is filled with burlesques of romantic or artificial art and literature. Again and again, in the course of his journey down the Mississippi, Huck Finn encounters frauds whose addiction to outworn styles
has led to complete abandonment of common sense and often to
things much worse. Huck's story begins and ends with the efforts of
Tom Sawyer, for whom "style" is everything, to import the exoticism
and excitement of romance into the mundane world of the antebellum
South, and Tom is hardly unique. Emmeline Grangerford's clichéd
crayon drawings and obituary verses are beautifully burlesqued, and
her family's suicidal prosecution of its feud with the Shepherdsons, in
the name of some dimly understood conception of honor, seems to
foreshadow Howells's dire warnings about the dangers of the "aristocratic spirit." So do the pretensions of the self-proclaimed Duke and
Dauphin, whose butchery of Shakespeare, in the Royal Nonesuch,
once again underlines the apparent connection between bogus aristocracy and bogus style.

Huck responds to such romantic excesses with deadpan common
sense. He subjects Tom's claims—for instance, that a group of children
is a band of Arabs, or that genies may be summoned by rubbing lamps
(because "all the authorities" say so)—to the test of practical experience:

I got an old tin lamp and an iron ring and went out in the woods and rubbed
and rubbed till I sweat like an Injun, calculating to build a palace and sell it;
but it warn't no use, none of the genies come. So then I judged that all that
stuff was only just one of Tom Sawyer's lies. I reckoned he believed in the
A-rabs and the elephants, but as for me I think different. It had all the marks
of a Sunday school. (17)[24]

As important as the apparent realism of Huck's experimental method here (or the realistic prudence of planning to sell the summoned castle) is the vernacular language in which he describes his experiment and his conclusions: "old tin lamp," "iron ring," "sweat like an Injun," "all that stuff." Such phrases inevitably deflate the romantic discourse with which "Tom Sawyer's lies" strive to legitimize themselves. A similar effect, to cite one more example, is produced by Huck's description of Emmeline Grangerford's sentimental drawings:

They was different from any pictures I ever see before; blacker, mostly, than is common. One was a woman in a slim black dress, belted small under the arm-pits, with bulges like a cabbage in the middle of the sleeves, and a large black scoop-shovel bonnet with a black veil, and white slim ankles crossed about with black tape, and very wee black slippers, like a chisel, and she was leaning pensive on a tombstone on her right elbow, under a weeping willow, and her other hand hanging down her side holding a white handkerchief and a reticule, and underneath the picture it said "Shall I Never See Thee More Alas." . . . These was all nice pictures, I reckon, but I didn't somehow seem to take to them, because if ever I was down a little, they always give me the fan-tods. (84)

Once again, the vernacular diction—"arm-pits," "cabbage," "chisel," "fan-tods"—discredits Emmeline's artificial, literary discourse.

While these examples are quite typical of the antiliterary, antiromantic burlesque that recurs throughout *Huckleberry Finn*, one might still wonder whether such burlesque necessarily serves the purposes of anything like Howellsian realism—whether it expresses anything like Howells's understanding of the moral function of literature. To what extent, for instance, are Tom Sawyer's "style" or Emmeline Grangerford's bathetic clichés mocked for being *irresponsible*? Or, to put the same question in a more interesting way, to what extent does Huck's much-discussed vernacular honesty express a Howellsian conception of *responsibility*? According to many readers of *Huckleberry Finn*, Huck's burlesques of "sentimentality & sloppy romantics" *are* ultimately based on a sense of responsibility; Huck's vernacular, in their view, is not simply a humorous device, undercutting the pretension it so neutrally describes, but a repository of positive moral value. Indeed, the notion that vernacular values lie at the heart of *Huckleberry Finn* has long been central to serious readings of the book, and especially to arguments that its achievement is tied significantly to the supposed tradition of American realism.[25]

The trouble with such readings, in addition to their apparent identification of Twain's values with Huck's, is that they ultimately distort Huck's character and behavior and even the nature of many of the targets of his humor. Although Tom Sawyer and the Duke and the Dauphin may be irresponsible, even to the point of cruelty, this is hardly the case with Emmeline Grangerford, for instance, who is simply ridiculous. More to the point, Huck himself, while he learns to avoid cruelty to others, notably Jim, is in all other respects most characteristically *irresponsible;* he does not seek to change society but repeatedly flees it—for the raft, where life is "free and easy and comfortable" (96), or, at the close, "for the Territory ahead of the rest" (229). And even when his voice functions as a burlesque or satirical device, Huck himself is mainly passive, seldom acknowledging in his own proper character the message implicit in his vernacular utterance. Thus Huck does not contest Tom's own belief in the "A-rabs"; his skepticism is merely personal ("but as for me I think different"); and even as he confesses his inability to "take to" Emmeline's drawings, Huck accepts the social judgment that they "was all nice pictures."

Even in chapter 31, when Huck tears up the letter that would send Jim back into slavery, the moral importance of his decision does not—at least for Huck—take the form of anything like Howellsian responsibility. "'All right, then,'" he proclaims, "'I'll *go* to hell.' . . . I shoved the whole thing out of my head; and said I would take up wickedness again, which was in my line, being brung up to it, and the other warn't" (169–70). While Huck rejects the course of behavior dictated by society, he does not dismiss society's valuation of this rejection; his decision remains for him a form of "wickedness," just as Emmeline's drawings remain "nice pictures." However much *we* may applaud Huck's behavior, he himself never takes overt *responsibility* for the moral superiority of his vernacular values; unlike the Howellsian realist, he never embraces "the office of the teacher." One might object, of course, that I am making too much of Huck's irresponsibility, that I am forgetting that *Huckleberry Finn* is, after all, a work of irony and humor, but this possible objection is really my point. The moral assumptions implicit in Huck's ironic humor (or in Twain's use of Huck for the purposes of ironic humor) are a far cry from the assumptions that form the basis of Howells's thinking about literary realism.

In this connection we should attend to the terms in which James Cox has brilliantly dissented from morally serious readings of Twain's humor. Cox states quite succinctly, for instance, the point I have just been trying to make: that, as he puts it, "since Huck's entire identity is based upon an inverted order of values . . . , he cannot have any recognition of his own virtue." Cox's main argument, however, rests on a

general consideration of the essential nature and function of "burlesque" humor, as opposed to "satire." "Criticism," he writes, "is not
so much the end as the means of burlesque. The end of burlesque must
be entertainment"—so that "although much of Mark Twain's burlesque has its roots in indignation, it moves the reader not toward guilt
but toward a laughter arising from recognition of the absurdity of the
world; and the laughter is not an acceptance of, or a guilt toward, but
a relief *from* responsibility." Turning to *Huckleberry Finn*, Cox insists
that "any 'positive' value we may wish to ascribe to the experience of
reading it" must depend upon "the logic of pleasure at the heart of the
book," whereas "most criticism of *Huckleberry Finn* . . . retreats from
the pleasure principle toward the relative safety of 'moral issues' and
the imperatives of the Northern conscience."[26] While Cox's argument
is inevitably oversimplified by so brief a summary, and while his approach remains controversial, it is nevertheless clear that an understanding of his approach at least problematizes the notion that Twain's
humor, in *Huckleberry Finn*, serves a serious satirical purpose.

There is a good deal of antisocial violence in Mark Twain's humor,
but to acknowledge its presence is hardly to establish that it operates
as social criticism. What Cox says about the Nevada sketches is true of
many of Twain's jokes: "all of them . . . were relatively direct ways of
discharging aggression."[27] "Discharging" is the key term here: extravagant humor, like extravagantly guilty self-accusation, was a means
of defusing or displacing anger, of turning it into "fun," as Twain well
knew. Sam Clemens apparently learned this lesson early, and its importance was personal long before it was literary. Paine tells the story,
for instance, of Clemens's 1854 return to his family, by then living in
Muscatine, Iowa, and depending now on the hopeless quest for prosperity of Sam's older brother, Orion. Sam had left the family a year
before, at the age of eighteen, to seek employment and experience in
the East. He had had to go; Orion, for whom he had been working as
a typesetter, had been unable to pay his wages and had refused him
even the money to buy a gun. So Sam arrived in Muscatine a year
later, unannounced; the family was at breakfast; Sam entered, carrying
a rifle he had purchased with money earned on his own, in the East.
Paine describes the scene:

"You wouldn't let me buy a gun," [Sam] said, "so I bought one myself, and I
am going to use it now, in self-defense."
  "You, Sam! You, Sam!" cried Jane Clemens [his mother]. "Behave yourself," for she was wary of a gun.
  Then he had had his joke and gave himself into his mother's arms.[28]

Some "joke," we might remark; the hostility and aggression are pain-fully clear. But what matters most is that, once the joke had worked, Sam Clemens "gave himself into his mother's arms," and jokes like this *kept* working. In 1863 Samuel Clemens confirmed his dedication to humor by adopting "Mark Twain" as his nom de plume; a short time thereafter—through the Eastern success of the "Jumping Frog" in 1865, and especially through the success of *The Innocents Abroad* in 1869—he gave himself, as it were, into the arms of America. Aggression openly proclaimed, Herman Melville discovered in the 1850s, led to popular oblivion. Aggression displaced or discharged into humor, Samuel Clemens discovered in the same decade, was aggression con-trolled; and in the 1860s, as Mark Twain, he discovered that it could capture the very audience Melville had lost as well as the prosperity Clemens's father and brother had failed to find. In these linked discov-eries lay the foundation of Mark Twain's literary identity.

Twain's humor, Cox writes, "arises from the art of exploiting the discrepancy between futile illusion—not merely his own, but those of society and history—and 'reality.'" So far this sounds more or less compatible with Howells's realist program, but we should pay atten-tion to the quotation marks around the key term "reality." "The humorist's creative role," Cox continues, "lay in inventing a 'reality' which would define the inadequacy of the given traditions, clichés, and illusions." In Twain's writing, as in Howells's program, "reality" indeed undercuts "literary" or "romantic" preconception; but, as Cox puts it, "the 'reality' which deflates the expectation is clearly not actuality, but an extravagant invention which, poised against the clichés, displaces them."[29] Once again, this is a far cry from the assumptions of Twain's friend Howells, for whom the essence of "real-ity," as guarantor of social responsibility, was that it was *not* invention.

Cox is mainly concerned with the claims made for the serious or satirical purpose of Huck's vernacular humor, and the production of humor is not, of course, the only function of this vernacular—nor even, perhaps, its most important function. The passages in *Huckle-berry Finn* that one remembers and rereads with the greatest fondness are probably not those devoted to burlesque deflation but those de-voted to sincere description and emotional expression, to the recrea-tion of feeling. The most memorable accomplishments of Huck's vernacular, this is to say, involve not the deflation but the *evocation* of sentiment. Think, for instance, of the description of a river dawn that opens chapter 19, coming just after Huck's and Jim's escape from the Grangerford-Shepherdson feud:

Two or three days and nights went by; I reckon I might say they swum by, they slid along so quiet and smooth and lovely. . . . Not a sound, anywheres—perfectly still—just like the whole world was asleep, only sometimes the bull-frogs a-cluttering, maybe. The first thing to see, looking away over the water, was a kind of dull line—that was the woods on t'other side—you couldn't make nothing else out; then a pale place in the sky; then more paleness, spreading around; then the river softened up, away off, and warn't black any more, but gray; you could see little dark spots drifting along, ever so far away—trading scows, and such things; and long black streaks—rafts.(96)

This passage is suffused with a combination of emotional contentment and imagistic precision; it is even impressionistic, if you will, in its insistence on perception ("a kind of dull line," "little dark spots drifting along," "long black streaks") preceding "objective" interpretation and naming ("the woods on t'other side," "trading scows, and such things," "rafts"). It would no doubt be plausible to describe such writing as realistic; one can certainly understand why Twain's prose in *Huckleberry Finn* mattered to Ernest Hemingway—who himself strove, as he put it, to get onto the page "the real thing, the sequence of motion and fact which made the emotion."[30] Still, this is a realism of vision and emotion, not of principle and action; such descriptions always occur, in *Huckleberry Finn*, in moments of respite from action, moments of "comfort," when no moral choices need to be made. It is surely significant that Huck is most open to impressions when he is completely free of responsibility: "free and easy and comfortable on a raft" (139). The "realism" of such descriptions, however we may wish to define it, has as little to do with Howellsian responsibility as does Huck's humor.

So it is still the case that if we wish to find some connection between the implicit values of *Huckleberry Finn* and the assumptions underlying Howellsian realism we must continue to look elsewhere—not only beyond Twain's explicit literary opinions but beyond, as well, both his humorous and evocative uses of vernacular—and the field of inquiry might seem, by now, to be rather hopelessly constricted. But one other area might still be explored. Among other things *Huckleberry Finn* is, or at least might appear to be, a novel of education, a story of its narrator's moral development. From his complicity in the effort to defraud the Wilks girls, from his similar complicity in Tom's cruel game of "freeing" Jim, and especially from his own earlier discovery of his ability to care for Jim, Huck would seem to learn something about love and kindness; he would seem to grow, and *Huckleberry Finn* would seem to be the story of this growth. How, then, might we compare what Huck learns or becomes to the values associated, by Howells, with literary realism?

Early in Howells's *A Hazard of New Fortunes* (1890), the complacency of Basil and Isabel March, who are in the process of moving from Boston to New York, begins to be upset by the harsh realities of Manhattan slum life and by the fact that they can only view these realities as spectators, from the outside. "The time had been," we are told, "when the Marches would have taken a purely aesthetic view of the facts as they glimpsed them in this street of tenement houses, when they would have contented themselves with saying that it was as picturesque as a street in Naples or Florence and with wondering why nobody came to paint it."[31] In the story that follows, the Marches are driven to seek some morally or politically serious alternative to their "aesthetic view" of urban poverty, and while it is far from clear that either of them ever finds it, their anxiety is important because it suggests a kind of paradigmatic plot implicit in realist thinking, at least in *Howells's* thinking about realism. The protagonist would move from irresponsibly aesthetic detachment to a position of morally and politically responsible realism, making the renunciation of the aesthetic itself a kind of badge of moral and political commitment. This admittedly ideal paradigmatic plot, with all its confusion of aesthetics and politics, matters because it crops up, again and again, in the fiction of Howells's contemporaries and immediate successors.[32] But how relevant is it to what happens in *Huckleberry Finn*?

My considered answer would have to be that it is not relevant at all. Huck Finn, for one thing, is not an aesthetic outsider (a status that depends at least as much on social class as on any specific devotion to things artistic); rather, in terms of the realist distinction between the (genteel) "aesthetic" and the (lower class) "real," he is very much an *insider*—part of that abstracted "reality" which people like the Marches, for instance, can only view from a distance. Moreover, since Huck, in Cox's phrase, "cannot have any recognition of his own virtue," since he never overtly recognizes his own moral superiority, he does not share the Marches's (and Howells's) *valuation* of the "real"; he is no spokesman, as are so many characters in realist or naturalist fiction, for "reality" as a moral or political norm. Finally, Huck's confrontation with the aesthetic views or pretensions of others (Tom Sawyer, Emmeline Grangerford, the Duke, and the Dauphin) has rather little to do with the story of his development or growth, and for a fairly simple reason. Already by the end of chapter 3, in a novel containing forty-three chapters, Huck has seen through "Tom Sawyer's lies"; unlike the Marches, he has nothing left, in this respect, to learn. What leads him to continue to participate in the "aesthetic" games of others—notably the Duke and the Dauphin, and, in the final episode, Tom Sawyer—is not a belief in their deceptions or self-deceptions but a varying mixture of fear, humility, and loneliness.

If we wish to understand the plot or action of *Huckleberry Finn* we need to distinguish, as serious or realist readers of the novel often fail to do, between Huck as a *device* (an ironic vehicle for Mark Twain's humor, or for expressing his opinions) and Huck as a *character*. And what moves Huck, the character, is neither a desire to escape a "purely aesthetic view" nor an impulse to expose aesthetic frauds. His primary motives are more personal and human, which is one of the reasons people still read *Huckleberry Finn*. Take, for instance, Huck's account of his reasons for participating in what he knows to be the ridiculous schemes of Tom Sawyer's gang. He recognizes that their "swords" are "only lath and broom-sticks," and he does not believe, in any case, that they "could lick such a crowd of Spaniards and A-rabs." "But," he adds, "I wanted to see the camels and elephants, so I was on hand next day" (16). Huck, this is to say, is *curious*. So, too, when Huck and Jim approach the sinking steamboat, the *Walter Scott*, Huck insists on boarding her, against Jim's strenuous objections: "I wanted to get aboard of her," he explains, "and slink around a little, and see what there was there" (57).

Huck soon mounts another argument for boarding the *Walter Scott*: "Do you reckon," he asks Jim, rhetorically, "Tom Sawyer would ever go by this thing?" (57) Again and again, to the dismay of serious readers, Huck seems to accept Tom's values; finally, at the Phelps farm, he even takes on Tom's name. Why, we have often asked, does Huck repeatedly adopt values he dismissed at the outset as "lies"? One answer would be that values (in the sense, for instance, of the realist distinction between the falsely literary and the genuinely human or "real") do not lie at the heart of Huck's story. Another answer appears in the book's opening chapter and suggests that behind even Huck's curiosity is a far deeper feeling. He is alone at night, in his room at Miss Watson's. "I set down in a chair by the window," he writes, "and tried to think of something cheerful, but it warn't no use. I felt so lonesome I most wished I was dead. . . . I got so down-hearted and scared, I did wish I had some company." It is at precisely this moment that Huck hears something "stirring" beneath his window. "I put out the light," he writes, "and scrambled out of the window onto the shed. Then I slipped down to the ground and crawled in amongst the trees, and sure enough there was Tom Sawyer waiting for me" (9). Huck's main reason for joining Tom is quite clear: he is lonely and frightened, and he wants distraction, companionship, friendship—ultimately, of course, love.

Jim, on Jackson's Island, is first of all Huck's replacement for Tom Sawyer. "I was ever so glad to see Jim," Huck writes. "I warn't lonesome, now" (38). And if Huck grows during the course of his story, he does so not because he is educated in "reality" (as opposed to the falsely aesthetic) but because he discovers, with Jim, the possibility of a love deeper than the distraction offered by Tom Sawyer's gang. This love involves responsibility, to be sure, but it is personal responsibility, not the sort of abstract social responsibility Howells would call for in *Criticism and Fiction*. Huck learns about personal responsibility when he betrays Jim's trust: when he puts a dead snake in Jim's bed in chapter 10, or when he pretends they were never separated by the fog in chapter 15. He learns even more from the moments, in chapter 16 and chapter 31, when he decides not to betray Jim. We might want to question the depth of Huck's love for Jim, since he often seems simply to forget about Jim when Jim is absent or presumed dead, but what matters here is that we recognize how little the story of Huck's growth in personal loyalty to Jim, in love for Jim, has to do with the assumptions of Howellsian realism, or with the paradigmatic plot implicit in these assumptions.

The much discussed problem of the ending of *Huckleberry Finn* is, most simply, that what happens at the Phelps farm seems to turn away from, or even to undermine, what Huck has experienced with Jim earlier; Huck's participation in Tom's cruel "evasion" seems an inexplicable betrayal of what Huck has already twice decided *not* to betray: his personal responsibility to Jim. I have no wish, here, to enter into the debate about whether the ending of *Huckleberry Finn* is or is not appropriate, but the dissatisfaction this ending has aroused in so many readers does indicate, once again, how irrelevant the literary ideals of William Dean Howells are to the achievement of Twain's novel. It is a nice paradox, for instance, that the ending perhaps especially troubles serious realist readers; for what happens in the final episode would seem to be what they should be looking for. Huck, the human character, is displaced once more by Huck the humorous device; it is on Huck's function as a device—on a serious, satirical reading of the novel's antiliterary burlesques—that the case for the realism of *Huckleberry Finn* is most often based; and what *is* this final episode if not a sustained (perhaps oversustained) antiliterary burlesque? That realist readers have nevertheless found the ending disappointing thus suggests that even *their* deepest response to the book has little to do with its supposed realism, with its burlesques of the romantic and literary. When Twain reverts, or seems to revert, to the distinction between life and literature, they too miss his earlier, powerful evocation of loneliness and love.

My overall point, in any event, is that the case for connecting *Huckleberry Finn* to the supposed tradition of American realism seems, at virtually every point, an exceptionally weak one, whether one is considering Twain's literary ideas, the function of burlesque humor in the novel, the effects of Huck's vernacular, or the book's plot or action. It might be objected, even granting this point, that to make the point at all appears to involve one in a curiously negative critical enterprise. Arguments about what *did* influence a writer, while they have a clear purpose, are often rather dry and pedantic; a person who argues about what did *not* influence a writer might seem to be maintaining the pedantic dryness while sacrificing the purpose. In fact, however, there are at least three lessons to be learned from recognizing the tenuousness of *Huckleberry Finn*'s relationship to the version of realism for which William Dean Howells was so fervent a spokesman. For one thing, this recognition might allow us to see our literary history with greater clarity, as something more complicated (and more interesting) than a series of homogenized, generational periods and movements; surely a term like "realist" ought to indicate something more important than the general dates of an author's career. Recognizing the fundamental irrelevance of Howellsian realism to *Huckleberry Finn* might also help us understand the specific achievement of this novel more clearly. In part, to be sure, this too is a rather negative enterprise, like clearing away an underbrush of accumulated preconception and misconception without ever quite getting to the positive task of exploring and appreciating the revealed terrain. Still, even this apparently negative enterprise has, in and of itself, a positive side; for to recognize the qualities in *Huckleberry Finn*—in its humor, its language, and its human action—that distinguish it from the dogmas of realism is already, after all, to describe some of the very qualities that make it the special sort of book it is.

The third lesson to be learned by disconnecting *Huckleberry Finn* from Howellsian realism has to do with the possibility such disconnection offers of clarifying our understanding of Mark Twain's development as a writer, and of the relationship of this development to the literary thinking of Twain's time. For it is not quite enough, in this context, simply to say that Twain was not a realist and to leave it at that. He may never have described himself as a "realist" or even have used the term, but it is still true that Howells was his close friend and that Twain read the "Editor's Study" essays faithfully from the time they began to appear in 1886. And Howells's ideas, however irrelevant they may be to *Huckleberry Finn*, *would* seem to be relevant to the first novel Twain published *after* Howells began his campaign for literary realism: *A Connecticut Yankee in King Arthur's Court*, which appeared in 1889. Twain's Yankee, unlike Huck Finn, repeatedly insists on the moral and political superiority of his own values, he openly attacks the romantic and literary, and he associates this attack, quite explicitly, with political reform. Is it any wonder that Howells thought *A Connecticut Yankee* the greatest of Twain's works and called it "an object-lesson in democracy"?[33]

A Connecticut Yankee in King Arthur's Court

"I am an American," Hank Morgan writes at the beginning of his story; ". . . I am a Yankee of the Yankees—and practical; yes, and nearly barren of sentiment, I suppose—or poetry, in other words" (8).[34] Henry Nash Smith has noted that this opening seems to echo the first sentence of Ulysses S. Grant's *Memoirs* (1885–86)—a book Twain published, and one with whose preparation for publication he was obsessed at the time he began *A Connecticut Yankee* in 1885.[35] Twain's novel climaxes in a spectacle of technological carnage—the Battle of the Sand Belt, with its grisly details and 25,000 casualties—and something like this violent catastrophe was apparently part of Twain's plan from the beginning; so the association of Hank with a general widely credited for having helped to invent the brutality of modern warfare should probably not surprise us.[36] But students of Mark Twain's relation to American realism might also recall that William Dean Howells lavishly praised Grant's *Memoirs* in the "Editor's Study" column of *Harper's* magazine (in an 1886 review reprinted in *Criticism and Fiction*)—as an alternative to "literary consciousness" and "style," to "preening and prettifying, after the fashion of literary men"—and they would likely think the most important aspect of Hank's self-introduction is his claim to be (like Howells's version of Grant) "practical," "nearly barren of sentiment . . . or poetry, in other words." For here, surely, we would seem to get what we do not get in *Huckleberry Finn*: a fictional embodiment of the "realist," a "real" man of practical attainments, who disdains literary falsehood and who therefore, to recall Howells's terms, champions "democracy in literature" in its struggle against the "aristocratic spirit" embedded in "pride of taste."[37] This shift raises two important (or at least interesting) questions. What, first of all, is the relationship between Hank's realism and the extraordinary violence of his ultimate confrontation with King Arthur's

Court—why is his campaign for realism like the American Civil War? And, second, what is the relationship between Hank's realism and what most readers have seen as the ultimate incoherence of his attack on Arthurian England?

In one sense, the answer to the first of these questions is pretty simple: Twain's attacks on such things as the "sentimentality & sloppy romantics" of Sir Walter Scott had always tended to be violent. For instance, in *Life on the Mississippi* (1883), Twain blames the bogus medievalism of the Louisiana State Capitol on the "debilitating influence" of Scott's "medieval romances," on Southern "admiration of [Scott's] fantastic heroes and their grotesque 'chivalry' doings," and this complaint leads to an expression of regret that the fire-damaged Capitol is being restored "when it would have been so easy to let dynamite finish what a charitable fire began, and then devote this restoration money to the building of something genuine." Here we have, in embryo, both the basic idea of *A Connecticut Yankee* and its outcome (or at least the outcome Hank claims to intend): dynamite the old (as Hank dynamites Merlin's tower in chapter 7) and build "something genuine" in its place. The only significant departure here from the Howellsian program is the insistence on explosives. Later in *Life on the Mississippi* comes Twain's famous assertion that Scott—having revived in the South the "sham grandeurs, sham gauds, and sham chivalries of a brainless and worthless long-vanished society . . . . the jejune romanticism of an absurd past that is dead"—was "in great measure" responsible for causing the War between the States.[38] Here we seem to see the logic of association that could lead Twain, when he was beginning his new novel, to associate his brash Yankee with Ulysses Grant, and to link a satirical attack on "jejune romanticism" to the mechanized butchery of the American Civil War.

It is important to remember, too, that Howells's campaign for a new standard in literature was repeatedly described as a "Realism War," and one might even argue that the Civil War itself had been in some innovative respects an expression of "realist" values. This is the perspective expressed, for instance, in Herman Melville's poem, "A Utilitarian View of the Monitor's Flight," which sees in the battle of the ironclads the triumph of "plain mechanic power," the replacement of "passion" by "crank, / Pivot, and screw, / And calculations of caloric." "War yet shall be," the poem concludes, "but warriors / Are now but operatives."[39] Hank Morgan, however, seems to feel none of Melville's regret over technological innovations in warfare; he is happy and proud to base his realist campaign on "calculations of caloric," on the *superiority* of "operatives" to "warriors." As James Cox

puts it, *A Connecticut Yankee*, "seen in a certain light, amounts to
fighting the Civil War again"—since "it is, after all, a tale of the
Yankee doing battle with chivalry."[40]

But this sense of violent military confrontation, setting modern
against medieval, practical North against superstitious South, the
building of "something genuine" against "jejune romanticism": Why
does all this apparent binary clarity lead so rapidly to incoherence and
confusion? Many readers have attributed the incoherence of *A Connecticut Yankee* to Twain's effort in the novel to convert his humor to
serious purposes. As Cox puts it: "Doubting his burlesque impulse,
Mark Twain . . . tried to make his book serious; determining to write a
satire, he . . . destroyed his humorous genius; seeking for truth and
ideology, he . . . deserted the pleasure principle. His Hank Morgan . . .
is trapped and destroyed in his effort to be a serious revolutionary."[41]
All I would want to add to this, from one point of view, is that the
form Twain's new seriousness took bore a remarkable similarity to the
ideas being proclaimed, under the banner of literary realism, by his
friend William Dean Howells. But I also would want to insist that
Twain's initial humor—the joke that led to the writing of *A Connecticut
Yankee*—was already essentially incoherent, long before it began to be
converted to the purposes of literary seriousness. Here, for instance, is
the now well known 1884 notebook entry that seems to be Twain's
first recorded idea for his new novel:

Dream of being a knight errant in armor in the middle ages. Have the notions
& habits of thought of the present day mixed with the necessities of that. No
pockets in the armor. No way to manage certain requirements of nature. Can't
scratch. Cold in the head—can't blow—can't get at handkerchief, can't use iron
sleeve. Iron gets red hot in the sun—leaks in the rain, gets white with frost &
freezes me solid in winter. Suffer from lice & fleas. Make disagreeable clatter
when I enter church. Can't dress or undress myself. Always getting struck by
lightning. Fall down, can't get up. See Morte DArthur.[42]

The humor here arises entirely from incongruous juxtapositions (for
instance, of the antithetical genres of idealized medieval romance and
childish talk about nose blowing and other forms of bodily discharge),
and it has nothing to do with satire or with serious meaning of any
kind. The inappropriate armor produces not meaning but inconven-
ience, embarrassment, increasingly extreme physical discomfort. The
joke works as a set of variations on an initial theme, and it is in fact
much funnier than Twain's development of the same theme, at far
greater length, in *A Connecticut Yankee* (particularly in the story of the
Boss's travels with Sandy in chapter 12).

Also notable in this entry, and perhaps more interesting, is what we might call its instability of reference or location. "The story," Twain wrote in 1886 of his work in progress, "isn't a satire peculiarly, it is more especially a *contrast*,"[43] and in the notebook as in the novel the contrast seems to derive in a rather straightforward way from juxtaposing an American "of the present day" with "the middle ages." But already in the notebook entry this historical distinction keeps getting confused, collapsed, or inverted. While a longing for pockets may be a distinguishing sign of nineteenth-century modernity, most of the "requirements of nature" with which armor here interferes are in fact (as the term "nature" would suggest) universal; they have no specific historical location. And take what is probably the best line in this extended armor joke: "Make disagreeable clatter when I enter church." Surely "church" conjures up the nineteenth century rather than the Middle Ages, and the joke requires that it do so; the humorous contrast, reducing martial panoply to "clatter," works here by *reversing* the initial contrast, relocating a *medieval* knight (even if he does contain, inside, an embarrassed nineteenth-century American) to a *modern* setting (a genteel Victorian Sunday service). A similar referential instability helps generate the incoherence of Twain's novel—in which the alleged evils of King Arthur's Court, for instance, can stand at the same time for medieval "superstition," for innate human depravity, and for the abuses of nineteenth-century industrial capitalism. So the original joke simply did not support the kind of "realist" meaning with which Twain soon sought to freight it—which is one reason the notebook entry is a lot funnier than the whole account of Hank Morgan's travels with Sandy.

From another perspective, however, the joke was a perfect vehicle for Twain's ideological realism, since his serious ideas about the political evils of "jejune romanticism" were every bit as incoherent as his initial meditation on the humorous possibilities of armor. *A Connecticut Yankee* is like fighting the Civil War again, according to Cox, because it is "a tale of the Yankee doing battle with chivalry." But what does it mean, exactly, to do battle with chivalry? Chivalry, after all, most essentially expresses itself in battle (hence the reliance on armor); so how can one do battle with chivalry, even in the name of realism, without becoming chivalric oneself? Or suppose Sir Walter Scott really *did* cause the Civil War; could one do battle with him without *becoming* him? What causes the Civil War, then: Southern "sham chivalries" or Northern *hatred* of "sham chivalries"? These are no idle questions; for all through *A Connecticut Yankee* moral and political oppositions—the binary pairings on which realist thinking depends—keep collapsing into equivalencies. "Somehow," Hank moralizes after his tournament victory over the Knights of the Round Table in chapter 39, "every time the magic of fol-de-rol tried conclusions with the magic of science, the magic of fol-de-rol got left" (227). The problem, of course, is that in its contest with magic, Hank's science *becomes* magic, a matter of deceptive and spellbinding effects. And in the book's conclusion, Merlin's magic, which Hank has repeatedly exposed as a sham, turns out to be genuine. Merlin's spell succeeds in putting the Yankee to sleep, and this sleep in effect turns the Yankee into his supposed opposite, Malory's King Arthur; for like Arthur, the once and future king, the spellbound Yankee lies sleeping in a cave until the moment for his return. And when he wakes up in the nineteenth century he speaks not American slang but archaic British English.

Another problem with Twain's appropriation of realist thinking in *A Connecticut Yankee*—perhaps the most important problem, and one that also leads to a collapsing of supposed oppositions—is that Hank Morgan and his story, his claims to the contrary notwithstanding, are by no means "barren of sentiment." There is the slave about to be separated from his wife, who "strained her to his breast, and smothered her face and the child's with kisses, and washed them with the rain of his tears"—this reaction standing in pointed contrast to the "hardened" indifference of the observing pilgrims (111); "I knew I should never get his picture out of my mind again," Hank writes, "and there it is to this day, to wring my heart-strings whenever I think of it" (112). As the old woman in the small-pox hut holds her dying daughter, Arthur's sentimental reaction certifies *his* inherent virtue: "I saw tears well from the king's eyes," Hank writes, "and trickle down his face" (165). In chapter 35, as the mother is about to be hanged for trying to save her child from starvation, she drenches the baby with tears, and "even the hangman," we are told, "couldn't stand it, but turned away" (207). Or think of Hank's reaction to the grandmother of the page murdered by Morgan le Fay: "I couldn't help seeing, in my fancy, that poor old grandam with the broken heart, and that fair young creature lying butchered, his little silken pomps and vanities laced with his golden blood" (91). Like much else in *A Connecticut Yankee*, this is not realism but sentimental protest, in the mode of *Uncle Tom's Cabin* (whose famous author, in the 1880s, lived next door to Mark Twain in Hartford). "I was the champion," Hank writes of his tournament with the Knights of the Round Table in chapter 39, "of hard unsentimental common-sense and reason" (221), but his political ideas, and even his ideological realism, are in fact *based* on sentiment. "A king is a mere artificiality," Hank proclaims in chapter 35, "and so a king's feelings, like the impulses of an automatic doll, are mere artificialities; but as a man, he is a reality, and his feelings, as a man, are real, not phantoms" (201). Reality *is* feeling, so that sentiment is not finally the object of Twain's realist political satire; on the contrary, Hank's overt attacks on aristocratic abuses almost always involve quite flagrant—and flagrantly conventional—appeals *to* sentiment.

Huck Finn, too, is in many respects a hero of sentiment, of feeling, but the sentimentality of *A Connecticut Yankee* is of a very different sort from the sentimentality of *Huckleberry Finn*. Both books rely on underlying economies or cycles of sentiment and humor, but they work out the relationship between these terms in quite different ways. When Huck describes the deaths of Buck Grangerford and his cousin, for instance, he says nothing about "fair young creatures" or "golden blood"; instead he writes: "It made me so sick I most fell out of the tree. I ain't agoing to tell *all* that happened—it would make me sick again if I was to do that" (94). Huck is characteristically reticent about feeling, seemingly embarrassed by it, and he reacts to moments of sentiment (or Mark Twain reacts through him) by reestablishing control—often through a kind of evasive humor. When Huck decides not to give Jim up to the white men in chapter 16, his recognition of feeling is quickly dissipated into joking: "Well, then, says I, what's the use you learning to do right, when it's troublesome to do right and ain't no trouble to do wrong, and the wages is just the same?" (76) Or there is the back-and-forth alternation of tone in Huck's memory of Mary Jane Wilks:

It made my eyes water a little, to remember her crying there all by herself in the night . . . ; and . . . I see the water come into her eyes, too. . . .
    You may say what you want to, but in my opinion she had more sand in her than any girl I ever see; in my opinion she was just full of sand. It sounds like flattery, but it ain't no flattery. . . . I hain't ever seen her since that time that I see her go out of that door; no, I hain't ever seen her since, but I reckon I've thought of her a many and a many a million times, and of her saying she would pray for me; and if ever I'd a thought it would do any good for me to pray for *her*, blamed if I wouldn't a done it or bust. (152)

The balance of feeling and reticence here looks forward to, among other things, hard-boiled detective fiction.[44]

This balance is even clearer in Huck's decision to tear up the letter to Miss Watson and "*go* to hell":

I shoved the whole thing out of my head; and said I would take up wickedness again, which was in my line, being brung up to it, and the other warn't. And for a starter, I would go to work and steal Jim out of slavery again; and if I could think up anything worse, I would do that, too; because as long as I was in, and in for good, I might as well go the whole hog. (170)

Huck repeatedly deflects feeling into jokes; he deflects the language of sentiment into the vernacular of humor: "the wages is just the same," "blamed if I wouldn't a done it or bust," "go the whole hog." We might even want to read the problematic ending of *Huckleberry Finn* as an extended, terminal deflection of the feeling built up in the first thirty-one chapters—into one last (and in this case finally tiresome) joke. We must recognize, however, that up until this long final "evasion," Mark Twain's humor is not at all directed *against* Huck Finn's sentiment; it functions, rather, to secure the authenticity of that sentiment, protecting Huck's feeling from the risk of emotional display and sentimental cliché.

Hank Morgan, unlike Huck, is *not* reticent about his feelings; he is, as I have already noted, quite openly sentimental. One price Twain pays for this shift is that Hank's feeling, and his language of sentiment, are for the most part unconvincing. Another is that the openness of Hank's sentimentality deprives Twain's humor, in *A Connecticut Yankee*, of one of the most important functions it served in *Huckleberry Finn*, and once the reciprocal relationship between humor and sentiment has been broken, they are both left to run wild, pretty much independently. It is more than a little difficult, for example, to reconcile Hank's sentimental outrage at Morgan le Fay's killing of her page with his complicity in the joke about the queen's composer and bandleader, whom she has sentenced to be hanged. "I . . . ended by having the musicians ordered into our presence to play that Sweet Bye and Bye again," Hank writes, "which they did. Then I saw that she was right, and gave her permission to hang the whole band" (85). Hank Morgan protests against the brutality of knight errantry and superstition, but his jokes have an escalating brutality of their own and generate a steadily growing body count.

Sometimes the brutality of these jokes is only metaphorical, as in Hank's account of the effect of his humorous story at a dinner in the Valley of Holiness: "[T]he fifth time I told it, they began to crack, in places; the eighth time I told it they began to crumble; at the twelfth repetition they fell apart in little chunks; and at the fifteenth they disintegrated, and I got a broom and swept them up." "This language," he hastens to add, "is figurative" (115–16)—but even here, the figurative surface scarcely conceals the violence that energizes it. Such language becomes decreasingly figurative in *A Connecticut Yankee*, and as the line between figurative and actual violence dissolves, humor becomes less and less a displacement and more and more an overt expression of aggression. Hank saves Arthur from two approaching knights with a dynamite bomb; "[D]uring the next fifteen minutes," he tells us, "we stood under a steady drizzle of microscopic fragments of knights and hardware and horse-flesh" (158). The tournament begins as a parody circus or Wild West Show, with the Yankee in tights lassoing the pride of the Round Table, but the shooting of Sir Sagramour—and ten others—with a Colt revolver would seem to change the nature of the joke; the excesses of a Roadrunner cartoon are in no obvious way compatible with a serious protest against the excesses of aristocracy, or romanticism, or whatever *A Connecticut Yankee* is protesting against. And what makes this episode and the ensuing Battle of the Sand Belt especially puzzling is that they directly follow the incident in which the Knights of the Round Table have *rescued* the Boss and the king from being executed as rebellious slaves. "I broke the back of knight-errantry that time," Hank reflects on his triumph in the tournament (227), but neither the plot of his novel nor the nature of his political ideas finally explains the violence of his (and his author's) aggression against Hank's recent benefactors.

The Battle of the Sand Belt begins with another joke, about Clarence having tested the glass-cylinder dynamite torpedoes by placing them in a public road—where they blew up a church committee:

"Did the committee make a report?"
"Yes, they made one. You could have heard it a mile."
"Unanimous?"
"That was the nature of it." (245)

But from here on the pretense that violence is funny drops away; the only laugh in this ending is the one produced on Merlin's face when he runs into one of the electrified fences after putting his spell on the Boss: "His mouth," Clarence writes, "is spread open yet; apparently he is still laughing. I suppose the face will retain that petrified laugh until the corpse turns to dust" (256). Some joke. It is as if Sam Clemens had returned to his family in 1854 from his travels in the East, had threatened them at breakfast with his new gun, and then, instead of having his joke and giving himself into his mother's arms, had shot her. By the end of *A Connecticut Yankee* Twain's humor, or what is left of it, has come completely unmoored from any satirical political purpose, realist or otherwise.

Does all this mean that Mark Twain, when he began to appropriate realist thinking in *A Connecticut Yankee*, failed to understand that thinking? I think not. On the contrary, in the confusion and instability of Hank Morgan's realism Twain brilliantly (however unwittingly or unconsciously) dramatizes what is already a fundamental instability in William Dean Howells's version of literary realism. For what is Howellsian realism, after all, but a lie that claims to be truthful, a form of literature that claims *not* to be "literary," a deployment of style that claims to *avoid* "style"—a species of magic, in short, that justifies itself as a righteous battle *against* magic? The fact that Hank in his conflict with Merlin keeps turning *into* Merlin does more than collapse the historical contrast between "the present day" and "the middle ages"; it also collapses the essential realist pretense. "Tolstoy," Howells writes in the final chapter of *My Literary Passions*, "awakens in his reader the will to be a man; not effectively, not spectacularly, but simply, really."[45] The problem is that a public and self-publicizing effort to evade spectacular effects is itself inevitably a kind of spectacle, a performance, an effect—and this is the problem Hank's realist crusade keeps illustrating. He is obsessed with effects, and even in the delirium of his death he cannot quite be simple:

With the first suggestion of the death-rattle in his throat he started up slightly, and seemed to listen; then he said:

"A bugle?. . . . . It is the king! The drawbridge, there! Man the battlements!—turn out the—"

"He was getting up his last 'effect,'" the narrator concludes, the idiom in his expression perhaps unwittingly calling attention once again to the spuriousness of Hank's manhood, "but he never finished it" (258).

The "will to be a man" was central to Howellsian realism, and from this perspective too, as from so many others, *A Connecticut Yankee* seems to show Mark Twain buying into his friend's ideas of literary seriousness—and into the problems, the always-collapsing binary oppositions, underlying these ideas. The most obvious arena for the display of true manhood was warfare—a fact of some embarrassment to writers who, like Howells and Twain (and Henry James), evaded combat in the Civil War—and we might see in both Howellsian realism and the excesses of the Battle of the Sand Belt attempts to deny or overcome this evasion.[46] Hank compensates for his noncombatant status by declaring war on the combatants, on chivalry. When he first arrives at King Arthur's court, he belittles his antagonists as "children," as "big boobies," "great simple-hearted creatures," as a brainless "nursery" (20), and these terms define the action or program he tries to place at the heart of his story. He will certify his own manhood by demonstrating his superior intelligence, his brains, his modern technological wizardry. He will educate these children into manhood, in what he calls his Man-Factory; or, this educational project failing, he will destroy the children: he will simply annihilate the combatants.

But the gender distinctions at the heart of Hank's demonstration of manhood prove no more stable than any of the other dichotomies on which he tries to base his literary-political campaign for "something more genuine." For one thing, Hank's belittlement scarcely conceals his knowledge that it may be the bravery of Arthur and his knights rather than his own scientific knowledge that represents the epitome of genuine manhood. One suspects that Hank attacks chivalry not because Arthur and his knights are children but because he fears the manhood of these literal combatants is more genuine than his own. It is also notable, and notably strange, that Hank's allies in his battle against the "nursery" of chivalry are all themselves literally children, and rather effeminate children: the army Clarence assembles for the Battle of the Sand Belt consists of "clean-minded young British boys" (246)—"a darling fifty-two!" Hank writes. "As pretty as girls, too" (248). Similar terms are used earlier to describe Clarence: when Hank first meets this future superintendent of his Man-Factory, Clarence is wearing "blue silk and dainty laces and ruffles," he has "long yellow curls" and is, according to Hank, "pretty enough to frame" (15); and of Clarence's behavior in a moment of excitement Hank writes later that he "pirouetted about the place in an airy ecstasy of happiness" (54). It is significant that Dan Beard's model for Clarence, in his illustrations for the first edition of *A Connecticut Yankee*, was a photograph of the actress Sarah Bernhardt.[47]

When they first meet, Hank thinks that Clarence, in his "shrimp-colored tights," looks "like a forked carrot" (15). This odd simile soon gets echoed by an even odder one: when Hank is stripped before the men and women of Arthur's court, in order to deprive him of the supposed power of his clothes, he is left, he writes, "as naked as a pair of tongs" (26)—surely a peculiar way to image the anatomy of revealed manhood. Hank's reaction to this experience is a combination of embarrassment and shock that, as he puts it, "I was the only embarrassed person there," and these reactions are typical; Hank consistently sets his own Victorian prudery in contrast to the "indelicacy" of King Arthur's court (26). He has already noted that the stories exchanged "by this assemblage of the first ladies and gentlemen of the land would have made a Comanche blush" (26), he continues to note instances of such supposed indecency, and he refuses to let Sandy help remove his armor "because it would have seemed so like undressing before folk. . . . I knew that when it came to stripping off that bob-tailed iron petticoat I should be embarrassed" (63). Genteel prudery also provides the only motive Hank offers for his marriage to Sandy, who has insisted on staying with her knight: "I was a New Englander," he explains, "and in my opinion this sort of partnership would compromise her, sooner or later. She couldn't see how, but I cut argument short and we had a wedding" (233). Hank is particularly shocked that medieval *women* are not bothered by the indecency of their society, and this reaction is significant; for it suggests that his own modern delicacy is, in his mind, a "feminine" quality. Hank wants to believe in his project of turning medieval children into nineteenth-century "men," but his habitual delicacy suggests that the citizens of Arthur's court, including the women, are significantly more "masculine" than their Victorian visitor.[48]

"The country," Hank insists, in one of the mini-essays that stud his narrative, "is the real thing, the substantial thing, the eternal thing; . . . institutions are extraneous, they are its mere clothing, and clothing can wear out, become ragged, cease to be comfortable, cease to protect the body from winter, disease, and death. To be loyal to rags . . . —that is a loyalty of unreason" (67). Here we get the ultimate ideological extension of the initial armor joke: reason and the real, "substantial" qualities, are opposed to the artifice of "mere clothing"; they are identified with nakedness—not the comfortable, lazy nakedness of Huck and Jim on the raft, but what we might call strenuous nakedness, nakedness with a serious purpose. One perhaps thinks of Thomas Jefferson's insistence, in his attack on novel reading, on "reason and fact, plain an unadorned,"[49] and Hank seeks to convert his attack on artificial clothing, finally, into a form of political revolution, a revolution whose fundamental action is a stripping down. This is the essential basis of his ideological realism. The trouble is, though, that being "unadorned"—having one's manhood (or perhaps the deficiencies of one's manhood) publicly exposed—is precisely what offends Hank's delicacy, so that Hank is left in a quandary. In his final tournament with the knights of the Round Table, he finds a solution to this quandary, at least a solution of sorts, in another species of imposture: he arrives dressed in "flesh-colored tights from neck to heel, with blue silk puffings about my loins" (222). This costume surely recalls the androgynous "shrimp-colored tights," the "blue silk and dainty laces and ruffles," in which Clarence first appears, but Guenever's reaction suggests a deeper meaning: "Alack, Sir Boss, wilt fight naked, and without lance or sword or—" (222). Of course, she is wrong; Hank's outfit is only a *simulation* of nakedness, of "the real thing, the substantial thing, the eternal thing"; it is more magic. She may be right, however, and in more ways than she intends, that the Boss is "without lance or sword." We recall that the first time he was rushed by a knight with lance lowered, by Sir Kay, Hank ran away; he climbed a tree. But now he has a pistol hidden in a holster—concealed, presumably, in the "blue silk puffings about my loins"—and his high-tech weaponry, here and in the Battle of the Sand Belt, accomplishes something like what his circus costume accomplishes: it is his simulation of, his substitute for, true manhood. It is thus a perfect expression of his literary-political realism.

Many explanations have been proposed for the transformation of Twain's writing between *Huckleberry Finn* and *A Connecticut Yankee,* and I have no wish to insist on a conversion to realist values as the sole or even the leading cause of the debacle of the book. "Conversion" implies a stability of behavior or intention few readers find in the novel, and the book's incoherence is in any case of a scope sufficient to contain multitudes of explanations. But Hank Morgan does seem to appropriate many of the ideas Howells was expressing in the "Editor's Study" column of *Harper's* magazine while Twain was writing *A Connecticut Yankee,* particularly ideas about the connection between literary "romanticism" and political tyranny, and this appropriation, fascinating as it may be, is in its results almost completely unfortunate. While Mark Twain's enduring contribution to American literature is his stylistic brilliance, his invention of an American literary language, the most obvious symptom of his confusion in *A Connecticut Yankee* is the deadness of the book's prose. Hank's language of sentiment is, like the feelings it asserts, wholly conventional, impersonal, ridden with clichés, and the novel's humor also repeatedly falls flat; again and again, like a stand-up comic who is losing his audience, Hank resorts to the desperate expedient of *explaining* his jokes.[50] I argued earlier that the supposed tradition of American realism is irrelevant to Twain's achievement in *Huckleberry Finn,* and what happened to Twain in *A Connecticut Yankee* should make it clear that this point is not merely a bit of pedantic information to be stored away in the dry databasement of literary history; it is also something for which lovers of Twain's masterpiece should probably be grateful. Twain's experiment in *A Connecticut Yankee* with what Howells called "democracy in literature" produces a strange mixture of violence and sentiment that manically displays the incoherence at the heart of realist thinking. But the price of this revelation is the suppression or distortion of almost all the qualities that lie behind the power of *Huckleberry Finn.*

3

Artist Fables

HENRY JAMES'S REALIST PHASE

"It goes without saying that you will not write a good novel unless you possess the sense of reality; but it will be difficult to give you a recipe for calling that sense into being."

Henry James, "The Art of Fiction" (1884)

"In a career in which she was constantly exposing herself to offence and laceration, [Olive's] most poignant suffering came from the injury of her taste. She had tried to kill that nerve, to persuade herself that taste was only frivolity in the disguise of knowledge."

James, *The Bostonians* (1886)

"'It has made this difference, that I have now a far other sense from any I had before of the reality, the solidity, of what is being prepared. I was hanging about outside, on the steps of the temple, among the loafers and the gossips, but now I have been in the innermost sanctuary—I have seen the holy of holies.' . . .

"'Then it *is* real, it *is* solid?' she pursued."

James, *The Princess Casamassima* (1915)

The middle 1880s mark a distinct phase, and quite self-consciously so, in Henry James's career as a fiction writer.[1] The long previous phase of his career, the development of his literary reputation through a set of variations on the much-discussed (and later to be revived) "International Theme," had culminated in *The Portrait of a Lady* (1881); in the mid-1880s he was trying something quite new. This brief but important period of James's career began with the now-famous manifesto, "The Art of Fiction" (1884), and it produced, most notably, two substantial novels: *The Bostonians* and *The Princess Casamassima*, both published in 1886. The middle 1880s were also, of course, the years in which James's friend, William Dean Howells, was beginning to call publicly for realism in fiction, and it is generally agreed that what James was trying out at this time was, precisely, realism. Leon Edel writes of "The Art of Fiction," for instance, that "never had the case for realism in fiction, and for the novel as social history, been put in the English world with such force"; and Richard Brodhead notes that "the compositional initiatives that group *The Bostonians* with *The Princess Casamassima*," which are "in no sense extensions of [James's] earlier writing," are "all well-marked features of nineteenth-century literary realism."[2] There can be no doubt that during the middle 1880s, as during no other period of his long and protean career, Henry James was setting out to transform himself into a realist.

But does consensus on this matter mean that James can conveniently be grouped with the so-called *American* realists among his contemporaries? Does it mean that he was a realist in the same way that his friend Howells was a realist? For the most part, to announce in advance the main argument of this chapter, the answer to these questions is no. Far more than Samuel Clemens, James was buffeted by the literary-intellectual currents that helped determine the literary ambitions of Howells and other so-called American realists; and I will soon be describing the marks of this buffeting on James's career, on his sense of his literary vocation, and on the two novels he produced in the mid-1880s. Nevertheless, there are many reasons (and at the outset fairly obvious ones) for regarding easy generalizations about James's relation to Howellsian realism with suspicion. For one thing, the onset of James's realist phase in fact *preceded* the beginning of Howells's public campaign for realism, since Howells did not inaugurate the "Editor's Study" column for *Harper's* until 1886—two years after James published "The Art of Fiction" and at a time when both *The Bostonians* and *The Princess Casamassima* were already in serialization. We should remember, too, that when James wrote his mainly appreciative essay on Howells in 1886, he ended by taking exception to the literary ideas Howells was by then beginning to promulgate in *Harper's*.[3] During his Paris residence of 1875–76, James had been introduced by Ivan Turgenev into the circle of Continental realists and naturalists surrounding Flaubert, but, as we will see, what he made of their example had almost nothing in common with Howells's idea of the realist as socially responsible moral instructor. James's pursuit of an American (or Euro-American) literary vocation led him to a conception of realism, and of the *function* of realism, apparently quite different from the realism Howells worked out in Boston.

A Different Road/A Different Realism

There is a minor tradition in American fiction of what we might call "artist-fables": stories that chronicle, often in a cautionary manner, the consequences of an "artistic" temperament. Nineteenth-century examples would include Washington Irving's "Buckthorne" and "The Young Italian"—the latter greatly admired by Edgar Poe[4]—and Nathaniel Hawthorne's "The Artist of the Beautiful." These stories typically focus on a sensitive and usually effeminate young man (in its main American manifestations, it is important to note, this is a distinctively male *genre*). Sometimes he is favored by his mother and scorned by his father; sometimes he is contrasted with a more "masculine" brother or rival; in the end, usually, he sacrifices the "real" satisfactions of the world (whether by choice or simply by a kind of pathological default) for the "insubstantial" enjoyments of art (unless, as in the most obvious variation on this formula, he instead pulls back from this sacrifice). Thus Hawthorne's artist, Owen Warland, loses his beloved Annie to the brawny blacksmith, Robert Danforth; while *they* make a real baby, Owen makes his artificial butterfly, and it is a little hard to know whether his renunciation represents an aesthetic triumph or a neurotic failure. Henry James wrote artist-fables of this sort throughout his career,[5] and the tradition of the artist-fable also provided the mold in which he would cast the main story of his own artistic development that runs through the autobiographical writings of his last years: *A Small Boy and Others* (1913), *Notes of a Son and Brother* (1914), and *The Middle Years* (the fragment published posthumously in 1917).

The Robert Danforth of these autobiographies, the figure who represents social normalcy and "masculine" force, is Henry's older brother, William. From the first William occupied, according to Henry, "a place in the world to which I couldn't at all aspire—to any approach to which in truth I seem to myself ever conscious of having forfeited a title." In contrast to William's Robert Danforth, Henry assigns himself the role of Owen Warland. As a child, he writes, he was one of those "whose faculty for application is all and only in their imagination and their sensibility"; he was one "in whom contemplation takes . . . the place of action," one whose only known "form of riot or revel . . . would be that of the visiting mind"; he was a "mere mite of observation." Social marginality, in this autobiographical artist-fable, leads to the habit of observation, to the cultivation of "impressions," and to the recognition or conviction that "to live by the imagination was to live almost wholly in that way."[6] These tendencies culminate, in *Notes of a Son and Brother*, in James's famous and notoriously vague account of his "obscure hurt," the mysterious injury that prevented (or relieved) him from serving in the Civil War.[7] "There was the difference and the opposition," James writes in *A Small Boy and Others*, " . . . that one way of taking life was to go in for everything and everyone, which kept you abundantly occupied, and the other way was to be as occupied, quite as occupied, just with the sense and image of it all." The point of his story, of course, is that he chose this "other way": he chose to "throw up the sponge for stoppage of the absurd little boxing-match within me between the ostensible and the real"; he followed what he calls "the aesthetic dream," and he was fortified in his choice, he writes, by the growing conviction "that fortune had in store some response to my deeply reserved but quite unabashed design of becoming as 'literary' as I might be."[8]

All of this might well recall William Dean Howells's autobiographical accounts of *his* childhood, of his marginal status in the games of boys (including in his case, too, a more "masculine" older brother), and of the process by which, in compensation, he turned to reading—until, as he puts it in *My Literary Passions*, "the love of literature, and the hope of doing something in it, had become my life to the exclusion of all other interests." But there is a very significant difference between the ultimate outcomes of the stories Howells and James tell about how they became writers. We might recall, for instance, Howells's account of his reasons for turning down a newspaper job in 1857: "I did not know then that life was supremely interesting and important. I fancied that literature, that poetry was so." Howells, though, presents himself as having in the years since 1857 *overcome* his initial "love of literature"—in order to reconnect himself with "life," with what he calls "the world of men's activities"—and I have argued that this gesture lay at the heart of his campaign for realism in the later 1880s.[9]

Henry James, by contrast, wants nothing to do with any such gesture, as he wants nothing to do with crude distinctions between "literature" and "life." He may present himself as having been socially marginal; he may constantly surround his childish identity with diminutives and episodes of comic inaptitude for "normal" tasks; but he is in no sense apologizing for or lamenting his early "design of becoming as 'literary' as I might be." On the contrary, he presents this design as having involved both passionate dedication and genuine satisfactions—satisfactions at least as real as those of "normal" activities, and depending precisely and wholly on the dedication's *being* "literary." "I imagined things," James writes of his early experience of the school-room, " . . . wholly other than as they were, and so carried on in the midst of the actual ones an existence that somehow floated and saved me even while cutting me off from any degree of direct performance, in fact from any degree of direct participation, at all." This does sound a bit like Howells's account of his boyhood, but what distinguishes James's story is that he *celebrates* his alienation from "normal" activi-ties, and even associates this alienation with a superior, and very *un*-Howellsian, "reality." While James writes that his teachers and fellow students were never "realities of relation, . . . playmates, inti-mates," he insists that they were in fact "something better . . .; they were so thoroughly figures and characters, divinities or demons, and endowed in this light with a vividness that the mere reality of relation, a commoner directness of contact, would have made, I surmise, com-paratively poor." And when, at Harvard, James abandoned the study of law to pursue literature, he was not retreating from reality; rather, he insists, "to get somehow, and in spite of everything, in spite especially of being so much disabled, at life, *that* was my brooding purpose."[10]

Henry James, in short, had no use for what in my first chapter I called the Boston compromise, for the anti-"literary" campaign to make authorship socially respectable that was perfected by Henry Wadsworth Longfellow and others and adopted by William Dean Howells. To Howells, we recall, the literary lions of Boston and Cam-bridge were in 1860 "the sum of greatness."[11] To James, significantly, they were nothing of the sort. In an 1872 letter to Charles Eliot Nor-ton, for instance, he describes Longfellow as "bland and mildly anec-dotical" and comments, a bit cattily, that "he is not quite a Tintoretto of verse." James Russell Lowell became a close friend in the 1880s, after Henry James had left the United States, but James continued to find in Lowell what he calls, in an 1881 letter to his father, "a simplicity as of childhood or of Brattle Street." Leon Edel writes of James's liter-ary opinion of Lowell that James thought Lowell's "poetry to be that of the outraged citizen smiting a lyre, rather than the poetry of the addicted artist."[12] Both James and Howells began their literary careers in Boston in the 1860s, where Howells, as assistant editor of the *Atlan-tic*, played an important role in helping to establish James's early repu-tation, but James could not share his friend's enthusiasm for literary Boston—which he himself, after all, fled for Europe as soon as possi-ble. James was unconvinced by Boston's ideal of "greatness." His pri-vate literary opinion of Howells, moreover, closely resembled his pri-vate opinions of Longfellow and Lowell. Howells, he wrote to Charles

Eliot Norton in 1871, "has little intellectual curiosity. . . . It's rather sad, I think, to see Americans of the younger sort so unconscious and unambitious of the commission to do the *best*." "For myself," he continues, "the love of art and letters grows steadily with my growth." To Norton's sister Grace, later the same year, James wrote of Howells that "he has passed into the stage which I suppose is the eventual fate of all secondary and tertiary talents—worked off his less slender Primitive, found a place and a routine and an income, and now is destined to fade slowly and softly away in self-repetition and reconcilement to the common-place." "But he will always be a *writer*," James adds, only somewhat more generously, "—small but genuine."[13]

We might well want to challenge James's view of Howells, or his claims for his own superior dedication to art, but accuracy is not really relevant here. What matters is that James came to cast Howells into something like the role he would always assign to his brother William: the necessary foil to his own supposedly single-minded pursuit of "the aesthetic dream." Thus it was that when Howells began to call for literary realism in the "Editor's Study" column of *Harper's*, in 1886, James dissented from his assertion that "the style of a work of fiction is something that matters less and less all the while"—and regretted that Howells "should appear increasingly to hold composition too cheap." When Howells published *A Hazard of New Fortunes* in 1890, his most "naturalistic" novel to date, James praised it sincerely both to Howells and in a letter to his brother William. But the letter to William contains a telling qualification: "His abundance and facility are my constant wonder and envy—or rather not perhaps, envy, inasmuch as he has purchased them by throwing the whole question of form, style and composition overboard into the deep sea—from which, on my side," Henry perhaps unnecessarily adds, "I am perpetually trying to fish them up."[14] All of which is to say that, while Henry James's "design of becoming as 'literary' as I might be" may ultimately have led him, in the 1880s, to a species of literary realism, it did not do so by bringing him any closer to the ideas and practice of William Dean Howells. Howells instead became another of the figures who functioned for James, in effect, as negative touchstones, helping him define his own sense of vocation and his own version of realism.

At the beginning of his professional career, in the middle 1860s, Henry James was as much a literary critic as a fiction writer, and in a loose and very general sense of the term we could say that his principles as a critic were the principles of a realist. At the end of an 1865 review, for example, he exhorts a novelist "to be *real*, to be true to something"; in a review of Louisa May Alcott's *Moods*, also in 1865, he disparages what he calls Alcott's "ignorance of human nature" and laments that "her play is not a real play, nor her actors real actors"; in an 1866 review he writes of another novel's sentimentality that it destroys the "appearance of reality; it falsifies every fact and every truth it touches." Later, in *Hawthorne* (1879), he repeatedly calls attention to his American predecessor's "want of reality." James's insistence on being "*real*" is by no means, however, an exclusive or even a dominant standard of judgment in his early critical writings. Hawthorne, after all, was a writer he greatly admired, and in spite of what James calls Alcott's "absurdities," his review of *Moods* praises the "beauty and vigor" of much of the book, qualities he attributes to the power of Alcott's "imagination." James tends, moreover, to be especially critical of books that reproduce "reality" in an *un*imaginative fashion; this is the overriding point, for instance, of his early reviews of Trollope. "Mr. Trollope is a good observer," James writes in an 1866 review of *The Belton Estate*, "but he is nothing else." "Life is vulgar," we are told in an 1865 review of Trollope's *Miss Mackenzie*, "but we know not how vulgar it is till we see it set down in his pages." Trollope's virtues, according to this review, "are all virtues of detail: the virtues of the photograph"—and the photograph, James adds, "lacks the supreme virtue of possessing a character."[15]

When James uses the actual term "realism" in his early criticism, he usually means by it something more specialized than "truth to nature" or a desire to "be *real*." In an 1866 essay on George Eliot, for example, he writes of "Janet's Repentance" (in *Scenes of Clerical Life*): "[T]he subject of this tale might almost be qualified by the French epithet *scabreux*. It would be difficult for what is called *realism* to go further than in the adoption of a heroine stained with the vice of intemperance." "Realism" refers here to low, scandalous material; it is a quality above all of *French* fiction (hence the italics), and while James does not condemn it out of hand he is hardly eager to identify *himself* as a realist in this sense. In a review of a novel by the younger Alexandre Dumas, also from 1866, he concludes that "since the taste of the age is for realism, all thanks for such realism as this"; but he has already complained that the "ultimate effect" of the novel is "to depress the reader's mind," and he has insisted that "to be completely great, a work of art must lift up the reader's heart," that "it is the artist's secret to reconcile this condition with images of the barest and sternest reality." Of a romantic novel by Victor Cherbuliez, James writes in 1873 that "its great merit in this age of dingy realism is that it is simply beautiful, and that the author has ventured to remember that it is not precisely amiss that a work of art should be lighted with a ray of idealism."[16]

James's ambivalence toward "dingy realism" is an abiding preoccupation of his many essays on the members of what he calls, in an 1884 essay on Turgenev, "the young French school . . . the new votaries of realism, the grandsons of Balzac." In 1874, for instance, he describes *Madame Bovary* as "a revelation of what the imagination may accomplish under a powerful impulse to mirror the unmitigated realities of life"; but he himself prefers mitigation, writing of Flaubert's novels generally that "the fatal charmlessness of each and all of them is an eloquent plea for the ideal." In the same year he describes Turgenev, by contrast, as a "searching realist" whose hand and touch are nevertheless guided by "imagination" (which "makes the artist worthy of the observer")—as a writer who "equals, and even surpasses, the most accomplished representatives of the French school of story-telling" and who is especially to be admired for his "closely commingled realism and idealism." James's quarrel with "the young French school" comes to a head in an 1880 review of Zola's *Nana*, which he attacks for being "inconceivably and inordinately dull," for its "monstrous uncleanness," and most fundamentally for violating the very principle of adherence to "reality" that Zola claims to espouse. "Does he call that vision of things of which *Nana* is composed," James asks of the novel's supposed naturalism, "*nature?*" "It is of high importance," he insists, now invoking the key term *against* Zola, "that realism should not be compromised," and he concludes by noting the paradox "that this last and most violent expression of the realistic faith is extraordinarily wanting in reality."[17]

James's skittishness in the presence of Zola's "uncleanness" might recall Howells's squeamishness about certain forbidden phases "of the physical or emotional nature," but we should be cautious about construing James's ambivalence toward "the grandsons of Balzac," or his more general comments about truth in fiction, into a coherent theory of realism or antirealism or into *any* very distinctive or original critical position. Whatever his personal beliefs, after all, James could hardly have identified himself with French realism in the pages of the *Nation* or the *Atlantic Monthly*, where most of his reviews and critical essays appeared. What he says about the difference between English and French novels was equally true of the difference between American and French literary journals: that while "the former are obviously addressed in a great measure to young unmarried women, . . . the latter directly count them out."[18] We should recognize, too, that while James repeatedly insists on "truth to nature" in works of fiction, and on balancing "realism and idealism," such insistence, by the mid-1860s, had long been thoroughly commonplace in American and British reviews of novels.[19] The most interesting notes in these early reviews and essays are struck, then, on somewhat different registers of the critical keyboard.

In 1875, for instance, in the first of the five essays on Balzac he produced during the course of his career, James describes the French master as a "realistic novelist," but he soon gives this definition a distinctive twist. The power of this "realistic romancer"—what allowed him to create figures "so definite, . . . so plausible, so real, so characteristic, so recognisable"—stemmed, James writes, from "the fertility of his imagination," from his "love of reality." For James's Balzac, this is to say, realism is a matter not of faithful imitation but of personal expression; the authority of "the real," for this Balzac, is its authority "for his imagination." On another front, in an 1874 review of *Far from the Madding Crowd*, James upbraids Thomas Hardy for forgetting "that a novelist is after all but a historian," and this idea reappears, in fuller form, in a well-known passage in the essay on Trollope James published in 1883, shortly after Trollope's death. James here laments that the author of *Barchester Towers* "took a suicidal satisfaction in reminding the reader that the story he was telling was only, after all, a make-believe"—and that he, as novelist, "could direct the course of events according to his pleasure." "It is impossible," James responds, "to imagine what a novelist takes himself to be unless he regard himself as an historian and his narrative as history. It is only as an historian that he has the smallest *locus standi* . . . ; to insert into his attempt a backbone of logic, he must relate events that are assumed to be real." A similar objection of course reappears in "The Art of Fiction," where James protests that Trollope's violation of the novelist's stance of "historian" is "a betrayal of a sacred office," a betrayal that "deprives him at a stroke of all his standing-room."[20]

We also should attend to the account of the French realists James includes in his 1884 essay on Turgenev, the friend who introduced him into the society of the "grandsons of Balzac." "The conviction that held them together," James writes, "was the conviction that art and morality are two perfectly different things, and that the former has no more to do with the latter than it has with astronomy or embryology. The only duty of a novel was to be well written; that merit included every other of which it was capable." While Turgenev had his differences with this group, James insists that "no one could desire more than he that art should be art; always, ever, incorruptibly, art"—and that he shared the realists' belief "that a novel could no more propose to itself to be moral than a painting or a symphony."[21] It is *this* belief, *this* conception of literary seriousness, and not the one

Howells inherited from Longfellow and others, that animates "The Art of Fiction," the manifesto James published only eight months after the Turgenev essay.

"The Art of Fiction" could certainly be described as a realist manifesto, and with good cause. "The only reason for the existence of a novel," James writes early in the essay, "is that it does attempt to represent life." But James proposes a version of realism very different from the one Howells sets forth in *Criticism and Fiction*. Unlike Howells, first of all, he insists that even realism gives us not unmediated reality but a "sense of reality"—that in fiction "reality" depends not on the truth of the writer's material but on the strength of his or her "sensibility" or "imagination." Howells, by contrast, identifies the "standard" of "realism" with "the simple, the natural, and the honest"; and these are not terms of art but clichés of conventional morality, social norms. James also insists that a plea for the seriousness of fiction must contest head on the conventional notion that "'Art' . . . [has] some vaguely injurious effect upon those who make it an important consideration, who let it weigh in the balance . . . [that] artistic preoccupations, the search for form . . . are too frivolous to be edifying . . . and . . . are moreover priggish and paradoxical and superfluous." It is on precisely this notion, we should recall, that *Howellsian* realism is based. Above all, finally, James insists that a plea for the seriousness of the art of fiction must be presented from the "point of view" of "the producer"—that "the deepest quality of a work of art will always be" not the supposed reality or morality of its subject but "the quality of the mind of the producer," that the novel will be fine "in proportion as that intelligence is fine." In short, if the artist wishes really to be taken seriously he must openly present himself *as an artist*. And Howells, in 1884, was already fully aware of his friend's position; as he had put it in his 1882 essay, "Henry James, Jr.": "[I]f we take [James] at all we must take him on his own ground, for clearly he will not come to ours."[22]

"The Art of Fiction" takes pains to reject a whole series of distinctions—for instance, between "character" and "incident," between "novel" and "romance"—that James sees as limiting both the novelist's freedom and the novel's air of reality. He asserts toward the close, in the vein of the 1884 Turgenev essay, that a work of art can be neither moral nor immoral—that "questions of art are questions (in the widest sense) of execution," while "questions of morality are quite another affair"—but his essay tends more generally to find the morality of the work of art *in* the quality of its execution, in the quality of the novelist's imagination. As James would put this idea in 1908, at the end of a famous passage in his preface to the New York edition of *The Portrait of a Lady:* "Tell me what the artist is, and I will tell you of what he has *been* conscious. Thereby I shall express to you at once his boundless freedom and his 'moral' reference." Once again, we note in passing, James's distance from Howells is striking. Even more fundamental to "The Art of Fiction" is a subversion of the traditional distinction between "art" and "life." "It goes without saying," James writes, "that you will not write a good novel unless you possess the sense of reality; but it will be difficult to give you a recipe for calling that sense into being," and he goes on to speak of novelistic "reality" as "a concrete image," not something reflected but something "produced." This line of thinking anticipates James's well known declaration of 1915 (in a letter to H. G. Wells, who had publicly satirized the supposedly lifeless artistry of James's late manner) that "it is art that *makes* life, makes interest, makes importance, . . . and I know of no substitute whatever for the force and beauty of its process."[23] All of this certainly seems to short-circuit the polarities propounded again and again in Howells's *Criticism and Fiction*, and we should also note the conjunction here of "force and beauty," a conjunction quite unimaginable in the case of Howells. For Howells the realist is a figure of power only to the extent that he succeeds in suppressing or at least transcending the "artistic." For James, by contrast, the power of the realist (a term, by the way, that he does not use in "The Art of Fiction") is made manifest *through* art, through imagination and execution. And it was just this sort of power that he set out to achieve or appropriate during the realist phase of his middle years.

If we fully believe the seeming confidence with which "The Art of Fiction" equates "art" *with* "life," and identifies the novelist with the historian, then we are likely to conclude that the terms of Howells's problem of literary vocation—of what I have called the problem of American realism—were simply irrelevant to James. The situation is hardly, however, so simple; there are grounds for at least a modicum of suspicion. It may be that the most radical ambition of "The Art of Fiction," at least as we have been conditioned to read it by our own historical vantage point, is to insist that the whole relation between novelist and reader is through the novel, through the achieved work of art. James never substitutes the language of social intercourse for the act of reading, as Howells so often does, and his insistence on the integrity and autonomy of the work of art now seems to establish him as a major progenitor both of literary modernism and of the New Criticism of the 1940s and 1950s. He wants us to talk about the *novel* (albeit as an expression of the author's sensibility) rather than about the *novelist*. Yet we should attend to the tone in which he speaks of "the novel" at the beginning of his essay:

> It must take itself seriously for the public to take it so. . . . It is still expected, though perhaps people are ashamed to say it, that a production which is after all only a "make-believe" (for what else is a "story"?) shall be in some degree apologetic—shall renounce the pretension of attempting really to represent life. This, of course, any sensible, wide-awake story declines to do, for it quickly perceives that the tolerance granted to it on such a condition is only an attempt to stifle it disguised in the form of generosity. . . . [H]istory also is allowed to represent life; it is not, any more than painting, expected to apologise. The subject-matter of fiction is stored up likewise in documents and records, and if it will not give itself away, as they say in California, it must speak with assurance, with the tone of the historian.[24]

This is the passage that leads immediately into the discussion of Trollope and his "betrayal of a sacred office," but what is most intriguing about it is the extent to which (as even a James-inspired New Critic would be bound to recognize) it *personifies* "the novel." This autonomous work of art, this impersonal formal structure, is apparently able to "take itself seriously" in an exemplary and self-justifying public performance; it seems to be capable of responding to the exhortation never to "apologise" (at least if it is "sensible" and "wide-awake"), since it "perceives" the price of such apology; it can be told not to "give itself away" but instead to "*speak* with assurance."

"The novel," here, is clearly functioning as a more or less allegorical proxy for the novelist in his confrontation with a hostile public, a public inclined to be insensitive and dismissive, a public rather similar in character to Hawthorne's Robert Danforth or to Henry James's own brother William (or at least to the role in which Henry cast William). Which is to say that we are still, here, in the realm of the artist-fable—even in a manifesto that seems to collapse the distinctions on which the artist-fable is based. And to recognize the "story" at the heart of James's manifesto may lead us to reexamine the apparently stark and total contrast between James's and Howells's literary ideas. The defiant behavior of James's personified "novel" is very different, to be sure, from the desire of the Howellsian realist to identify himself with his imagined audience, but the confrontation James imagines is just as personal as Howells's ingratiation; it too is a form, finally, of social interaction. And this passage reveals another affinity of sorts between James and Howells: namely, that the former's realism is in the last analysis no less a pretense, no less a *pose*, than the latter's—however different the apparent intentions behind the poses. James (and in this he is still significantly different from Howells) is rather disarmingly open about the imposture: the novel must "take itself seriously," his passage makes clear, not because it is inherently serious but so the public will "take it so," and the realism that will save it from the need to "apologise" is a *"pretension* really to represent life." The apparent claim of power here is also significantly qualified: envied history is only *"allowed* to represent life," it is not *"expected* to apologise"—so that even in the case of history "the public" is apparently still very much in control. And what may be most telling is the fact that the personified "novel" can maintain its pretense of representative power only "if it will not give itself away, *as they say in California.*" In 1884, what giving oneself away would have meant in California (at least from James's more than moderately stereotypical perspective) would presumably have had to do with poker, with revealing inadvertently that one was betting beyond one's cards, that one was bluffing. So it seems that "to speak with assurance" is finally, for the Jamesean realist, to bluff, to assume (or ventriloquize) "the *tone* of the historian."

"In a digression, a parenthesis or an aside," James complains of what he calls Trollope's "want of discretion," "he concedes to the reader that he and this trusting friend are only 'making believe.' He admits that the events he narrates have not really happened, and that he can give his narrative any turn the reader may like best"—and this, James adds, "is what I mean by the attitude of apology."[25] The joke, of course, is that Trollope may well be in the right against James, since his indiscretion is in fact a good deal more truthful than what James immediately goes on to call the novelist's "sacred office." After all, the novelist and the reader *are*, in truth, only "making believe"; the events in a novel have *not* really happened; the novelist *can* indeed give his narrative any turn he or she (or the reader) might like. As a number of so-called American "metafictionists" recognized (or at least proclaimed) in the 1960s, self-reflexive "apology" may be the truest form, and perhaps the only true form, of fictional realism. But James was of course in on the joke; why else would he have associated the novelist's confidence with the composure of California—only seven years (worth noting if one is committed to connections) after Mark Twain had scandalized an *Atlantic Monthly* dinner in honor of John Greenleaf Whittier's seventieth birthday by converting Longfellow, Emerson, and Holmes into California cardsharps?[26] What finally matters, though, is that even in this critical essay, in this supposed "realist" manifesto, the realist pretense so rapidly produces a Jamesean "situation," an incipient story. Introducing the personified "novel" generates, by way of one sort of contrast, a hostile or indifferent "public"; it then generates, by a different sort of contrast, a "bad" counternovelist, a role assigned to Anthony Trollope. "We must grant the artist," James writes in a now-famous passage in his essay, "his subject, his idea, his *donnée*: our criticism is applied only to what he makes of it."[27] Literary realism mattered to James, in the last analysis, less as doctrine than as *donnée*, and the story of the fiction of his "realist" phase is the story, finally, of what he made of this *donnée*—or of what it made of him.

In *The Bostonians* and *The Princess Casamassima*, according to Richard Brodhead, James undertakes a deliberate experiment with realism only to discover "that realism is after all not his style," that "he cannot practice this sort of work on its own terms, and that it will not work on his." In both of these experimental novels, Brodhead writes, James fails to graft the vision of literary realism onto the conventions of Hawthornesque "romance."[28] One could worry that Brodhead's account of James's realist phase might tend to perpetuate some of the very distinctions James rejected (for instance between the "novel" and the "romance"); that it risks buying into the rigid distinction between the "literary" and the "political" that has characterized so much American criticism, particularly American criticism of James; and that it seems to assume, for instance with Howells, some necessary relationship between being "realistic" and being "political."[29] Still, Brodhead seems to me fully persuasive in his account of James's experimental appropriation of realism *as a style*.

There are other ways, however, of discussing the relation of *The Bostonians* and *The Princess Casamassima* to literary realism, to what I have been calling realist thinking—ways perhaps more pertinent to my own concerns. In the late nineteenth century, Brodhead writes, realism possessed a "well-consolidated legitimating mythology," but James had no interest in this mythology: "[F]ully conscious of realism's self-naturalizing arguments, James is remarkable for the extent to which he abstains from putting forth such arguments himself, and for the uninterest—really it is more like disdain—with which he regards such arguments in others."[30] This is certainly an accurate account, as we have seen, of James's discussions of realism and naturalism in his critical writings. But does James's overt disdain for the extraliterary rationales offered by realists necessarily mean that these rationales, and the assumptions and anxieties that underlay them, were irrelevant *to his fiction*, to the two big novels he produced during his realist phase? I believe the answer to this question is no. Moreover, to ask this question may lead us to another, a question made particularly intriguing by the fact that so few commentators on James's realist phase have thought it important or visible enough to ask. Why, we might wonder, did James's experiment with literary realism lead him, in *The Bostonians* and *The Princess Casamassima*, to the subcultures of Boston reformers and London revolutionaries? If James had no interest in the self-legitimating mythology of realist thinking, why did both of his realist experiments lead him to the subject, for him so uncharacteristic, of politics? The answer, I believe, is that conventional realist thinking proved harder to escape than the apparently easy bravado of James's critical essays might suggest.

Realism and Reform

In April 1883, after copying into his notebook a prospectus for what would become *The Bostonians,* James added an account of the process that had led him to his subject: "I wished to write a very *American* tale, a tale very characteristic of our social conditions, and I asked myself what was the most salient and peculiar point in our social life. The answer was: the situation of women, the decline of the sentiment of sex, the agitation on their behalf."[31] While the causal connection between the desire to write "a tale very characteristic of our social conditions" and the subject of feminist agitation is not, here, exactly transparent, it is certainly true that the politics of *The Bostonians* are above all sexual (or gender) politics, and we might see in this subject some connection to the gender anxieties underlying Howellsian realism. The novel's sexual situation, however, seems quite different from the situation implied in Howells's critical writings: the "problem" in *The Bostonians* is apparently not effeminate men but mannish women, and the masculinity of James's male protagonist seems to be quite unattended with anxiety—often, indeed, to the point of ludicrous excess.[32]

Basil Ransom is introduced, on the first page of *The Bostonians,* in a kind of phallic flurry: the conceit that Mrs. Luna looks him up and down "as if he had been a long sum in addition" leads to the notation that "he was very long, . . . like a column of figures," that "his head had a character of elevation," that his hair gave this head "a leonine manner," that he had (the enumeration goes on for almost a full page) a "superior head," an expression of "hard enthusiasm"; and it seems almost superfluous for the narrator to inform us, apparently to justify the length of his descriptive excursion, that this young man "is, as a representative of his sex, the most important personage in my narrative" (35–36).[33] But just what, in this war of the sexes, does Basil's sex *represent*? According to Lionel Trilling, James's masculine Southerner stands (like the later Southern Agrarians) for "a kind of realism which the North, with its abstract intellectuality, was forgetting to its cost";[34] but whatever we think of Trilling's ideal of the Agrarians, "realism" seems just exactly the wrong term for James's Southerner. On the contrary, Ransom clearly stands for (as his last name nearly anagramatizes) *romance*.[35] In the 1883 prospectus for his "American tale," James made this character a Westerner, but he shifted his home to the South, to Mississippi, for fairly obvious reasons. This region of origin helps explain Ransom's conservatism, especially his conservatism with respect to the position of women; it accentuates his conflict with his Northern cousin, Olive Chancellor, who lost her two brothers to the Civil War; and it also, of course, links Basil's conservatism to Southern "chivalry," to the conventional association of the Confederacy with pseudomedieval romance. Thus when Ransom thinks of Selah Tarrant as a "varlet" we are told, by way of explanation, that he "generally" used "terms of opprobrium extracted from the older English literature" (82); Basil thinks of Verena Tarrant, at Miss Birdseye's, as a "half-bedizened damsel" (84); and we later learn that "it was not merely a humorous idea with him that whatever might be the defects of Southern gentlemen, they were at any rate remarkable for their chivalry. He was a man who still, in a slangy age, could pronounce that word with a perfectly serious face" (202). Romance, for this Southerner who always seems to be picking up old books or carrying them about, is above all a matter of words, old words.

We are assured that "the artistic sense in Basil Ransom had not been highly cultivated" (45), but he nevertheless often takes things, as we might say, artistically, as objects of taste rather than of judgment. This is in any case how he generally takes women, as in his reaction to what he sees as Olive Chancellor's physical coldness—or in his reaction to Verena Tarrant's first improvisatory oration in defense of women's rights, the performance that leads both Basil and Olive to fall in love with Verena. "The necessity of her nature," the observing and appreciative Basil thinks to himself of Verena on this occasion, "was not to make converts to a ridiculous cause, but to emit those charming notes of her voice, . . . to please every one who came near her, and to be happy that she pleased" (85). The reason Basil's "artistic sense" is not cultivated, we might surmise, is because it is innate. And taste, for this representative of romance, is finally an instrument of power: the attribution of beauty to this "damsel," the attribution of an idealized wish to "please" rather than a self-actualizing and potentially disruptive desire to "convert," is for him (as it turns out) a tactic of possession—not in the sense of the witchcraft with which Olive is early associated (37) but in the sense of ownership, of control—and on all of this the narrator (a far cry from the supposed nonintrusive Jamesean norm) is quite clear, or at least quite loquaciously expository. "I know not," he writes of Basil's response to Verena's improvisation, "whether Ransom was aware of the bearings of this interpretation, which attributed to Miss Tarrant a singular hollowness of character; he contented himself with believing that she was as innocent as she was lovely, and with regarding her as a vocalist of exquisite facility, condemned to sing bad music. How prettily, indeed, she made some of it sound!" (85).

Olive Chancellor is herself, of course, by no means innocent of impulses to ownership and control, and the main difference between her and Basil Ransom in this connection, at least with respect to Verena, is that where Olive ultimately fails, Basil ultimately succeeds: he "gets the girl." But acknowledging the significant affinity between these antagonists, the effective similarity or even identity of their desires, should not obscure what is for us a more immediate question. If Basil Ransom stands for something like romance, for romance as a means of control and ownership, for what does Olive Chancellor stand? There is a hint toward an answer, or part of an answer, in Richard Brodhead's discussion of James's persistent evocation in *The Bostonians* of Hawthorne's *Blithedale Romance*, through which James implicitly presents himself as a sophisticated modern writer powerful enough to "repair" Hawthorne's primitive "representational style." In this stance, Brodhead notes, James asserts his "methodological superiority" to his American predecessor; "[B]y bringing the realist style to Hawthorne's conceits James can pose as something like Hawthorne's perfecter," reforming the errors or deficiencies of Hawthornesque romance.[36] Might we not find an analogue of this pose, at least provisionally and speculatively, in the political program of the New England reformers in *The Bostonians* who, instructed by the supposed superiority of their modern understandings, work to repair the historical evils of male domination? "You hate it!" Olive exclaims to Basil of her own political program, just before they enter Miss Birdseye's apartment. "Miss Birdseye," he replies, "will convert me" (54). Is it possible that this confrontation between Basil and Olive, this belated renewal of the American Civil War, is in some sense, at least in part, a confrontation between romance and realism?

We should pay attention, here, to some information we acquire about Olive Chancellor that might at first glance seem somewhat extraneous. Taste, first of all, is as important to her as it is to Basil, and in her case the "artistic sense" has in fact been a good deal "cultivated." What Basil first notices in her parlor, for instance, is "the presence . . . of so many objects that spoke of habits and tastes" (45). Olive's refined taste is repeatedly offended by the surroundings into which her political activities carry her; at Miss Birdseye's, for example, Mrs. Farrinder's assumptions about "the ladies of Beacon Street" strike a "false note," making that reformer seem "provincial" to Olive—who then goes on to reflect that "there was something provincial, after all, in the way she did her hair too" (61). Olive's visit to Mrs. Tarrant's home in Cambridge leaves "no doubt . . . as to her being vulgar," and "Olive Chancellor," we are told, "despised vulgarity" (129). Particularly interesting in this context is Olive's reaction to the musical evening at Henry Burrage's rooms in Cambridge. Before this occasion Verena asks "whether taste and art were not something," to which Olive has her ready answer that "taste and art were good when they enlarged the mind, not when they narrowed" (163). As Burrage begins to play Schubert and Mendelssohn, however, Olive's composure is threatened (and the extended passage is worth sampling at some length):

Olive was extremely susceptible to music, and it was impossible to her not to be soothed and beguiled by the young man's charming art. . . . It was given to Olive, under these circumstances, for half an hour, to surrender herself, to enjoy the music, to admit that Mr Burrage played with exquisite taste. . . . Civilization, under such an influence, in such a setting, appeared to have done its work; . . . human life ceased to be a battle. She went so far as to ask herself why one should have a quarrel with it; the relations of men and women, in that picturesque grouping, had not the air of being internecine. (166)

She soon recovers herself, of course; when Verena asks, outside, if Mr. Burrage is to be respected, Olive replies: "Yes, very much—as a pianist!" (168). Much earlier, at the first evening at Miss Birdseye's, the narrator writes that Olive's "most poignant suffering" in her political work "came from the injury of her taste," and that "she had tried to kill that nerve, to persuade herself that taste was only frivolity in the disguise of knowledge" (57). For Olive Chancellor, this is to say, as for the Howellsian realist, to be *serious* requires the suppression, the mortification, of the "artistic."

Olive displays other affinities with the kinds of thinking Howells would soon be expressing in his "Editor's Study" column in *Harper's*. While she despises "vulgarity," she nevertheless convinces herself that "the toilers and spinners, the very obscure, these were the only persons who were safe from it" (129), and we have also been told that "she had long been preoccupied with the romance of the people," having "an immense desire to know intimately some *very* poor girl" (62). This desire, thwarted up till now, Olive hopes finally to realize with Verena—whose "bright, vulgar clothes" and Bohemian air appear "to make her belong to 'the people'" (101). All of this strikingly anticipates Howells's desire to equate "pride of caste" with "pride of taste," to ally realism, "democracy in literature," with the aspirations of "unaffected people everywhere,"[37] and James's analysis of such thinking is acute and, in its consistent double entendre, both funny and rather nasty. Olive's earlier attempts to make the acquaintance of "pale shop-maidens" had come to nothing, the narrator writes, because "they had seemed afraid of her. . . . She took them more tragically than they took themselves; they couldn't make out what she wanted them to do" (62).

We need to recognize that Olive is herself an artist, or an artist of a sort. "I want," she explains to Mrs. Farrinder (and the nasty double entendre is still in force), "to enter into the lives of women who are lonely. . . . I want to be near to them. . . . I want to do something—oh, I should like so to speak!" But, she adds, "I can't speak; I have none of that sort of talent. I have no self-possession, no eloquence" (63). This assertion is immediately belied by an extended interior meditation on "the suffering of women"—which is eloquent (for instance in its reliance on alliteration) to the point of something like the pastiche of the chapter endings in Joyce's *Portrait of the Artist as a Young Man:*

Ages of oppression had rolled over them; uncounted millions had lived only to be tortured, to be crucified. They were her sisters, they were her own, and the day of their delivery had dawned. This was the only sacred cause; this was the great, the just revolution. It must triumph, it must sweep everything before it; it must exact from the other, the brutal, blood-stained, ravening race, the last particle of expiation! (64)

"You are quite a speaker yourself!" Verena later remarks, following one of Olive's private lectures on masculine perfidy. "You would far surpass me if you would let yourself go" (152). "We know that she was without belief in her own eloquence," writes the narrator, later still, "but she was very eloquent when she reminded Verena how the exquisite weakness of women had never been their defense" (191). Olive *can* speak, she has an innate gift for oratory, but she will not let herself go; eloquence, being "artistic," is something else she must mortify in her dedication to the political.[38] The stylistic signature of *The Bostonians*, particularly of the first and longest of its three Books, is narrative cruelty, and no character is treated more cruelly than Olive Chancellor—as in the famous comparison of her faint smile to "a thin ray of moonlight resting upon the wall of a prison" (39). But behind this cruelty, and perhaps animating its excess, one suspects an anxious identification; one suspects that Olive stands for a good deal that Henry James is trying to stand for, or at least thinking about standing for.[39] I have no desire to reduce *The Bostonians* to some sort of realist or antirealist allegory; Olive is far too complex a character to allow so reductive a reading, and the novel is hardly coherent enough to support *any* stable allegorical interpretation. But part of what gets embodied in Olive does seem to be associated with her author's fears about the implications of his new realist ambitions. James may have disdained realism's self-justifying rationales, but they still show up, in *The Bostonians*, in Olive's mortification of her taste, in her suppression of her susceptibility to beauty, in her "romance of the people," in her deliberate self-immersion in "vulgarity."

But if the contest between Olive and Basil is in some sense a contest between realism and romance, it is a little difficult to know what the *outcome* of this contest means. What is ultimately at stake between Olive and Basil is the power to define Verena's "character," to "inscribe her," as Claire Kahane puts it, "in the narrative of culture"[40]— to determine, for instance, whether her name alludes to the realist's truth (*veritas*), to the romancer's feminine beauty (*venus, venerean*), or perhaps to nothing at all. Basil of course "wins": he forces Verena to become a character in his romance-narrative. But this narrative becomes, in the process, so self-contradictory and peculiar as to make his victory meaningless as anything more than an arbitrary assertion of (or unaccountable capitulation to) brute power. As Basil arrives at the Burrages' evening entertainment in New York, he thinks of Verena as "a touching, ingenuous victim, unconscious of the pernicious forces which were hurrying her to her ruin. With this idea of ruin there had already associated itself in the young man's mind, the idea . . . of rescue" (251). Here is one of the hoariest of romance plots, much the same as the one to which Sandy commits the Boss in Mark Twain's *Connecticut Yankee in King Arthur's Court*: the Knight rescues the imprisoned damsel from the tower, the Ogre's Castle (with Olive Chancellor, in this case, assigned the role of the Ogre); and it is to the contours of this romance narrative that Basil bends, for instance, Verena's image of woman trapped inside the glass box of patriarchy. "He said that he had come to look at her through the glass sides," we are told, "and if he wasn't afraid of hurting her he would smash them in. He was determined to find the key that would open it, if he had to look for it all over the world" (313).

Yet even while Basil casts himself as would-be rescuer he also, at the same time, assumes the role of the Ogre, the monster/enchanter. Thus we are told, as he details his "monstrous opinions" to Verena in Central Park, that "there was a spell upon her as she listened; it was in her nature to be easily submissive, to like being overborne" (322). To the extent that Basil plays the Ogre, moreover, he makes a space for *Olive* to become the Knight: "[S]he pitied Verena now with an unspeakable pity, regarded her as the victim of an atrocious spell, and reserved all her execration and contempt for the author of their common misery" (395). By the time of the final "rescue" at the Boston Music Hall, these dissonant narrative paradigms (or dissonant applications of the same narrative paradigm) have managed to generate an almost manic incoherence. Basil's enemy has now come to encompass, for him, all detested democracy—"the ferocity that lurks in a disappointed mob," the mob he means to deprive of "its entertainment, its victim" (416)—but Basil turns his attack, he inflicts "inevitable agony," not on this mob nor on Olive, nor even on the central-casting policeman Olive has hired, but on *Verena*, the captive damsel. And the account of his behavior, as many readers have noted, sounds less like a rescue (or a "ransom") than a rape: "[H]e saw that he could do what he wanted, that she begged him, with all her being, to spare her." We are then told, in a wonderfully contradictory sentence, that "the *spell* upon her—thanks to which he should still be able to *rescue* her—had been the knowledge that he was near" (425, my emphasis). Verena pleads with Basil, "just as any plighted maiden might have asked any favour of her lover," but what she wants is hardly the conventional "favour" of romance. She is begging him, rather, as the damsel would more naturally beg the monstrous Ogre, to "go away" (429).

The incoherence of Basil's deployment of romance does not, however, guarantee the coherence of Olive's counternarrative. The emphasis of this narrative is clear enough: Olive seeks to demystify romance in order to deprive it of its "spell"—in order to free women in general, and Verena in particular, from masculine power. It is in this sense that Olive's feminism is most essentially congruent with literary realism, the sort of realism Howells would soon be espousing; and her campaign against Basil Ransom's "chivalry" is in fact remarkably similar in its main intentions to the Connecticut Yankee's campaign against Merlin's bogus "magic." The problem is that Olive's campaign against romance, like Hank Morgan's, keeps getting infected with the very disease it sets out to cure. To a considerable degree, we recall, her political commitment has been inspired by "the romance of the people," and to the extent that she plays the role of Knight in opposition to Basil's Ogre she is not dismissing the aura of romance but buying into it. Her problem may be inevitable, since a narrative in which romance is to be deprived of its power, its "spell," is itself, after all, a romance-narrative. And nowhere are the self-contradictions in Olive's program clearer than in the way her narrative attempts to define Verena. Verena is to express and embody Olive's campaign of demystification, her campaign against aesthetic and erotic susceptibility, but Olive's attraction to Verena has everything to do with such susceptibility: she invests Verena, from the first, with all the qualities she has sought to suppress in herself, and she then falls in love with them. No more than Basil Ransom does Olive Chancellor value Verena for the substance of her speeches, which Olive herself apparently writes (230); like Basil, she loves Verena for her "gift," for her pretty music. It is thus sardonically appropriate that Olive—who has suppressed her susceptibility to, for instance, Burrage's performance on the piano— plans to launch her feminist-realist campaign, with Verena as star, from the stage of the Boston *Music* Hall. Nor should we be surprised to be told, as Basil surveys the scene, that behind this stage "the huge organ . . . lifted to the dome its shining pipes and sculptured pinnacles, and some genius of music or oratory erected himself in monumental bronze at the base" (414).

Critical debate over the meaning of *The Bostonians*, like debate about Twain's *Connecticut Yankee*, finally comes down to a fairly simple question: With which of his antagonists does the author side? Whose position does he endorse as his own? But in *The Bostonians* as in *A Connecticut Yankee*, and for rather similar reasons, this question is ultimately unanswerable, and it may even be meaningless. For all its apparent polemical energy, James's novel is, like Twain's, simply too disjointed and inconsistent to articulate any coherent position.[41] The narrator's habit of intruding judgmentally and even abusively only advertises a pronounced instability of judgmental *location*: we can find him, at different times and occasionally at the same time, both supporting and abusing almost *all* the characters and positions in the novel. And behind the embattled conflict of *The Bostonians*, behind the persistent imagery of military preparation and combat, the boundaries between opposed "sides" can in fact be notably indistinct, shifty, and porous. Olive and Basil have almost as much trouble maintaining distinct positions as do Hank Morgan and Merlin, and sometimes it is even as if one were watching the firing of heavy artillery at mirrors. There are plenty of plausible explanations to account for the ultimate incoherence of *The Bostonians*—James was at a turning point in his career, both of his parents had just died, he was embarking on his first

full-length fiction dealing entirely with an American subject and location—and all of these factors were no doubt significant. It is nevertheless also important to remember that *The Bostonians* was the initial
product of James's decision to make himself over into a realist. This
first fruit of his realist experiment is surely a better book than James's
American contemporaries thought it; like *A Connecticut Yankee*, again,
it is at the very least a fascinating mess. As a token of what being a
realist was likely to mean, however, the book's instability and incoherence can hardly have been heartening to its author. Still, James was
not deterred; he only waded in farther, farther into the amalgam of
realism and politics, farther away from his own experience—wading in
ultimately, some would say, over his head.

Naturalism, Impressionism, Revolution

In his 1909 preface to the New York edition of *The Princess Casamassima*, James insists that this novel of the mid-1880s was a product not
of the kind of research associated with Continental naturalism but of
personal impressions gathered in evening walks "during the first year
of a long residence in London"—that his story grew out of "the assault
directly made by the great city upon an imagination quick to react." As
for "the question of one's 'notes,'" he claims (and Zola, for instance,
was famous for taking notes on the subjects of his novels), "my notes .
. . were exactly my gathered impressions and stirred perceptions, the
deposit in my working imagination of all my visual and all my con-
structive sense of London." And this claim leads to the closing observation that "if you have n't, for fiction, the root of the matter in you,
have n't the sense of life and the penetrating imagination, you are a
fool in the very presence of the revealed and assured; but . . . if you *are*
so armed you are not really helpless, not without your resource, even
before mysteries abysmal."[42] All of this is very "Jamesean"—it pulls
The Princess Casamassima into the orbit, for instance, of the special
realism of "The Art of Fiction"—but the pose of the preface is also
more than a little disingenuous. The truth is that no other work by
James had so many sources outside of his direct personal observation:
for instance, in popular crime writing, in newspaper accounts of ter-
rorist activities, and especially in the work of other novelists.[43] Indeed,
given James's complete personal inexperience of his subject, of the
world he had chosen to write about, reliance on such outside
sources—whether or not we choose to call such reliance research—
was pretty much inevitable.

Of all James's literary sources for *The Princess Casamassima*, the most immediate and pervasive was undoubtedly, as several commentators have noted, Ivan Turgenev's *Virgin Soil*—which James had reviewed in French translation in 1877, a year after its first appearance in Russian.[44] Turgenev's novel, like James's, deals with members of a secret society of radical conspirators, members of an underground who receive orders from a mysterious absent superior, and the similarities between the two novels go far beyond their nearly identical subjects. James's confident revolutionary, Paul Muniment, has much in common with Turgenev's Solomin. There is a minor character in *Virgin Soil* named Paklin who, like James's diminutive Hyacinth Robinson, "could never resign himself to his small stature. . . . He felt it the more because he was passionately fond of women and would have given anything to be attractive to them." But far closer to Hyacinth, except in stature, is Turgenev's protagonist, Alexai Dmitrich Nejdanov. Nejdanov is the illegitimate son of an aristocrat; we are told that "everything about him betokened his origin" and that he "secretly took a delight in art, poetry, beauty in all its manifestations"; he composes verses while frequently lamenting "his hopelessly aesthetic nature"; and he loathes, he says, the "irritability, sensitiveness, impresssionableness, fastidiousness, inherited from my aristocratic father."[45] At the close, having lost what was even at its most intense only a wavering commitment to the cause of revolution, Nejdanov commits suicide; like James's Hyacinth, again, he shoots himself with a revolver. James's pilfering of Turgenev's novel is so assiduous as to constitute something far more obtrusive and deliberate than influence or even theft, something closer to a sustained reference, a continuous allusion. In the same sense that *The Bostonians* seems to be James's revision of Hawthorne's *Blithedale Romance*, so *The Princess Casamassima*, for all its appropriation of the styles of such urban realists as Balzac and Dickens, seems above all—at least in its subject, situation, and story—to be a revision of Turgenev's *Virgin Soil*.

The thrust of this revision is already clear in the 1877 review of Turgenev's novel, for instance, in its account of the motives behind Nejdanov's suicide. "Of course," James writes, "his career receives the final tragic stamp; the 'aesthetic' young man, venturing to play with revolution, finds it a coarse, ugly, vulgar, and moreover very cruel thing; the reality makes him deadly sick." This is in fact not at all what happens to Nejdanov in Turgenev's novel; or it is at the very least a strong misreading of the precursor text. Nejdanov, who has all the playfulness of a lead ingot, could not "play" with revolution if he wanted to, and he has little experience of its "reality." Rather what makes him sick (all too literally) is his consumption of large quantities of vodka (which James in his review calls, gloriously, "pestilent brandy")[46] while trying, in a frenzy both despairing and ridiculous, to organize a group of scornful peasants. Nor does Nejdanov recoil from revolution because it is "coarse" and "ugly." He instead loses his always marginal political will *along with* his marginal aesthetic will and his marginal romantic will (he burns his poetry and renounces his claim to the heroine, Mariana) out of a sense of general paralysis, a weary capitulation to the existential complexity of his motives and desires. He is not excessively aesthetic but excessively cerebral, anticipating the sort of modernist intellectual antihero (derived in part, of course, *from* Turgenev's fiction) who is repeatedly if gently mocked in the early films of Woody Allen. James's review, seeing an "aesthetic" hero succumbing to the cruelty of the "vulgar," converts Turgenev's existential political psychology into something more like aesthetic pathology, relying on a finally neurotic conflict between the "reality" of political commitment and the refined cultivation of artistic taste. James reads *Virgin Soil*, this is to say, as if it were an American artist fable, with Nejdanov, the inspiration for Hyacinth Robinson, playing the role of the sensitive, alienated artist figure.

While Olive Chancellor's radicalism often recalls the realism of Howells or Zola, or at least James's unsympathetic understanding of their literary principles, her thinking is quite different from the realism James himself sets forth in "The Art of Fiction"; that essay's impressionism finally seems irrelevant to *The Bostonians*. But in *The Princess Casamassima*, in the figure of Hyacinth Robinson, the ideas of "The Art of Fiction" enter quite directly into the action. "What was most important in life for [Hyacinth]," we are told, "was simply his impressions" (157–58); he inherits from his aristocratic father the "finest sensibilities" (169); he is "quick . . . to perceive and appreciate" (516).[47] Among the highest literary gifts, James writes in "The Art of Fiction," is "the power to guess the unseen from the seen, to trace the implication of things, to judge the whole piece by the pattern." "I perceive things," Hyacinth explains, "I guess things, quickly. That's my nature" (549). "Try," James writes in "The Art of Fiction," in a celebrated piece of advice to aspiring writers, "to be one of the people on whom nothing is lost."[48] Hyacinth, we are told early in his story, in what must be a direct reference to the 1884 essay, is "a youth on whom nothing was lost" (164). So we could see in the conflict between Hyacinth and the revolutionaries a struggle between something like the antiaesthetic realism or naturalism of Howells and Zola and something like James's own idea of impressionistic realism. Or, more interestingly, we could locate this struggle *within* Hyacinth, reading *The Princess Casamassima* as a chronicle of his growth from the one kind of realism to the other, or of his inability to reconcile these competing versions of realism.[49]

The trouble is that these readings, even though James clearly encourages them, are finally undercut by much of what we learn about Hyacinth. For one thing, he is not converted to art by his glimpses of aristocratic culture; he is innately "aesthetic," in the manner of the sensitive hero of the artist fable, from the outset. We also have good reason to wonder just how internally conflicted Hyacinth really is. Once he has made his promise to the conspirator Hoffendahl, his promise to engage in an act of terrorism when called upon, Hyacinth thinks and speaks as if he were losing a genuine earlier commitment to the revolution: "Isn't it enough, now, to give my life to the beastly cause," he asks the Princess Casamassima, who murmurs at the term "beastly," "without giving my sympathy?" (336) But his sympathy has *always* been at best limited; his taste has *always* been offended by the "beastly" life of the people. When Pinnie objects, early on, that Millicent Henning thinks Lomax Place "abominably low," Hyacinth replies, long before his first meeting with the princess: "So it is; it's a beastly hole" (103). Nor, finally, is Hyacinth's political commitment *ever* very strong, or very convincingly evoked. As early as chapter 7 we are told that "he had deviations and lapses, moments when the social question bored him" (123), and even when he imagines himself "absorbed in the struggles and sufferings of the millions whose life flowed in the same current as his," he still reflects that these millions "constantly excited his disgust, and made him shrink and turn away" (160).

What Hyacinth desires, even and perhaps especially in his moments of alleged political commitment, is not to *act* but to *see;* he cares far less about the goals of the conspiracy than about gaining some immediate perception of its secrets. When Paul Muniment accuses him of having gotten a political phrase, "the party of action," from the newspapers, Hyacinth replies: "If you'll show me the thing itself I shall have no more occasion to mind the newspapers" (151). Just before he makes the impassioned speech that leads to his selection by Muniment to kill for the movement, we are told that Hyacinth "was in a state of inward exaltation." Why? Because "he was seized by an intense desire to stand face to face with the sublime Hoffendahl, to hear his voice, to touch his mutilated hand" (291). "Should you like," Muniment asks, as they set off for the fateful meeting, "to see the genuine article?" (295). Hyacinth Robinson, the Jamesean realist, bearer of the values of "The Art of Fiction," wants not revolution but experience, *observed* experience. We have been told earlier of his longings—and it is not entirely clear whether this generalization applies to his asserted longing for revolution, to his longing for "luxury," or to both—that "it was not so much that he wished to enjoy as that he wished to know; his desire was not to be pampered, but to be initiated" (164).

I will return shortly to Hyacinth's initiation, and to the relevance of this initiation to the thematizing of competing realisms in *The Princess Casamassima*. But for the moment what matters is simply that Hyacinth's insistence on internal conflict is not borne out by his actual behavior and beliefs; he never seems to feel the democratic sympathies he claims. His oft-asserted internal division also gets rapidly displaced from the arena of motivation to the realm of genetic determinism, to the secret of his birth, to his supposedly conflicting inheritances from his aristocratic British father and his murderously revolutionary French mother. "It might very well be his fate," Hyacinth reflects, "to be divided, to the point of torture, to be split open by sympathies that pulled him in different ways; for hadn't he an extraordinarily mingled current in his blood?" (165). James's concern with the influence of Hyacinth's parentage has been linked to the naturalists' interest in heredity, and this aspect of conventional naturalism is no doubt at least part of what James had in mind in detailing the family backgrounds of so many of the characters in *The Princess Casamassima*.[50] But even admitting the foolishness of most of what passed for "science" with self-proclaimed naturalists (a subject to which I will be turning in Part Two), all the talk of the "mingled current" in Hyacinth's "blood" is grotesquely unscientific. It is also, in the context of the novel, strangely inconsequential.

The melodramatic circumstances of Hyacinth's birth—so portentously established in the visit to his dying mother in Millbank Prison in chapter 3—seem not only excessive but in many respects irrelevant to the story that follows. A young man of Hyacinth's position could surely come to be torn between sympathy for revolution and longing for aesthetic gratification without such secret origins, and for much of the novel (after the visit to Millbank Prison) Hyacinth's birth is pretty much forgotten. Also, while Hyacinth regards his secret with fascination and shame, other characters, when they learn of it (and it is a very poorly kept secret), seem hardly to care. When Hyacinth finally confides in Millicent, for instance, he is struck "with the fact that his base birth really made little impression upon her; she accounted it an accident much less grave than he had been in the habit of doing" (532). "There was no peace for [Hyacinth]," we are told late in the novel, "between the two currents that flowed in his nature, the blood of his passionate, plebeian mother and that of his long-descended, super-civilized sire" (479). This is not determinism but allegory—allegory, moreover, that is only tenuously related to the actual details and circumstances of Hyacinth's story. All this talk of "currents" and "blood" functions at best as a *substitute* for motivation: it has nothing to do with psychology—except, perhaps, as a symptom of something deeper, something concealed; it functions less as explanation, one suspects, than as sublimation.

The Princess Casamassima, James's second and last deliberate experiment in literary realism, is every bit as confused as *The Bostonians*, but its confusion is of a very different kind. Where *The Bostonians* is finally unstable, *The Princess Casamassima* is mainly inert: it is made up of chunks of antithetical materials, and antithetical modes, that will not combine. Large portions of the novel, for example, rely on an essentially comic mode, on something like a class-based variation on the International Theme. Upper class characters—recalling *The Bostonians* and anticipating Tom Wolfe's *Radical Chic*—fulfill their fantasies of the "real" by visiting the haunts of "the people," while actual representatives of "the people" fulfill *their* fantasies through contact with the aristocrats. James's development of this comic mode can be quite perceptive and funny, as in the princess's ironic but quite accurate observation to Hyacinth that he, though poor, knows far less about the poor than does Lady Aurora Langrish, the philanthropic *aristocrat* (425). James also works up this comedy of class into quite elaborate formal patterns. In chapter 15, for instance, a "slumming" visit by Captain Sholto to the lodgings of Paul and Rosy Muniment, where he asks prying questions about their habits and means of livelihood, is then symmetrically balanced by Hyacinth's visit to Sholto's flat, where Hyacinth sees "no reason why he, on his side, should not embrace an occasion of ascertaining how, as his companion would have said, a man of fashion would live now" (229). By chapter 26, we have two cross-class couples (Hyacinth and the princess, Millicent and Sholto) formed by recombining the members of two same-class couples (Sholto and the princess, Hyacinth and Millicent). Hyacinth's visit to Lady Aurora at the end of Book Five seems a bit implausible—she has hardly been an important figure in his emotional life—but it makes perfect sense in formal, comic terms: they are the "jilted" cross-class leftovers of the new cross-class conjunction of the princess and Paul Muniment.

One problem raised by this comedy of class-crossing is that it tends to corrode one of the scaffoldings on which James has apparently built his realist project. "I want to know London," the princess declares to

Hyacinth; "it interests me more than I can say—the huge, swarming, smoky, human city. I mean real London, the people and all their sufferings and passions; not Park Lane and Bond Street. Perhaps you can help me—it would be a great kindness: that's what I want to know men like you for" (201). The princess's designs on Hyacinth recall Olive Chancellor's designs on Verena Tarrant; hers seems to be yet another case of the "romance of the real." But her desire to know "real London" is also uncomfortably similar to the project of Henry James in the novel that bears the princess's name. James, like the princess and the naturalists, seems to equate "reality" with poverty, or he is at least aware that this equation is a convention of the naturalism with which he is experimenting. He also seems to be a bit uncomfortable with this simplification of the complex realities of class. Lionel Trilling writes that in *The Princess Casamassima* "James represents the poor as if they had dignity and intelligence in the same degree as people of the reading class"; "[F]ew of our novelists," he adds, "are able to write about the poor so as to make them something more than the pitied objects of our facile sociological minds."[51] While this observation is no doubt accurate, and a sign of James's fundamental moral decency, facile sociological condescension of the sort Trilling deplores has nevertheless always been, as we will see more fully in Part Two, a persistent feature, a generic signature, of conventional literary naturalism. Thus to the extent that James's social comedy deflates the distinction between the aristocrats and "the people," it seems to deprive him of the very distinction on which much of his novel apparently is based.

To make this point is of course only to repeat what has often been said: that James had little sympathy for the underlying ideas of his realist and naturalist contemporaries, ideas with which he was nonetheless flirting in the mid-1880s. A deeper problem with James's comic treatment of class divisions and interactions in *The Princess Casamassima* is that it is by no means consistently sustained, and the comic mode of much of the novel seems wholly unrelated, and even antagonistic, to the handling of Hyacinth's initiation. This theme also has its relevance to James's experiment with realism. "It has made this difference," Hyacinth says to the princess of his meeting with Hoffendahl, "that I have now a far other sense from any I had before of the reality, the solidity, of what is being prepared. I was hanging about outside, on the steps of the temple, among the loafers and the gossips, but now I have been in the innermost sanctuary—I have seen the holy of holies." "Then it *is* real," the princess asks, "it *is* solid?" (330) This interchange might remind us of the princess's earlier remarks about "real London," but nothing in the text registers or encourages such connections.

Reading *The Princess Casamassima* is a bit like reading two quite distinct novels—one veering toward farce, the other in deadly earnest—that just happen to have been wedged into the same book. And Hyacinth's statement, with its insistent overtones of religious conversion and initiation, identifies just the sort of realist narrative James is apparently attempting to derive from the ideas of "The Art of Fiction"—where, we will also recall, the novelist's profession is described as "a sacred office."[52] Hyacinth Robinson, the "youth on whom nothing was lost," will move from outside to inside, from "gossip" to "reality" and "solidity," from guessing the "unseen" to seeing it directly.

Yet even as *The Princess Casamassima* insists on this movement, on this paradigmatic realist narrative, it also keeps sabotaging it. Surely one of the most peculiar qualities of this peculiar novel is its habit of building up to great revelations and then skipping over them, eliding them, representing them, if at all, only in retrospect. The first three chapters climax with the visit to Hyacinth's mother in Millbank Prison, a visit whose impact supposedly changes little Hyacinth's life, but we see it from Pinnie's point of view rather than the child's. We then, between chapters 3 and 4, skip over the next ten years, and we do not begin to learn about Hyacinth's reaction to the prison visit until chapter 11, at the end of Book One. Book Two ends with Hyacinth on the way to his meeting with Hoffendahl, but this momentous event is also elided: Book Three begins with Hyacinth waking up (we eventually learn it is three months later) at Medley, the princess's rented country house, and almost a full chapter passes before he thinks back (very vaguely and briefly) to his visit to the conspiracy's "innermost sanctuary." Similarly, to cite only one more example, at the end of chapter 44, having retrieved Hoffendahl's commission from Shinkel and the Poupins, and having convinced Anastasius Vetch to go home (processes that consume two full chapters), Hyacinth finally, we are told, "approached the nearest gas-lamp and drew from his breast-pocket the letter that Shinkel had given him" (565). But we are not privy to what follows: this sentence ends the chapter; at the beginning of the next Hyacinth is calling on the princess; and even in memory, here, he continues to elide the actual experience of this last contact, however textually mediated, with Hoffendahl.

According to John Carlos Rowe, narrative disruptions in *The Princess Casamassima* "draw on the suspense of the adventure novel and popular romance" in order to undermine "the customary expectations of realistic narration," to "undermine the unity of form in realism," "the characteristic organicism and development of realistic narration."[53] We might wonder whether suspense is actually all that incompatible with the conventions of "realistic narration," and we must recognize that narrative elision in *The Princess Casamassima* goes far beyond effects of suspense. For instance, even Hyacinth's mind-opening but hardly suspenseful tour of Europe is effectively elided; all we get to "see" of it (in chapters 29 and 30) is an evening in a Paris café, during which Hyacinth recalls his travels (and in fact mainly thinks back on his relations with Millicent Henning and Paul Muniment following his return to London from Medley)—and then a letter to the princess from Venice, in which Hyacinth again recalls the impressions he has gathered on his travels. Even in Europe, apparently, the experience of Europe can only be *remembered*. But Rowe is certainly correct, in general terms, that there is a connection in *The Princess Casamassima* between disrupting narrative and disrupting realism. For what James repeatedly disrupts is precisely the realist narrative he has extrapolated from "The Art of Fiction"; what he elides, again and again, are Hyacinth's most momentous experiences—his encounter with his dying mother, his discovery of his ancestry, his meeting with Hoffendahl, his tour of Europe, his reading of the letter that seals his doom. This is a strange procedure for a realist, particularly for the sort of realist James is trying to project into the narrative of Hyacinth's initiation. Every time Hyacinth moves into the supposed "sanctuary," James's narration remains doggedly, even compulsively, "on the steps of the temple," turning "reality" and "solidity" back into "gossip," working hard not "to guess the unseen from the seen" but to conceal what *has* been seen.

This strange sabotaging of realism in *The Princess Casamassima*, this disruption of the narrative of Hyacinth's initiation, may stem in part from James's recognition of a contradiction at the heart of his project. The gift of guessing the unseen from the seen is one thing as an aesthetic ideal; it is something quite different as a *donnée*, implying not imaginative contemplation but literal penetration. Indeed, the literalness is the problem: to penetrate into the realm of the "unseen" is to turn it *into* the "seen"—and thus to deprive it of the very quality that called for imaginative play in the first place. A sense of this problem emerges toward the end of James's preface to the New York edition of *The Princess Casamassima:*

My scheme called for the suggested nearness . . . of some sinister anarchic underworld, heaving in its pain, its power and its hate; a presentation not of sharp particulars, but of loose appearances, vague motions and sounds and symptoms, just perceptible presences and general looming possibilities. . . .
    . . . [T]he value I wished most to render and the effect I wished most to

produce were precisely those of our not knowing, of society's not knowing, but only guessing and suspecting and trying to ignore, what "goes on" irreconcileably, subversively, beneath the vast smug surface.[54]

We may well doubt this retrospective claim of intention, which just happens to provide a convenient excuse for any vaguenesses or errors of fact in the novel's handling of its political subject. But James's preface presumably gives a true enough account of the *outcome* of his final experiment with full-dress literary realism, an outcome that makes the story of Hyacinth's initiation into sacred mysteries at the very least irrelevant. If "The Art of Fiction" implied a narrative, James discovered, it was not a narrative of penetration. What we get, then, is not discovery, not a movement *in*, but endless evasions and deferrals, displacements, uncanny repetitions.

We may also be getting hints that the special realism or impressionism of "The Art of Fiction" is by no means the deepest force behind Hyacinth's compulsive evasions—and that even the apparent allusions to "The Art of Fiction" end up functioning mainly as another form of evasion. For what is repeated and elided with particular insistence, over the course of Hyacinth's story, is not the development of artistic sensitivity but a series of variations on a scene in which Hyacinth spies, more or less guiltily, on a heterosexual couple. In chapter 12, having been introduced by Captain Sholto into the princess's theater box, and having been captivated by her beauty, Hyacinth proceeds to gaze up at Millicent and Sholto conversing in the balcony he has just left. In chapter 20, entering a pub to change a sovereign, Hyacinth meets Sholto and gradually recognizes (being a "youth on whom nothing is lost") that he is interrupting an assignation between Sholto and Millicent. The most spectacular variation on the scene occurs in chapter 20, when Hyacinth calls on the absent princess only to encounter (for the second time) her estranged husband, with whom he then conceals himself outside to watch the princess return with Paul Muniment and to watch them, after a significant hesitation, enter her house together. "All that Hyacinth saw," we are told, "was the door just closing; the Princess and Muniment were on the other side of it"; he walks away in silence, leaving the prince "in the darkness, to direct a great helpless, futile shake of his stick at the indifferent house" (520). Or there is the episode in chapter 47 (the last episode, before his suicide, in which we are privy to Hyacinth's point of view) when Hyacinth enters the haberdasher's where Millicent works and discovers her with her back to him, facing Sholto, who stands "with his eyes travelling up and down the front of [her] person," as he rubs "his lower lip slowly with his walking-stick" (585). Sholto then returns Hyacinth's gaze with a hard look, a look that drives Hyacinth away—and apparently to his death. Here we have the clearest echo of Hyacinth's own parents, of his aristocratic father and plebeian mother, whose coupling reverberates throughout the novel. It reverberates most suggestively, perhaps, in the mysterious off-stage acquaintance of the Princess Casamassima and the conspirator Hoffendahl—both of whose names, we might note, recalling the "indifferent" destination of the princess and Muniment, contain the word for "house" (*casa* and *hoff*) in their respective languages.

The unseen conspiracy, these uncanny repetitions hint—the "sinister anarchic underworld, heaving in its pain, its power and its hate," known only through "vague motions and sounds and symptoms"—is finally more sexual than political; and the repetitions suggest, too, the true meaning of the secret of Hyacinth's birth, the forbidden knowledge he sublimates into pseudoscientific ideas about the "extraordinarily mingled current in his blood." The unseen secret at which Hyacinth guesses, even as he and his author elide all moments of actual recognition, looks more and more like the primal scene, the coupling whose reality Hyacinth was forced to confront as a child as he descended into the depths of Millbank Prison (a visit arranged by yet another "parental" couple, Pinnie and Mr. Vetch). Hyacinth apparently has quite personal reasons for disrupting narratives of penetration, for "not knowing, but only guessing and suspecting and trying to ignore, what 'goes on' irreconcileably, subversively, beneath the vast smug surface"—since he must confront in the act of his own begetting the murder of his father, stabbed to death by his mother. Perhaps this is why, to return to one of Hyacinth's more peculiar sets of distinctions, "it was not so much that he wished to enjoy as that he wished to know," why "his desire was not to be pampered but to be initiated." For as long as Hyacinth can substitute knowing for enjoying, as long as he can remain the observer, he can avoid confronting the guilty knowledge at the secret heart of his desires.[55] This approach to Hyacinth's voyeurism takes us a considerable distance from the subject of *The Princess Casamassima* and realism, but this distance is of course precisely my point. The deepest themes of this realist experiment would seem to have nothing to do with realism; the realities elided by the novel's narrative disruptions would seem to have no bearing on literary realism per se.

There is still, however, one other kind of connection we might consider. The suppressed but fascinating story of Hyacinth's mother, Florentine Vivier—this secret everyone seems to be in on, this lurid tale of illicit sex, murder, and imprisonment—is exactly the kind of subject James objected to in the work of the "grandsons of Balzac," the kind of subject that led him to deplore the "brutal indecency," the "monstrous uncleanness," of Zola. And it may be this subject, more than the legacy of the Revolution, that is evoked by Florentine Vivier's French nationality; she would be a perfect Zola heroine. But the point even of this connection, if it is one, is that in *The Princess Casamassima* the story of Florentine Vivier *is* elided, displaced, sublimated; like the intimacy of the princess and Paul Muniment it is kept on the other side of the door. Above all, we must recognize the considerable chasm between the psychological mechanisms of displacement and sublimation that seem to drive *The Princess Casamassima* and the idea of literary impressionism that is set forth in "The Art of Fiction."

In *The Princess Casamassima*, as in *The Bostonians*, the realist project self-destructs. Here the effort to understand the impressionism of "The Art of Fiction" as a species of literary realism collapses, if not all the way back to the family romance of psychoanalysis, then at least as far back as the allegorical, pathological melodrama of the artist fable. At ten Hyacinth is small for his age, and he remains "little Hyacinth" throughout his story; there can be few other novels in which the vertical impairment of the protagonist is so repeatedly insisted upon. When Hyacinth reappears at the age of twenty, in chapter 4, he has "a short pipe in his teeth," and the now-buxom Millicent, looking him over, somewhat strangely exclaims: "Gracious, Hyacinth Robinson, is *that* your form?" (101) We soon are told that he looks "like a little Frenchman," that "he was as small as he had threatened," that "he had a very delicate hand," and that "a painter (not of the heroic) would have liked to make a sketch of him" (102–4). In telling contrast to Hyacinth—the Robert Danforth to his Owen Warland, or the William James to his Henry—stands the forceful and practical revolutionary, Paul Muniment. Hyacinth notes of Paul at their first meeting that "there was nothing French about *him*" (125); Paul is "tall and fair" (127); he "probably," Hyacinth thinks to himself, "had a tremendous head" (128); he is not "delicate" but performs his "work in the world . . . by the simple exercise of a rude, manly strength" (134–45). And just as Hawthorne's Owen Warland loses Annie Hovenden to Robert Danforth, the "real" man, so Hyacinth loses the princess to Paul Muniment; she is more interested in "his powerful, important head," which makes him "one of the most considerable men she had ever known" (449), than in the decorative artistry of little Hyacinth's bookbinding. The artist fable, this is to say, runs true to formula, and we need once more to recognize that this formula—with its rigid distinction of the

aesthetic and the manly, of art from "reality," from life—is the very
opposite of the special realism, the impressionism, of "The Art of
Fiction."

James ends his novel with something of a reversal of the standard
story. First of all, the "real" man, having won the woman away from
his rival, dismisses *her* as well: Paul reveals to the princess in chapter
46 that he has been in correspondence with her husband and that,
since the prince is withdrawing her allowance, she is of no more use to
the conspiracy. He also, at this interview, reveals that Hyacinth has
already received his commission from Hoffendahl, a fact Hyacinth
had manfully concealed from the princess at their last interview. In
this masochistically self-justifying variation on the conventional conclusion of the artist fable, the woman recognizes the superior virtue of
the sensitive artist, but too late. The princess arrives at Hyacinth's
lodgings to find at the door not Hyacinth but another of his many
father figures, Shinkel, "smoking his big pipe and looking up and
down" (586). And then the princess proceeds to act out the drama of
penetration that has so often, up to now, been elided—but no longer.
She insists that Shinkel break down the locked door of Hyacinth's
room:

The door collapsed. . . . The light . . . was so poor that for a moment she
made out nothing definite. Before that moment was over, however, her eyes
had attached themselves to the small bed. There was something on it—something black, something ambiguous, something outstretched. Shinkel held her
back, but only for an instant; she saw everything, and with the very act she
flung herself beside the bed, upon her knees. Hyacinth lay there as if he were
asleep, but there was a horrible thing, a mess of blood, on the bed, in his side,
in his heart. (590)

The princess is punished for her misjudgment of Hyacinth, for her
preference for Muniment—punished by the very kind of direct vision
Hyacinth himself, or at least James as he has narrated Hyacinth's story,
has so persistently avoided: "She saw everything." This is not realism,
however, but fantasy, the child's fantasy, in his "small bed," of that
self-destruction that might at once atone for his own guilt and wreak
vengeance on the mother for the secret of his birth, for her inatten-
tion, for her conspiracy with the child's rival, the father. Which is to
say that the James of *The Princess Casamassima*—for all the book's
density of notation and description, and in spite of his high-realist or
naturalist intentions—may finally have more in common with a writer
like Poe than with writers like Zola or Flaubert, or Turgenev, or
William Dean Howells. The competing versions of realism, impres-

sion, and naturalism that James deploys in the book seem to function, ultimately, not as modes of representation but as additional means for masking and eliding the psychological realities, the forbidden fantasies, at the heart of Hyacinth's story.

Leon Edel writes of James's attempt to turn himself into a popular dramatist, in the 1890s, that it was "doomed to failure," since James never overcame his scorn for the form he was seeking to appropriate. "No citadel," Edel writes, "can be assaulted through mere contempt for the conditions of the assault; no original creativity is possible when it is mixed with so much distaste."[56] We could say much the same thing about James's attempt to turn himself into a realist in the mid-1880s; for here, too, James could neither accept nor simply dismiss the conventions, and conventional associations, of his project—of the ideas to which he would soon be objecting in his criticism of Howells's "Editor's Study" column in *Harper's*. In *The Bostonians*, James focuses his contempt and distaste for realist thinking, for its assumptions about the "reality" of politics and the frivolity of "taste," in the figure of Olive Chancellor and then sets out, in effect, to destroy her; and this was hardly a promising beginning for a writer seeking to *become* a realist. What happens in *The Princess Casamassima* is more complicated, and stranger. Here the narrative distance of *The Bostonians*, so well suited to expressing James's scorn, is replaced by what seems a far more sincere investment in the rendering of social and political reality. But the book sets in motion such different kinds and conceptions of realism—social comedy, heavily descriptive and deterministic naturalism, the impressionism of the sensitive protagonist—that they hardly seem to belong in the same novel. And then, as the ostensible logic of discovery and revelation gives way to an underlying pattern of repression and evasion, these supposedly competing realisms become both more or less interchangeable and more or less irrelevant. James's experiment in literary realism was by no means as disastrous as the fiasco of his dramatic career; neither *The Bostonians* nor *The Princess Casamassima* is, to use Edel's terms, without "original creativity," and they are both deeply fascinating, perhaps especially in their incoherences and confusions. But it is still true that both of them seem, in the context of the realist project of which they are a part, not only doomed to failure but *designed* to fail.

PART TWO

The Problem of Naturalism

FRANK NORRIS

STEPHEN CRANE

THEODORE DREISER

It is a virtual axiom of our literary history that during the 1890s realism in American fiction gave way to naturalism.[1] Such new writers as Stephen Crane, Frank Norris, and Theodore Dreiser turned from the parlor to the slum, from middle-class manners to urban squalor, from polite society, the arena of realist fiction, to the brutal struggles of business and the underclass—from genteel courtship to what keeps being called, as if it were a species of *sushi*, "raw" sex. Darwin, so the story goes, had revealed the animalistic struggle underlying all human behavior, and Zola had shown how this "scientific" vision might be expressed in fiction. For these new writers the "more American" aspects of life were hardly, as they were for Howells, the "more smiling," quite the contrary; and there were deeper differences. Howells's sense of moral responsibility grew out of a belief that his characters were free, within the limits of inevitable human complication, to choose between right and wrong, and to learn from the experience of such choices. In the work of our so-called naturalists, so the story has gone, a thoroughly different sense of character emerges: dehumanized, determined, moved by inner and outer forces beyond conscious moral control.[2]

This story of the naturalists' break with their immediate predecessors was originated by the naturalists themselves. In 1901, for instance, Frank Norris dismissed "Realism" for its "meticulous presentation of teacups, rag carpets, wall paper and haircloth sofas, stopping with these, going no deeper than it sees, choosing the ordinary, the untroubled, the commonplace." He called instead for a fiction that would explore "the unplumbed depths of the human heart, and the mystery of sex, and the problems of life, and the black, unsearched penetralia of the soul of man."[3] Howells, albeit from the other side of the fence, described the difference between the new fiction and his own ideal of realism in rather similar terms. In an 1899 review of Norris's *McTeague* he expresses admiration, but with reservations: the book's "true picture of life," he complains, sounding a bit like James on Zola, "is not true, because it leaves beauty out. Life is squalid and cruel and vile and hateful, but it is noble and tender and pure and lovely, too." *McTeague* is not a faithful "reflection of reality," Howells contends, now choosing a very un-Jamesean figure, because it lacks "the impartial fidelity of the photograph."[4]

Critical arguments for a tradition of American naturalism operate with at least one significant advantage over discussions of realism; for while the qualities attributed to realism often constitute little more than a vague set of intentions or attitudes, those associated with naturalism would seem to add up to something far closer to an actual literary *genre*. There are the customary subjects or concerns linked with naturalism: lower-class life, the play of "brute" forces (both external and unconscious), the futility of human endeavor. Even more important to works we have come to associate with naturalism, as June Howard persuasively argues, is a characteristic formal strategy, a narrative arrangement that views "brutal" characters, characters whose lives are subject to determinism, through the eyes of middle-class observers or omniscient third-person narrators who are to a large extent exempt from determinism but who are frequently bound by a kind of spectatorial paralysis.[5] Howard's understanding of *genre* is at once rigorously formalist and deeply historicist, and the writers traditionally grouped as American naturalists have proved interesting to a number of so-called new historicists. Among the great virtues of the new historicists' approach to this literature are an ability to maintain a distance from the claims of the supposed naturalists and a penetrating sense of the presence of history or culture *in* form, in conventions of *genre*.[6]

Nevertheless, generalizations about American naturalism can still present problems. For instance, while the differences among Crane, Norris, and Dreiser are perhaps not as striking as the differences among Howells, Twain, and James, it is hard to imagine any coherent "school" that could include the authors of *The Red Badge of Courage*, *McTeague*, and *Sister Carrie*. Nor did all of these men even conceive of themselves as "naturalists": Crane, for instance, never used the term, and it is worth noting that he plays only a small role in Howard's *Form and History*. In the context of the present study, the most important of the widely accepted ideas about American naturalism is the claim that it was above all or first of all a departure from realism. This is a claim in which new historicists tend not to be interested, and with good reason; for it is far from clear that American declarations of allegiance to naturalism represented all that sweeping a rejection of William Dean Howells, and these declarations in fact perpetuate many of the deepest assumptions, confusions, and evasions of *Criticism and Fiction*. For instance, if the naturalists' insistence on "force" functions, as Mark Seltzer argues, "as a counter to female generativity," as a masculine alternative to the feminine, is this not equally a prime function of *Howells*'s thinking about literature?[7] And in the last analysis, as we will see, American writers who embraced the identity of naturalist would seem to have done so for many of the same reasons that lay behind Howells's campaign for realism: the label allowed them to claim that they were not really "artists," concerned with form and style, but were full participants in what Howells called "the world of men's activities." One might note, in this connection, the terms in which Norris concludes his naturalist manifesto, "The Novel with a 'Purpose'" (1902):

Fiction may keep pace with the Great March, but it will not be by dint of amusing the people. The muse is a teacher, not a trickster. Her rightful place is with the leaders, but in the last analysis that place is to be attained and maintained not by cap-and-bells, but because of a serious and sincere interest, such as inspires the great teachers, the great divines, the great philosophers, a well-defined, well-seen, courageously sought for purpose.[8]

The prose here is more jingoistic than Howells's—Norris, after all, identified with Teddy Roosevelt and the strenuous life rather than with the subtler politicians of Ohio—but what matter most are the sentiments. The distinction between "teacher" and "trickster," the identification of the writer not with artists but with "leaders," "teachers," "divines," "philosophers" (with, that is, "real" men): these sentiments are all vintage Howells. The obvious and important differences between Norris and Howells—the latter of whom, for example, never identified himself with the turn-of-the-century cult of the "he-man"—should not obscure the equally important, if less obvious, continuities between their ways of thinking and writing about literature.

This is not to say that what Norris espoused was not a version of naturalism but only that we should recognize how naturalist thinking, like realist thinking, could function as a way for a writer to suppress his "artistic" identity. And small wonder: the seminal manifesto of Continental naturalism, Emile Zola's "The Experimental Novel" (1880), was admirably suited to such purposes. Zola's equation of the novelist with the experimental scientist anticipates similar comparisons in Howells, and Zola's pseudoscientific prose develops the analogy to the point of unwitting burlesque. Moreover, Zola is very close to Howells in what he has to say about style, about "the question of form." "This," he admits, "is what gives literature its special quality. Not only does genius reside in feeling, in the *a priori* idea, but also in the form, in the style. However," he adds (and this turns out to be quite a "however"), "the question of rhetoric and the question of method are distinct. And naturalism, I repeat, consists uniquely in the experimental method, in observation and experiment applied to literature. Rhetoric for the moment has no place here."[9] An American convert to Zola would scarcely have needed, as proof of his conversion, to renounce the most basic assumptions of *Criticism and Fiction*. However extreme their differences with respect to the appropriate *material* of realistic fiction, on the desirability of excluding questions of style from discussions of the importance of literature Howells and Zola were in fundamental agreement.

In terms of its deepest assumptions and tendencies, the new idea of literary naturalism that arose in America in the 1890s represented neither an escape from nor a resolution of what I have been calling the problem of American realism. For its proponents, rather, naturalist thinking was a translation of this problem, the problem of a theory of literature based on a radical desire to suppress the "literary," into new and sometimes grotesquely exaggerated terms. While we could investigate the effect of these terms on the works of quite a few authors, I have chosen to concentrate on three—Frank Norris, Stephen Crane, and Theodore Dreiser—because of all those conventionally claimed as naturalists they produced the work now regarded as the most enduring; they have come to stand at the center of the so-called naturalist canon. Chronology would suggest beginning with Crane, who was the first of the three to publish, and the first to die. I have chosen to begin instead with Norris because no one, among the writers of this generation, was more outspoken in advocating literary naturalism, and this fact makes his example especially instructive, at least as a

starting point. In Norris's case I ask what the effect of naturalist thinking was on the work he produced in the name of naturalism: What
effect did his growing commitment to what he took to be naturalism
have on the shape of his brief career? In the cases of Crane and Dreiser
I pursue a somewhat different line of inquiry. Both of them would
seem to have relied on what June Howard sees as the distinguishing
generic feature of literary naturalism: aloof, omniscient narrators who
understand their characters as the characters can never understand
themselves—and who therefore seem largely exempt from the conditions that determine the characters' brutal lives. To what extent, I ask,
does this apparent *stylistic* affiliation with naturalist conventions indicate a corresponding affiliation with naturalist *thinking*? My answer,
briefly, is that it indicates far less affiliation than one might at first
suppose. Naturalist thinking, I argue, was ultimately irrelevant to
Dreiser, and Crane quite deliberately appropriated naturalist conventions in order to undermine naturalist assumptions.

4

The Revolt Against Style:
FRANK NORRIS

"Had you given the Prize to Mr. Dreiser, you would have heard groans from America; you would have heard that his style—I am not exactly sure what this mystic quality 'style' may be, but I find the word so often in the writings of minor critics that I suppose it must exist—you would have heard that his style is cumbersome, that his choice of words is insensitive, that his books are interminable."
Sinclair Lewis, "Nobel Prize Acceptance Speech" (1930)

"I detest 'fine writing,' 'rhetoric,' 'elegant English'—tommyrot. Who cares for fine style! Tell your yarn and let your style go to the devil. We don't want literature, we want life."
Frank Norris to Isaac F. Marcosson (1899)

Frank Norris has become for many literary historians perhaps *the* representative American naturalist—particularly, in the 1980s, in the work of the so-called new historicists—and for clear and good reasons. For instance, when Mark Seltzer proposes in "The Naturalist Machine" (1986) that "production, both mechanical and biological, . . . troubles the naturalist novel at every point" and that the naturalist novel devises "a counter-model of generation," he insists that such a model "operates in a wide range of naturalist texts." But he has chosen to focus on Frank Norris, he explains, because Norris is "the American novelist who most conspicuously and compulsively displays both these anxieties about generation and the aesthetic machine designed to manage them."[1] Norris, for the new historicists, is a kind of cultural seismograph, his compulsions and anxieties nicely registering the wide

115

variety of ideological formations and cultural practices that he shared with his era, and it is also important that he was the most conspicuous and overt proponent, among his American contemporaries, of literary naturalism. Yet for all his historical centrality, Norris is one of the most incompetent practitioners of his craft across the whole range of the American canon. I am referring here simply to his *writing*, his labored and lugubrious *style*. I will be fleshing out this observation shortly, and the point is hardly controversial; all I would add to it for the moment is that Norris's style in fact gets worse over the course of his brief career, more prone to clichéd purple prose, to unintentionally hilarious bathos, to strangely inappropriate (yet often hideously extended) metaphor.

In arguing for Norris's centrality, it should be recognized, new historicists are by no means arguing for the literary *value* of his work; nor, of course, is there any necessary contradiction between Norris's growing incompetence as a writer of English and his current status as representative American naturalist. Restraint is probably not the first quality one looks for in a seismograph, and it well may be Norris's ineptitude that allows his compulsions and anxieties to play so freely and conspicuously across the surface of his prose. But I want to argue for a more direct connection: I want to argue that the obvious defects of Norris's style were, in effect, *learned* and that this deliberate learning was a product of growing commitment to what he took literary "naturalism" to be. Norris, it is important to recognize, was a representative naturalist even to himself; he strove to *become* a representative naturalist; and what commitment to naturalism entailed for him was above all a kind of deliberate literary self-impairment, a revolt against "style."

The Road to Naturalism

Benjamin Franklin Norris, Jr., was born in 1870.[2] His mother was "artistic"; she had been an actress before her marriage, and while matrimony ended her career it did not abate her devotion to literature and culture. Norris's father, by contrast, was a man of practical affairs, a self-made business success who had little use for art or literature and who wanted his eldest son and namesake to follow in his footsteps. This contrast between a "feminine" world of culture and a "masculine" world of "real" business dominated Norris's childhood and adolescence and left its mark on nearly everything he wrote before his untimely death in 1902—not only on his fiction but also on his essays about the nature and function of literature, about the need for naturalism in fiction. Norris spent the 1894–95 academic year at Harvard, studying writing with Lewis E. Gates. Here he worked on a novel begun earlier, finally published in 1899 as *McTeague;* he also wrote a draft of *Vandover and the Brute*, which was not published until the manuscript was discovered in 1914. He produced five more novels before his death. *Moran of the Lady Letty*—his first novel to be published, although it was third in order of composition—appeared in 1898. *Blix* was published in 1899, soon after *McTeague*, and was followed by *A Man's Woman* in 1900. Norris then embarked on what he called his "Wheat series," a projected trilogy with one volume to be devoted to production (and set in California), a second devoted to distribution (and set in Chicago), and a third devoted to consumption (and set in Europe). The first of these volumes, *The Octopus*, appeared in 1901, bringing its author his first real taste of fame. Norris died shortly after finishing the second volume, *The Pit*, which was published posthumously in 1903. The third volume was never begun.

In the course of a very brief career, then, Norris wrote seven novels, producing at the same time numerous stories and essays. This is an impressive performance, and it would seem to indicate the triumph of his mother's influence over his father's, of the "artistic" woman over the "practical" man of business. Yet even while he fulfilled his mother's ambitions, Norris fully shared his father's (and his father's culture's) devaluation of the "literary" as feeble and effeminate. "Life," he declared again and again, "is more important than literature. . . . Life is better than literature" (7:179).[3] Artists, in his fiction, are almost always treated with contempt and ridicule, and he delighted in the idea that his own novels were anything but "literary." His characteristic stance is clear in a letter he wrote in 1899, thanking Isaac F. Marcosson for his favorable review of *McTeague:* "What pleased me most was the 'disdaining of all pretentions to style.' It is precisely what I try most to avoid. I detest 'fine writing,' 'rhetoric,' 'elegant English'—tommyrot. Who cares for fine style! Tell your yarn and let your style go to the devil. We don't want literature, we want life."[4] This stance, moreover, constitutes the central plank in Norris's campaign for literary naturalism. "I've lived by doing things," announces one of his characters, "not by thinking things, or reading about what other people have done or thought; and I guess it's what you do that counts, rather than what you think or read about" (3:234). To put it crudely but accurately, a naturalist for Norris is a writer who "counts."

"Zola," Norris writes in "A Plea for Romantic Fiction" (1901), "has been dubbed a Realist, but he is, on the contrary, the very head of the

Romanticists." Whereas "Realism . . . notes only the surfaces of things," and confines itself to "the drama of a broken teacup, the tragedy of a walk down the block, the excitement of an afternoon call, the adventure of an invitation to dinner," Zolaesque "romance" breaks through this surface to explore "the unplumbed depths of the human heart, and the mystery of sex, and the problems of life, and the black, unsearched penetralia of the soul of man" (7:164–65, 167–68). Five years earlier, in 1896, Norris set forth much the same argument in an essay in the San Francisco *Wave*, "Zola as a Romantic Writer." "Naturalism," Norris here insists, "is a form of romanticism, not an inner circle of realism." Because Zola deals with "the lower—almost the lowest—classes," his work is not "purely romantic"; but neither is it "realism." "It is a school by itself," Norris concludes, "unique, powerful beyond words. It is naturalism."[5]

Norris's principal contribution to the definition of naturalism is his notion that it is a synthesis of "romance" and "realism," but if we wish to understand what this synthesis meant to him we must recognize that the key terms, as he used them, had far less to do with literary theory, with a discrimination of fictional modes, than with a personal effort to transform the meaning of his identity as a writer. For instance toward the end of *Moran of the Lady Letty* the terms "real" and "romance" are used in a quite suggestive way as virtual synonyms. After discovering his manhood at sea and in the thrill of killing a man in hand-to-hand combat, the hero, Ross Wilbur, returns to San Francisco, to discover that he no longer fits into its feminized social world. "He had known romance," we are told, "and the spell of the great, simple, primitive emotions." A few pages earlier Wilbur himself expresses the same idea in somewhat different terms. "We've come back to the world of little things," he announces. "But we'll pull out of here in the morning and get to the places where things are real" (3:314, 309). The meaning of "real" here has little to do with any philosophical definition of reality; rather the ocean is more "real" than the city because it is bigger, because life on it is more exciting. This is why Norris can equate the "real" with "romance," and to say in this sense that something is "real" is merely to say that it is an exotic antithesis of the ordinary routines of middle-class life—which is precisely the sense in which Norris advocated the rejection of Howellsian realism in favor of romantic naturalism.

The trouble with Howells, Norris writes in the 1896 essay on Zola, is that his characters "live across the street from us, they are 'on our block.'" "One can go even farther," he adds. "We ourselves are Mr. Howells's characters, so long as we are well behaved and ordinary and bourgeois, so long as we are not adventurous or not rich or not unconventional." What, by contrast, is the appeal of Zola? Norris says nothing about such things as "experimental" method or determinist philosophy, qualities normally associated with naturalism; what matters instead is that Zola's characters "are not of our lives . . . because we are *ordinary*." The expansion of this point tells us a good deal about just what naturalism meant to Norris, and why it appealed to him:

> To be noted of M. Zola we must leave the rank and the file, either run to the forefront of the marching world, or fall by the roadway; we must become individual, unique. . . . Terrible things must happen to the characters of the naturalistic tale. They must be twisted from the ordinary, wrenched out from the quiet, uneventful round of every-day life, or flung into the throes of a vast and terrible drama that works itself out in unleashed passion, in blood, and in sudden death. The world of M. Zola is a world of big things; the enormous, the formidable, the terrible, is what counts; to teacup tragedies here.[6]

Here as always Norris understands naturalism entirely in terms of the writer's material, but this is the least of the passage's interest. Ross Wilbur, we recall, turns to "romance" from "the world of little things" and in so doing becomes a "real" man. Norris turns to naturalism for precisely the same reason: it offers him, he seems to believe, a connection to "a world of big things," and the concern with size is suggestive. Norris's version of naturalism sounds like nothing so much as a prospectus for a body-building course, promising to turn the ninety-eight-pound literary weakling into a dynamic he-man, one who "counts" in the domain of masculine "reality." Thus did naturalism offer Norris what he apparently needed and wanted: a way of following his mother's footsteps, as it were, in his father's boots.[7]

Donald Pizer writes that "although . . . Norris's critical essays are poorly written, repetitive, and occasionally plain silly, they nevertheless contain a coherent critical attitude of some importance."[8] No one can doubt the importance of Norris's ideas—they are typical of a good deal of the thinking that characterized American literary modernism in the 1890s and early twentieth century—but the truth is that nothing in Norris's essays is sillier than the critical attitude that underlies them, and even to describe Norris's call for naturalism *as* a critical attitude may be to invite misunderstanding. For the terms in which he espouses the new fiction are not finally terms of criticism; they are rather the terms of crude fantasy, the fantasy of a writer haunted by the specter of "effeminate" irrelevance, dreaming of a virile fiction that "counts" because it dismisses the "literary" in order to keep step with "the marching world." There is of course nothing wrong with a

writer wishing to rescue literature from the excessively "literary"—
wishing to return it to "reality," to the life and language of actual
people. This has been the project of many writers, of Wordsworth, for
instance, or Whitman. Yet what distinguishes Norris's ambition from
theirs, even more than an obvious difference in achievement, is the
crudeness of his idea of reality. It is almost always tinged, or more than
tinged, with sexism and racism; white, Anglo-Saxon males always
seem to have a corner on the "real." The art of the novelist, according
to Norris, is "of all the arts . . . the most virile. . . . It is not an affair of
women and aesthetes" (7:158–59).[9]

An even more basic problem is that Norris cannot invoke his idea
of "reality," in his essays or in his fiction, without resorting to a language of sodden and inflated cliché. One thinks of such things as
"flung into the throes of a vast and terrible drama that works itself out
in unleashed passions, in blood, and in sudden death"—or "the unplumbed depths of the human heart, and the mystery of sex, and the
problems of life, and the black, unsearched penetralia of the soul of
man." Such language hardly convinces one that its author has a very
precise sense of the reality to which he thinks literature should turn;
instead, it indicates clearly what should be clear by now in any case,
that Norris's conception of literary naturalism was based on the crudest sort of *fantasy* of the "real." Behind such rhetoric there lurked a
serious dilemma, a dilemma inevitable once Norris had accepted the
assumptions on which his idea of naturalism was based. To insist on the
distinction between "literature" and "life," and to choose "life" over
"literature," was not to solve the problem of his vocational identity but
to compound it—by cutting off the very bough on which he himself
had chosen to perch. In another literary essay, "The Novel with a
'Purpose,'" Norris briefly glimpses his predicament: "The artist," he
writes, "has a double personality: himself as a man and himself as an
artist." As a "man" he may care about his materials, but to the "artist"
in him they "must be . . . a matter of the mildest interest" (7:23–24).
Thus even the naturalistic novelist, the novelist with a "purpose," is
finally beset by a fundamental schizophrenia, torn between the antithetical identities of "man" (identifying with his "big" characters and
materials) and "artist" (regarding both with aloof detachment); moreover in order to function as an "artist" he must at least temporarily
cease to function as a "man." Norris soon retreats from this insight,
ending his essay with the passage quoted in the prologue to Part Two
of this study, the passage in which fiction is allied with "the Great
March" and the novelist is grouped with "leaders," "teachers," "great
divines," and "great philosophers"—all united in their muscular pur-

suit of "a well-defined, well-seen, courageously sought for purpose" (7:26). This retreat is hardly surprising, since to have followed his insight to its logical conclusion would have been to undermine the whole rationale for a fiction that "counts" in the world on the world's own terms.

The confusions and fallacies rampant in Norris's writings about naturalism are obvious, and it may seem mean-spirited to pick on him. Nevertheless, it is of the utmost importance that we understand the nature and basis of his thinking about literature. We must recognize that the ultimate significance of naturalism for Norris, like the ultimate significance of realism for Howells, was far more centrally personal than literary. We should recognize, too, that Norris's assumptions have been shared, in one form or another, by a great many so-called American naturalists—who have sought, like Norris, to neutralize suspicions of the irrelevance of literature by suppressing the "literary" and insisting on the primacy of a fantasy of masculine "reality." In any case, understanding the nature and basis of Norris's thinking about literature allows us to ask what may be the most important question about his example: How, exactly, did his confused idea of naturalism, and the personal and vocational conflicts that lay behind this idea, affect the fiction he wrote during his brief literary career?

Naturalism and Style

Toward the end of 1898 Norris wrote to Howells, who had seen promise in Norris's first published novel, that its successor, *McTeague*, would be quite different: "It is," he explained, "as naturalistic as *Moran* was romantic." A year later he wrote to Isaac Marcosson that the novels published immediately following *McTeague*—*Blix* and *A Man's Woman*—had been diversions, but that he now vowed to change: "I am going back *definitely*," he wrote, "to the style of MacT. and stay with it right along. . . . The Wheat series will be straight naturalism with all the guts I can get into it."[10] Literary historians and critics have come to regard *McTeague* and at least the first volume of the "Wheat series," *The Octopus*, as Norris's most important novels, and they have agreed, by and large, that part of what distinguishes them is their cultivation of naturalism. It is far from clear, however, just what qualities in the novels this classification refers to. For instance, if we understand naturalism mainly as indicating a certain kind of subject matter—the underclass rather than the middle class, the brutal and sordid rather than the genteel—the label certainly would seem to suit *McTeague*, Norris's tale of an uneducated San Francisco dentist whose increasingly sadistic relationship with his wife culminates in her murder, but it hardly seems to suit *The Octopus*, whose rancher heroes, locked in struggle with the railroad, are wealthy capitalists, middle-class entrepreneurs. To Norris's contemporary readers the world of *The Octopus* might have seemed exotic, but it would not have seemed sordid.

If we follow Zola's lead, and see naturalism as "scientific" or "experimental" fiction, the term seems even less appropriate as a description of Norris's practice. There are in his novels scattered gestures toward the idea of determinism, but they remain gestures: Norris's "science," in this sense, is at bottom melodramatic and moralistic. He frequently indulges in meditations on the supremacy of amoral "forces"—most notably toward the end of *The Octopus* when the poet Presley, shocked by the railroad's victory over his friends the ranchers, comes to an "explanation of existence" couched in what popular thinking in the 1890s might have taken to be "scientific" terms:

Men were naught, death was naught, life was naught; FORCE only existed— FORCE that brought men into the world, FORCE that crowded them out of it to make way for the succeeding generations, FORCE that made the wheat grow, FORCE that garnered it from the soil to give place to the succeeding crop. (2:343)

But such meditations are seldom pertinent to what actually happens in Norris's fiction; throughout *The Octopus*, for instance, the railroad has been driven to combat the ranchers not by any demonstrated laws of nature or of the marketplace but by the conventional and melodramatic villainy of characters like the jowly railroad agent, S. Behrman. In the last analysis, Norris has little interest in exploring the actual mechanism by which "forces" and "conditions" influence human behavior; on this score, too, the conventional notion that his fiction is naturalistic would appear to rest on rather shaky ground.

Yet all of this may be beside the point. Norris, like Zola, dismissed considerations of style from the discussion of naturalism, yet as Larzer Ziff has observed, "one cannot have *no* style," and Norris in fact cultivates a number of distinguishable styles. "Disregard for style," Ziff writes, "is, as Norris unconsciously shows, in constant danger of being bad style, bad art," and it is not difficult to find in Norris examples of perfectly dreadful writing; he had, as John Berryman put it, "a style like a great wet dog."[11] Still, it is not enough simply to say that Norris had a "bad" style; there are more important matters to be pursued. What, for instance, are the precise qualities of Norris's various styles? In what sense or senses might we describe these characteristic styles as being "naturalistic"? What, finally, is the relationship between Norris's stylistic practice and his own conception, however vague or confused, of literary naturalism?

Let us begin with the most obviously "naturalistic" prose in Norris. In *McTeague*, for example, dentistry is described in a technical language clearly acquired through research. McTeague makes "'mats' from his tape of non-cohesive gold"; he makes "'blocks' to be used in large proximal cavities," "'cylinders' for commencing fillings," and so on (8:15). Still, while dentistry provides a fund of convenient symbols in a novel whose main characters are obsessed with gold, the factual details of dentistry, the actual procedures and the specialized language used to describe them, remain at best tangential to Norris's concerns; and once the real business of the novel gets going the language quickly veers away from the obvious naturalism of technical terminology and detail. For instance, when McTeague is first attracted to Trina Sieppe we are told that "suddenly the animal in the man stirred and woke; the evil instincts that in him were so close to the surface leaped to life, shouting and clamouring"; a kiss leads to an authorial meditation on "the changeless order of things—the man desiring the woman only for what she withholds; the woman worshipping the man for that which she yields up to him"; of Trina's response to this kiss we are told that "the Woman within her suddenly awoke" (8:26, 73, 77). This is the sort of language to which Norris always resorts, in his fiction as in his critical essays, when he wants to describe the "reality" he conceived to be the true subject of naturalistic fiction. This language has little to do with factual detail, with observation, or with any scientific effort to understand and explain physical or emotional processes; instead, it relies relentlessly on melodramatic metaphor and abstract assertion. The activities of McTeague's "evil instincts" are purely (and more or less inconceivably) metaphorical—"leaping," "shouting," "clamouring"—and this reliance on metaphor, and the epithet "evil," tell us a good deal about the depth of Norris's commitment to scientific objectivity. Finally, important nouns here are characteristically preceded by the definite article—"the man," "the animal," "the woman"—and they are likely as well to come out capitalized—as in "the Woman." This is a language not of scientific description or explanation but of abstract, melodramatic cliché. In *The Octopus* and in its sequel, *The Pit*, Norris gave this language free rein.

For *The Octopus* Norris researched wheat ranching and California politics; for *The Pit* he went through a crash course in the intricacies of commodity speculation; but in both books the nominal subjects are repeatedly swamped in waves of abstraction and melodramatic metaphor. While a description of a wheat harvest near the end of *The*

Octopus mentions such things as "header knives," "beltings," "the separator," "the agitator," along with "cylinders, augers, fans, seeders, and elevators, drapers and chaff-carriers" (2:325), the next to last paragraph of the book is far more typical of Norris's treatment of his subject:

> *But the* WHEAT *remained.* Untouched, unassailable, undefiled, that mighty world-force, that nourisher of nations, wrapped in Nirvanic calm, indifferent to the human swarm, gigantic, resistless, moved onward in its appointed grooves. . . . [T]he great harvest of Los Muertos rolled like a flood from the Sierras to the Himalayas to feed thousands of starving scarecrows on the barren plains of India. (2:360)

Norris's political research for *The Octopus*, unlike his research into wheat ranching, does play an important part in the book's action, providing the details for the story of the ranchers' unsuccessful effort to elect their own railroad commission and thus resist punitive increases in the rate charged for shipping their crop to market. Yet even here the details of political manipulation and countermanipulation keep dissolving into the abstract rhetoric of the "big" and "vital." For instance, when the ranchers unite to resist the railroad, the narrator enlarges considerably on the significance of their action:

> It was the uprising of The People; the thunder of the outbreak of revolt; the mob demanding to be led, aroused at last, imperious, resistless, overwhelming. It was the blind fury of insurrection, the brute, many-tongued, red-eyed, bellowing for guidance, baring its teeth, unsheathing its claws, imposing its will with the abrupt, resistless pressure of the relaxed piston, inexorable, knowing no pity. (1:271)

Except for the curious addition of a "relaxed piston" (which in spite of its relaxation still exerts "pressure") this eruption of "the brute" sounds a lot more like what happens to McTeague, and to so many of Norris's characters, than it sounds like any conceivable political meeting. Here "The People," capitals and all, are virtually interchangeable with such things as "the man," "the animal," or "the Woman," and the "resistless pressure" of this force (the word "resistless" occurs twice in this brief passage) makes it sound more than a little like the wheat itself, at the close, "gigantic, resistless, moved onward in its appointed grooves." The problem, of course, is that this rhapsodic description bears no relation whatever to its supposed subject, the formation of the Ranchers' League to combat the railroad. These capitalists are not in any sense "The People"—nor, for that matter, is any actual "mob" (let alone "*the* mob") involved in their coalition or in any of their subsequent actions.

The same sort of movement, from concrete detail to a quite irrelevant assertion of large "force," also characterizes Norris's last novel, *The Pit*. Much of the book's action turns on details of speculation in grain futures: Curtis Jadwin corners the market in May wheat only to destroy himself by trying to extend this corner to a July harvest made much larger by his own inflation of wheat prices, and in the story of his rise and fall we learn about such things as "bulls" and "bears," "selling long" and "selling short," or "covering" contracts to deliver grain on a specified date. These things matter in *The Pit* in ways that the details of dentistry, for instance, do not matter in *McTeague*. Still, these details, too, are finally tangential to the direction of Norris's deepest concern; what ultimately matters about Jadwin is that he is another "big" man who unleashes the "forces" in himself only to be beaten by even larger "forces." It is thus no surprise that the complex machinations of commodity trading are repeatedly buried beneath Norris's characteristic language of melodramatic metaphor. To cite only one example, here is some of the narrator's account of Jadwin's difficulty holding to a vow to stay out of speculation:

Try as he would, the echoes of the rumbling of the Pit reached Jadwin at every hour of the day and night. The maelstrom there at the foot of La Salle Street was swirling now with a mightier rush than for years past. Thundering, its vortex smoking, it sent its whirling far out over the country, from ocean to ocean, sweeping the wheat into its currents, sucking it in, and spewing it out again in the gigantic pulses of its ebb and flow.

. . . The great Fact, the great Result which was at last to issue forth from all this turmoil was not yet achieved. Would it refuse to come until a master hand, all powerful, all daring, gripped the levers of the sluice gates that controlled the crashing waters of the Pit? He did not know. Was it the moment for a chief?

Was this upheaval a revolution that called aloud for its Napoleon? (9:247–48)

To believe that this is in any sense naturalism is to believe that Napoleon rose to power as water commissioner of Paris, after a period of severe flooding.[12]

My point here is not simply that Norris's stylistic excesses are ridiculous, although the impulse to raucous laughter is often irresistible. The main importance of Norris's persistent cultivation of rhetorical melodrama, rather, is that it indicates quite clearly what is going on at the heart of his fiction. He cares very little if at all for factual or "scientific" detail—for specialized language or, what is far more important, for the specific biological, mechanical, economic, or political processes this language describes. He always shifts from the literal to the metaphorical, and he draws his metaphors—unlike Melville, say, or Thoreau, or Pynchon—not from the process he is supposedly describing but from a severely limited stock of conventional and interchangeable clichés about the emergence of vague, "resistless" forces: "the brute," "the mob," "the crushing waters," whatever. It would thus appear that Norris's conception of naturalism affected the style of his fiction in a rather direct way: one can easily understand the appeal of such metaphors to a writer who wanted something "big," who longed to escape "the quiet, uneventful round of everyday life" in order to join "the throes of a vast and terrible drama that works itself out in unleashed passions, in blood, and in sudden death." Even the abstract vagueness of this language would seem to be functional: Norris's was, after all, a *fantasy* of "reality," of "force," and detailed understanding does have a way of dampening ardors for the exotic. Still, to associate the style that emerges from Norris's needs and fantasies with what has normally been meant by "naturalism" is to throw critical seriousness to the winds—or, as Norris himself might have preferred it, into the smoking vortex.

The story of the effect of Norris's ideas on his style does not end here, however, for Norris has another arguably "realistic" or "naturalistic" style, at least in his earlier fiction. For instance, in *Vandover and the Brute*, written during Norris's year at Harvard in 1894–95, there is an interesting description of the home of Ida Wade, a "fast" young woman whom the hero, Vandover, eventually ruins:

The front door stood at the right side of the parlour windows. Two Corinthian pillars on either side of the vestibule supported a balcony; these pillars had iron capitals which were painted to imitate the wood of the house, which in its turn was painted to imitate stone. The house was but two stories high, and the roof was topped with an iron cresting. There was a microscopical front yard in which one saw a tiny gravel walk, two steps long, that led to a door under the front steps, where the gas-meter was kept. A few dusty and straggling calla-lilies grew about. (5:59)

Here, suddenly, is a Norris halfway between Mark Twain and Nathanael West, relying not on melodramatic inflation but on ironic understatement. The progression from "Corinthian pillars" to the "gas-meter" is very nice, and those "iron capitals . . . painted to imitate the wood of the house, which in its turn was painted to imitate stone," could be straight out of West's *The Day of the Locust*. For the reader accustomed to the inflated Norris, the deft and quiet irony of such passages is positively astonishing. It is not simply that they grow out of observation of the world Norris knew, rather than the out of the "big" world he fantasized, although this fact is important.[13] What is most surprising is that a writer in whose work irony (at least intended irony) is usually absent cultivates it here quite deliberately and skillfully. The Wades's world is seen on its own terms and yet is judged in quite other terms; narrator and reader stand aloof, seeing in the quietly reported details of this world what its inhabitants could never see themselves.

There is a fair amount of this sort of writing early in *Vandover,* although it soon retreats before the advance of the "serious" Norris, with his story of how Vandover "rushed into a career of dissipation, consumed with the desire of vice, the perverse, blind, and reckless desire of the male" (5:181). In *McTeague*—written for the most part, like *Vandover*, in the mid-1890s—the ironic style is sustained longer, which is surely one of the reasons the book now strikes many readers as Norris's most successful novel. For instance, we are told that on one wall of his Dental Parlors McTeague has hung "a steel engraving of the court of Lorenzo de' Medici, which he had bought because there were a great many figures in it for the money." We are later told about Trina Sieppe's taste in pictures, about her admiration for "the 'Ideal Heads,' lovely girls with flowing straw-coloured hair and immense, upturned eyes. These always had for title, 'Reverie,' or 'An Idyll,' or 'Dreams of Love.'" At a theater with Trina and her mother and brother McTeague is much impressed with the performance. "That's what you call musicians," he announces, "gravely." "'Home, Sweet Home,' played upon a trombone," adds the narrator, impersonating the admiration of the naive spectators. "Think of that! Art could go no farther" (8:3, 170, 87–88). The whole account of this visit to the theater, while the humor is sometimes a bit overdone, is a comic tour de force, as is the account of McTeague's and Trina's wedding, managed with military precision by Trina's blustering father. "Not Stanley penetrating for the first time into the Dark Continent," writes the narrator, "not Napoleon leading his army across the Alps, was more weighted with responsibility" (8:131). Significantly, the heroic analogies here used ironically are precisely the sort that Norris will later use seriously and straightforwardly—for instance, in *The Pit*, when Curtis Jadwin wonders whether the "maelstrom" is calling aloud for its "Napoleon."

In *McTeague*, moreover, this ironic aloofness is not confined to moments of comedy or satire. After a visit to Trina's family McTeague stays the night, sleeping in Trina's room (which she has vacated). He stands in front of her open closet, staring in fascination at her clothes.

"All at once," we are told, "seized with an unreasoned impulse, McTeague opened his huge arms and gathered the little garments close to him, plunging his face deep amongst them, savouring their delicious odour with long breaths of luxury and supreme content" (8:69). Such things as "savouring," "delicious odour," "luxury," and "supreme content" sound, in their excessiveness, like Norris's own purple rhetoric, but here they work because their excessiveness is the point: these terms express McTeague's emotions, not the narrator's, and in recognizing their ironic function we recognize our distance from McTeague, from his moment of fetishistic indulgence, a distance we share with the narrator. The same sort of narrative aloofness characterizes one of the best-known passages in *McTeague*—the description of Trina's death, after she has been beaten into insensibility by her husband:

Trina lay unconscious, just as she had fallen under the last of McTeague's blows, her body twitching with an occasional hiccough that stirred the pool of blood in which she lay face downward. Toward morning she died with a rapid series of hiccoughs that sounded like a piece of clockwork running down. (8:320)

There is a good deal of Norris's customary rhetoric in *McTeague*— abstract, melodramatic, overly insistent, and utterly without irony— but what gives the book its power is Norris's ability for the most part to maintain the distinction between himself and his characters, between the artist and his materials, between, as we might put it, "literature" and "life." The most curious fact about Norris's career, in this connection, is that what he discovered in the mid-90s, in *Vandover* and *McTeague*, he rapidly unlearned; in *The Octopus* and *The Pit* there is almost nothing like the aloof irony of *McTeague* at its best. At the beginning of the second volume of *The Octopus*, as the setting shifts briefly from the San Joaquin valley to the genteel world of San Francisco, we have a momentary eruption of satire, directed mainly at an "artistic" woman named Mrs. Cedarquist who surrounds herself with a coterie of cultural charlatans, but it is hard to find much irony of this sort elsewhere in the book. Descriptions of nature are "poetic" in the worst sense, while descriptions of habitations and their decoration, in both *The Octopus* and *The Pit*, are almost uniformly without either irony or point. To understand Norris, then, we must try to understand what happened to him between the writing of *McTeague* in the mid-1890s and the writing of *The Octopus* and *The Pit* at the end of the decade.

In this light we should look at the initial description of Norris's most obvious surrogate in *The Octopus*, the poet Presley, who conforms with almost ludicrous precision to the conventional stereotype of the "artist." He has "the forehead of the intellectual," along with "a delicate and highly sensitive nature"; "one guessed," we are told, "that Presley's refinement had been gained only by a certain loss of strength" (1:6). An important part of the "artistic" baggage he must slough off in order to discover himself as a "man" is an effete lack of sympathy with "the people"—meaning, in this case, not the big ranchers but those far below them in the economic hierarchy. "These uncouth brutes of farm-hands and petty ranchers," the narrator tells us, "grimed with the soil they worked upon, were odious to [Presley] beyond words. Never could he feel in sympathy with them, nor with their lives, their ways, their marriages, deaths, bickerings, and all the monotonous round of their sordid existence" (1:3). This whole issue of sympathy with the "sordid" might remind us of Olive Chancellor's need to mortify her taste, in Henry James's *Bostonians;* but in terms of what happens in *The Octopus*, this issue is a red herring—since very few "farm-hands and petty ranchers" appear in the book and none of them is an important character, especially to Presley. Norris's raising of the issue of sympathy is important, however, because it reveals how closely, by the time he wrote *The Octopus*, he associated lack of sympathy with artistic alienation, with the irrelevance of literature to life. And what matters is that such lack of sympathy was precisely the hallmark of the irony in *McTeague*, signaling again and again the aloofness of the narrator, his distance from the "sordid existence" of his characters. Given Presley's need to identify with "the people," is it any wonder that such irony is almost totally missing from *The Octopus* and *The Pit*?

By the time he wrote *The Octopus*, Norris had apparently convinced himself that he could be a "man" only if he could identify with his materials, with "the world of big things," and while such a belief may have helped assuage his personal and vocational anxieties, it left little room for satire and irony—which could hardly be used, in any significant way, to describe the ranchers who were after all Norris's projections of his own fantasy of "reality." To put it bluntly, then, Norris's theory of naturalism would seem to have destroyed his power as a writer. It compelled him to turn away not only from the *idea* of style but from the actual style and stance of his best novel, a novel largely written before its author began to theorize about fiction. Norris's insistence on the absolute distinction of "life" and "literature" set forth the terms of a self-fulfilling prophecy. Proclaiming again and again that he was a "man," Norris ultimately ceased to be an "artist." Lionel Trilling complained, years ago, about "the chronic American belief that there exists an opposition between reality and mind and that one must enlist in the party of reality."[14] This belief lies at the heart of Norris's essays and novels: dismissing "style" and the "literary," he ended up writing a style that is literary in the very worst sense of the term, and he turned from the irony of his best early fiction to a "reality" that is in fact a tissue of the very crudest fantasy. Norris's faults, this is to say, are not incidental; they are the products of what he conceived naturalism to be and to require. He wanted above all to enlist in the "party of reality," to join "the marching world," and in this respect his example is prophetic of a good deal of what has passed for naturalist thinking, in American fiction and criticism, in the years since his death.

5

Irony, Parody, and "Transcendental Realism"
STEPHEN CRANE

"Maggie lost herself in sympathy with the wanderers swooning in snow
storms beneath happy-hued church windows. . . . To Maggie and the rest of
the audience this was transcendental realism. . . . Viewing it, they hugged
themselves in ecstatic pity of their imagined or real condition."
Stephen Crane, *Maggie: A Girl of the Streets* (1893)

"He felt a quiet manhood, nonassertive but of sturdy and strong blood. He
knew that he would no more quail before his guides wherever they should
point. He had been to touch the great death, and found that, after all, it was
but the great death. He was a man."
Crane, *The Red Badge of Courage* (1895)

Frank Norris died in 1902, at the age of thirty-two; Stephen Crane
had died two years earlier, five months before his twenty-ninth birthday.[1] So when William Dean Howells sat down to write his 1902
eulogy, "Frank Norris," he quite naturally found himself comparing
the two ill-fated luminaries of their American literary generation.
Norris, he wrote, "gave one the impression of strength and courage
that would hold out to all lengths. . . . I never met him but he made
me feel that he could do it, the thing he meant to do, and do it robustly
and quietly, without the tremor of 'those electrical nerves' which im-
parted itself from the presence of Stephen Crane." This personal contrast dramatizes, for Howells, what he sees as a fundamental contrast
between Norris and Crane as fiction writers. He praises "the epical
breadths of Norris's fiction," "the full music of his . . . aspiration, the
rich diapason of purposes securely shaping themselves in perform-

ance," and this hackneyed and overwrought prose, so uncharacteristic of Howells generally, even sounds a bit like Norris's own "serious" style. Crane's fiction, on the other hand, is characterized for Howells by "physical slightness," reflecting "the delicacy of energies that could be put forth only in nervous spurts, in impulses vivid and keen, but wanting in breadth and bulk of effect."[2] Howells's contrast is typical of the quite different ways in which Norris and Crane, who would come to be classified as the two major American naturalists of the 1890s, were perceived by many of their contemporaries: Norris, exuding "strength" and animated by "purposes securely shaping themselves in performance," is very much a man; Crane, inspired by "impulses vivid and keen, but wanting in breadth and bulk of effect," and beset by "electrical nerves," is finally an "artist"—even, in Howells's account, something like a female hysteric. And whatever we think of Howells's specific judgments of Norris and Crane, the virtually allegorical emphasis of these portraits tells us a good deal about American literary culture in the 1890s.

I do not mean to deny that Norris and Crane wrote very different kinds of fiction; what strikes one from first to last is precisely the contrast between their works and stances. Crane cared not at all for "big" ideas, at least not in the way that Norris cared for them; he produced no literary essays, no manifestos; and except for a few very general statements about the importance of sincerity to literary excellence, mostly in private letters, one must infer his aesthetic principles from his fiction. In this fiction, moreover, he does not intrude in his own voice to provide mini-essays or pseudoscientific digressions; in an 1897 letter about his admiration for Tolstoy, for instance, he objects—with calculated colloquialism—to "the lectures he sticks in" and adds: "I like my art straight."[3] Digressions about the play of "forces" do sometimes appear in Crane's fiction, but they are located dramatically in the consciousnesses of characters (for example, the correspondent in "The Open Boat") and are hardly to be taken as expressions of authorial meaning or philosophy.[4] Also unlike Norris, at least Norris after *McTeague*, Crane achieves his effects through a pervasive narrative and verbal irony; what distinguishes Crane from Norris above all is that he cares about style, that he cultivates a style that deliberately calls attention to itself as a style.

The ironic self-consciousness of Crane's prose, which is what most clearly distinguishes his work from Norris's, is just as clearly the source of Howells's sense that Crane was excessively literary or artistic, cut off from life and therefore from "breadth and bulk of effect"; and Howells's complaint was hardly unique. A hostile British reviewer of *The*

Red Badge of Courage denounced the book's "serio-comic effect" and "grotesqueness of fancy"; Civil War General A. C. McClurg dismissed the novel as "a mere work of diseased imagination"—although the author "constantly strains after so-called realism," he added, "the result is a mere riot of words"; and even the New York *Times*, in a generally favorable review, complained of some "unpleasant affectations of style which the author would do well to correct"—Crane's "natural talent is so strong," the *Times* continued, "that it is a pity its expression should be marred by pretty tricks."[5] It hardly matters that many modern readers would see at least a bit of justice in these estimates; the point is that conventional American and British literary opinion in the 1890s, especially opinion committed to some sort of realism in literature, could respond to Crane's self-conscious stylistic irony in no other terms. If life and literature were antithetical, how could a writer be "realistic" and yet openly advertise a concern for style?

The same question haunts those who have sought more recently to classify Crane as a naturalist.[6] One of the deepest appeals of so-called naturalism in America has been its promise of a reality unmediated by language, instantly accessible to the reader, a direct transmission of "real" life in which style remains transparent. In this view, the author may be quite intrusive as a "scientific" voice, but anything that makes us aware of the writer as writer—or, perhaps equally important, makes the writer aware that he *is* a writer, a mediator—damages the goods. I have no desire to revive the debate about whether Crane's fiction is or is not "naturalistic"; but to dismiss this debate, or at least to bracket it, is by no means to dismiss or bracket the rather different question of the importance of naturalist thinking to Crane, the question of his relation to the ideas underlying the theory and practice of a novelist like Norris. Crane was not, of course, influenced by Norris, whose first published novel appeared five years after *Maggie: A Girl of the Streets* (1893) and three years after *The Red Badge of Courage* (1895), and who began preaching naturalism to a national audience only in the year following Crane's death. Still, the ideas to which Norris gave utterance had been current for some time, especially in circles interested in literary realism, and Crane could scarcely have escaped them; after all, they also lay at the heart of the critical writings of his most influential mentor, William Dean Howells.[7]

Both Norris and Howells set out to reconcile fiction writing with some of the ideas dominant in their culture: that to be "literary" was to be effeminate and unreal, that "real" life was essentially masculine, that the novelist proved his seriousness and power by dismissing style and identifying with his materials—especially, in Norris's case, with "big" materials. It is not enough to insist that a literary naturalism so conceived did not include Stephen Crane among its proponents or practitioners. What I wish to argue is not only that Stephen Crane was not a naturalist in this sense but that he quite consciously rejected such a view of literature and, what is most important, that he worked out his own literary practice in deliberate opposition to it. Crane used formal strategies conventionally associated with literary naturalism in order to undermine the deeper assumptions behind the American application of these strategies. His risk was that in rejecting the prevalent and supposedly avant-guard image of the writer as "man" he might seem to be acting out a caricature of the writer as "artist," and this is clearly how Howells and others understood his career. Crane's challenge (mostly, one gathers, to himself) was to produce a fiction which, by steering clear of both of these inane stereotypes, would be true to experience and be literary at the same time, and it is hardly surprising that those committed to the assumptions of American naturalism expressed by Frank Norris have had little understanding of, or sympathy for, what Crane was trying to accomplish. But what matters most is that naturalism for Crane, to the extent that it means anything to describe him as a naturalist, involved first of all not the discovery of authentic material but the fashioning of an authentic *style*, an authentic *language*.

The Language of the Street

The classification of Stephen Crane as a naturalist has been based largely on the setting and subject of his first novel, *Maggie: A Girl of the Streets:* the harsh world of the slums, the heroine's descent from innocence to prostitution, her mother's alcoholism, and so on.[8] Given the evident differences among Norris, Crane, and Dreiser, critics who argue for a school of naturalism in American fiction have been gratified that these three writers at least started out with fictional portrayals of lower-class brutality or amorality; *Maggie*, from this perspective, is Crane's *McTeague*, his *Sister Carrie*. Such critics have found further support for their view of Crane in the fact that he portrays slum life in *Maggie*, from the first chapter on, as a battle, arguably a Darwinian struggle.[9] They also have placed considerable weight on the inscription Crane wrote in a number of presentation copies of *Maggie* in 1893:

It is inevitable that you be greatly shocked by this book but continue, please, with all possible courage to the end. F'or it tries to show that environment is a tremendous thing in the world and frequently shapes lives regardless. If one proves that theory, one makes room in Heaven for all sorts of souls (notably an occasional street girl) who are not confidently expected to be there by many excellent people.

It is probable that the reader of this small thing may consider the Author to be a bad man, but, obviously, this is a matter of small consequence to

The *Author*[10]

These evidences of the supposed naturalism of *Maggie* are, however, at best equivocal. For one thing, as many readers have noted, Crane's inscription hardly describes what actually happens in his book: Maggie, who "blossomed in a mud puddle" (16), is not a product of her environment but a strange anomaly, like Verena Tarrant in James's *The Bostonians;* she is a deterministically inexplicable innocent in a world of corruption.[11] Nor does the inscription itself, if one reads it with care, turn out to be a straightforward declaration of naturalist intention. The apparent determinism of "shapes lives" is immediately qualified by "frequently" and "regardless" (indicating that environment does not always shape lives and that it is apparently not the only force to do so) and by the next sentence's sarcastic concern with "room in Heaven" and "excellent people." We should also recognize that if there is any overt statement of determinism in the inscription it occurs in the *first* sentence: "It is inevitable that you will be greatly shocked by this book." Crane, this is to say, is concerned here less with the general effect of environment on his heroine's behavior than with the specific way in which readers, confident that they are "excellent people," have been conditioned to react to his story. His inscription is thus less a naturalistic manifesto than a curious mixture of sardonic defiance ("this is a matter of small consequence to/The *Author*") and authoritarian instruction ("continue, please, with all possible courage to the end"). The sentences about "environment," considered in the context of the whole inscription, are, finally, not a rationale for *writing* the book but a mocking rationale, offered to the reader who may lack even "possible courage," for *reading* it. This inscription is not a manifesto but a taunt.

Crane does of course portray the life of the slums as a battle—even, perhaps, as a struggle—but the presentation of this struggle, the language in which it is described, is not exactly Darwinian. *Maggie* opens in the midst of a fight between two gangs of slum boys:

A very little boy stood upon a heap of gravel for the honor of Rum Alley. He was throwing stones at howling urchins from Devil's Row who were circling madly about the heap and pelting him.

His infantile countenance was livid with fury. His small body was writhing in the delivery of great, crimson oaths.

"Run, Jimmie, run! Dey'll get yehs," screamed a retreating Rum Alley child.

"Naw," responded Jimmie with a valiant roar, "dese micks can't make me run." (3)[12]

The effect of this description clearly depends on an ironic discrepancy between the elevated language of the narrator and the coarseness of the events he is describing.[13] Most obviously, it depends on the discrepancy between his language and the language of his characters: little Jimmie Johnson could hardly describe an "infantile countenance" as being "livid with fury," and there is a similar incongruity in the juxtaposition of "a valiant roar" and the speech to which it refers: "dese micks can't make me run." What we have here is mock heroic in the manner, say, of Fielding, and this is hardly a mode we associate with naturalism or Darwinian science; Darwin's prestige, after all, was not based on his reputation as a humorist.

There *is* a sense, however, in which we might take the discrepancy between the language of the narrator and the speech of his characters as a stylistic token of Crane's naturalism. In an 1896 review of the revised version of *Maggie*, Frank Norris complained that the heroine's downfall "strikes one as handled in a manner almost too flippant for the seriousness of the subject." "The reader," his review continues, "is apt to feel that the author is writing, as it were, from the outside. There is a certain lack of sympathy apparent. Mr. Crane does not seem to *know* his people." This judgment may recall the growing importance of sympathy to Norris's own version of literary naturalism, as he came more and more to identify with his "big" materials, but we must also recognize that writing "from the outside" may be *the* stylistic signature of works conventionally grouped under the rubric of naturalism. Thus June Howard has reminded us that while "the menacing and vulnerable Other," the "brute" at the center of so many naturalist texts, "is incapable of acting as a self-conscious, purposeful agent, he can only be observed and analyzed by such an agent"; and she notes that this distinction lies at the heart of the defining narrative arrangement of naturalistic fictions. "Although we explore determinism," she writes, "we are never submerged in it and ourselves become the brute"; the narrator is capable of just the sorts of understanding and analysis that are unavailable to the characters—so that in Crane's *Maggie*, for example, "the incongruity of Homeric language in a description of urchins fighting in the street provokes the reader to think, but also widens the chasm between the ignorance and brutality of the slum dwellers and the literary sensibilities of the narrator and reader."[14]

Although Howard seems to me wholly persuasive in her account of the narrative "chasm" at the heart of naturalist fictions, we might wonder about her use of *Maggie* as an example of this paradigm. There can be no doubt of the stylistic obtrusiveness of the novel's omniscient narrator, but does this obtrusiveness, for all its displayed sophistication, really express superior *understanding*? What, in this context, is the function of the narrator's persistent *mockery* of the characters, a mockery so different from the essayistic and often sodden sobriety more typical of naturalist narration? Few readers have been able to ignore the verbal irony of *Maggie*—the disparity between what Norris called its "flippant" manner and "the seriousness of its subject"—but there has been little agreement about the ultimate intention or effect of this irony. As is the case with all mock heroic, it has been hard to know what, exactly, is being mocked: Does the narrator's elevated diction satirize the squalor of his common characters, or does the coarseness of these characters and of their language deflate the narrator's heroic, euphemistic elevation? According to John Berryman, in no American work before Crane's *Maggie* "had the author remained so invisible behind his creation."[15] How can we account for such a statement, from so intelligent a reader, about a book in which the narrator's voice seems so obtrusive? What seems to be at issue here is the *authority* of the narrator's ironic language. From the very outset of *Maggie* the reader is obliged to wonder which, if any, of the book's rival languages, the language of the narrator or the language of the street, is authorized by the author, "Stephen Crane," and this sort of anxiety, we should note, is quite *un*characteristic of texts conventionally considered to be examples of literary naturalism.

Nowhere in *Maggie* is the question of the authority of the narrator's language more pressing than in the brilliantly comic account, at the end of chapter 5 and the beginning of chapter 6, of the heroine's growing infatuation with her brother Jimmie's "glamorous" friend, the bartender Pete:

As Jimmie and his friend exchanged tales descriptive of their prowess, Maggie leaned back in the shadow. Her eyes dwelt wonderingly and rather wistfully upon Pete's face. . . . Pete's aristocratic person looked as if it might soil. She looked keenly at him, occasionally, wondering if he was feeling contempt. But Pete seemed to be enveloped in reminiscence.

"Hully gee," said he, "dose mugs can't phase me. Dey knows I kin wipe up deh street wid any t'ree of dem."

When he said, "Ah, what deh hell," his voice was burdened with disdain for the inevitable and contempt for anything that fate might compel him to endure.

Maggie perceived that here was the beau ideal of a man. Her dim thoughts were often searching for far away lands where, as God says, the little hills sing together in the morning. Under the trees of her dream garden there had always walked a lover.

. . . .

　Pete took note of Maggie.

　"Say, Mag, I'm stuck on yer shape. It's outa sight," he said, parenthetically, with an affable grin. (18–19)

The operative contrast here derives once again from a juxtaposition of apparently antithetical languages. "Tales descriptive of their prowess" and "enveloped in reminiscence," for instance, stand in incongruous proximity to their referent, Pete's "Dey knows I kin wipe up deh street wid any t'ree of dem." And the stilted sentimentality of the account of Maggie's feelings is planets apart from Pete's considerably more colloquial language of esteem—"I'm stuck on yer shape. It's outa sight"—which is then followed, in its turn, by the self-conscious decorum of "he said, parenthetically, with an affable grin."

　Yet it simply makes no sense, here or elsewhere in Crane, to identify the elevated language of narration with the perspective or understanding of the author—the sort of identification normally encouraged by the narrative structure of naturalist texts. In fact, this language of euphemistic inflation is only in a rather limited sense even the language of the *narrator*; for while the diction and deliberately artificial syntax are beyond the means of the characters, as will be the case again in the chronicle of Henry Fleming's consciousness in *The Red Badge of Courage*, the thoughts and feelings to which the heightened diction and syntax give expression are the characters' own. Moreover, and this point is crucial, even the narrator's artificiality of expression reflects an analogous artificiality in the ways these characters view themselves and others: Maggie really does see Pete as "the beau ideal of a man," even if she might not be able to put it quite this way; nor do we imagine that "Stephen Crane" shares her admiration; and when Pete says, "Ah, what deh hell," he really is striving to produce an effect of "disdain for the inevitable and contempt for anything that fate might compel him to endure"—while the deliberate fanciness of this prose produces a precise equivalent of Pete's cheap, flashy clothes and cocky self-regard. So, too, the mock-heroic elevation of the novel's opening reflects the way the dirty little denizens of Devil's Row and Rum Alley themselves conceive of their struggle.

　All of which is to say that the authority behind Crane's ironic narrative language, the "reality" to which it gives expression, is not the judgment or understanding of the author, as is usually the case in naturalist fictions, but the self-delusions of the characters. This is why

Berryman could say that in *Maggie* Crane remains "invisible behind his creation": the narrator's language, for all its apparent obtrusiveness, lacks the sort of authority naturalist texts usually invest in the outside narrator's perspective. "Reality," in such a context, is little more than the discordant sum of the de-authorized conceptions or inventions of it that keep colliding with one another, and so comprehensive an irony is a far cry, needless to say, from Norris's or Howells's ideal of fiction as a conduit providing unmediated access to the "real."[16] Another way of describing the undermining of naturalist narrative authority in *Maggie* would be to say that Crane's verbal irony is essentially parodic. I do not mean, necessarily, deliberate satire of specific literary works or genres, although there is plenty of this sort of parody in Crane's fiction.[17] More basically, parody—whether or not it is satiric in intention, or whatever its intention—depends on stylistic imitation, and the universal condition of the world of Crane's fiction, perhaps especially the world of *Maggie*, is that all of its styles are imitations, tawdry recyclings of outworn and ill-understood originals. Nothing, here, can be experienced in itself, at least not without greater difficulty than most people seem willing to expend; the terms of experience have already been set in place, before the fact.[18] Thus Maggie, for instance, can only perceive Pete in the preestablished mode of sentimental romance: "Under the trees of her dream garden there had always walked a lover."

To speak of Crane in this way, in terms of his profound skepticism of outworn styles of expression, makes him sound a bit like the Howells who declaimed against the popular preference for "the artificial grasshopper," and this is clearly an aspect of Howells—it may be *the* aspect of Howells—to which Crane responded with sympathetic recognition and gratitude. The crucial difference between them, however, is that Crane appreciated far more than Howells the dreadful power of established styles to determine consciousness, and he was thus incapable of Howells's assurance that one could rather easily discover "the simple, honest, and natural grasshopper."[19] Crane apparently recognized that if environment shapes lives it does so, above all, by predetermining perception, by granting so much authority to the styles in which others' perceptions have been expressed that these styles come to constitute, in effect, the only experience there is; and in this sense, as Crane also recognized, the "artificial grasshopper" was perhaps a good deal *more* "real" than his "simple, honest, and natural" cousin.

In *Maggie*, parody is ultimately as much a matter of vision as of technique: the very "reality" of the book is itself inherently parodic, as most behavior, whether public or private, takes the form of self-conscious stylistic display. For instance when Pete recounts his heroic exploits what he stresses is his *verbal* prowess:

"Yer insolen' ruffin," he says, like dat. "Oh, gee," I says, "oh, gee, go teh hell and git off deh eart'," I says, like dat. See? "Go teh hell an' git off deh eart'," like dat. Den deh blokie he got wild. He says I was a contempt'ble scoun'el, er somet'ting like dat, an' he says I was doom' teh everlastin' pe'dition an' all like dat. "Gee," I says, "gee! Deh hell I am," I says. "Deh hell I am," like dat. An' den I slugged 'im. See? (19–20)

When Maggie "falls," her mother works up her stock of appropriate, mail-order feelings in a language of barely understood religious cliché: "May Gawd curse her forever. . . . May she eat nothin' but stones and deh dirt in deh street. May she sleep in deh gutter an' never see deh sun shine agin" (32). Maggie is treated with more sympathy than the other characters, largely because her addiction to imitation is so passive and unwitting, but she too has no style of her own. "Her dim thoughts," we are told, "were often searching for far away lands where, as God says, the little hills sing together in the morning" (19). That Maggie's deepest fantasies are conducted in unconscious pastiche of the language of the Psalms is finally not humorous but horrifying, and the most chilling detail of all is that interpolated tag, "as God says"; these people can imagine nothing of their own.

The distance achieved by Crane's irony, the distance between the reader and the characters, stems from our recognition of the parodic emptiness of the characters' conceptions of reality. A play is described, involving "wanderers swooning in snow storms beneath happy-hued church windows" (and we should attend to the carefully overwrought alliteration and assonance here); "to Maggie and the rest of the audience," we are told, "this was transcendental realism" (27). It is not enough to say that these characters are trapped by the styles they imitate; for the most part they are eager to indulge in the ferocious exuberance of empty stylistic display, and such indulgence is all that really "happens" in *Maggie*. There is no social interaction here, only a collision of self-referential performances, as if each of the characters were doing exercises in front of a mirror. We conclude with no resolution, and how could we? The book ends, instead, with one last performance. Maggie's mother, sardonically enough named Mary, is informed of her daughter's death; then there enters "a woman in a black gown." "Ah what ter'ble affliction dis is," she proclaims, while the narrator comments (in a rare and probably unnecessary moment of "naturalistic" explanation) that "her vocabulary was derived from mission churches" (57). This vocabulary, studded with such clichés as "She's gone where her sins will be judged" and "Deh Lord gives and deh Lord takes away," gives Mary her cue. "Yeh'll fergive her, Mary!" the woman in black pleads; "Oh, yes," Mary replies, assuming the appropriate role and discourse for the occasion, "I'll fergive her! I'll fergive her!" (58). This speech concludes *Maggie* only in the sense that it epitomizes the world of the novel; like everything else in this world it is a pure performance, totally devoid of any connection to felt experience.

In Crane's best-known fiction, from *The Red Badge of Courage* on, his characters struggle to redeem outworn styles and clichés from abstraction, to revive the experiences to which these styles and clichés once gave expression. They reject the external authority with which abstractions have been invested or, as is more often the case, circumstance shatters their belief in this authority; they are thus driven to test abstractions by the authority of personal experience. Sometimes, like the survivors in "The Open Boat" (1897), they seem to succeed in becoming genuine "interpreters"; sometimes, like the Swede in "The Blue Hotel" (1898), they succumb to the power of preconception; they are unable to de-authorize the myth. But they have the courage, or the recklessness, to try. No one in *Maggie*—or in Crane's other Bowery writings, including *George's Mother* (1896)—has this sort of courage. "The root of Bowery life," Crane wrote to a correspondent in 1896, "is a sort of cowardice. Perhaps I mean a lack of ambition or to willingly be knocked flat and accept a licking."[20] The characters of *Maggie* remain performers, holding to the authority of the established languages they reiterate endlessly, as if by rote.

In his 1969 essay, "A Literature of Law and Order," Richard Poirier describes a predicament confronted repeatedly in modern and postmodern literature:

The kind of energy that now threatens to overwhelm individual minds is . . . the energy implanted in myths and metaphors, styles and fashions, in images that insinuate themselves in back of the eyes and ears, there to direct, unless we consciously combat them, even our acts of silent self-imagining. . . . Styles and formulations have accumulated which precede us even to those experiences we think most private and original.[21]

This is the situation of Crane's Bowery characters, and for this reason we might describe *Maggie*, in which no one consciously combats the situation, as the most modern or postmodern of Crane's writings. The book's irony reveals, in any case, the fundamental condition of Crane's world, the context within which his later characters will strive to restore some sort of authenticity to their "acts of silent self-imagining."

What needs to be stressed above all is that the world of *Maggie*, the strange world brought into being by its discordant languages and styles, has little in common with the worlds of Howells's realism or Norris's naturalism—and even seems to function, in part, to subvert the assumptions on which men like Howells and Norris depended. It is not just that Crane, unlike Norris, has no desire to identify with his materials, although this difference is important. Crane's implicit creed differs most profoundly from the explicit pronouncements of Howells and Norris in the attention it pays, and the "real" power it grants, to style. *Maggie* ultimately discredits both of the generic marks of naturalism on which it seems to rely: the explanatory authority and understanding of the outside observer and the notion that the life of the streets, the realm of the brutal Other, is the repository of some sort of raw "reality," unmediated by style. To move from the study to the street was not, for Crane, to move from literature to life, from the artificial to the real, but simply to shift from one perspective, one style, to another—with neither being any more "authentic," nor any less, than the other. It is no doubt true, as June Howard puts it, that the narrative language of *Maggie* "widens the chasm between the ignorance and brutality of the slum dwellers and the literary sensibilities of the narrator and reader";[22] but as it does so, it renders this chasm more or less meaningless.

Words of War

When Frank Norris proclaimed that "fiction may keep pace with the Great March," when he placed the characters of serious fiction at "the forefront of the marching world,"[23] he was invoking a powerful language; these were clichés with a broad appeal. Fantasies of manly heroism were much in demand in the 1890s, and their most obvious context was military. William Randolph Hearst knew that wars sold papers, war correspondents became popular stars, and when Theodore Roosevelt led the charge up San Juan Hill in 1898 he was celebrated because he was acting out a national myth. This myth is the subject of *The Red Badge of Courage*, a fact that undoubtedly had a good deal to do with the widespread fame the book brought to its author. At the close, for instance, we are told what Henry Fleming has learned, or thinks he has learned, from his experience of battle:

He felt a quiet manhood, unassertive but of sturdy and strong blood. He knew that he would no more quail before his guides wherever they should point. He had been to touch the great death, and found that, after all, it was but the great death. He was a man. (109)[24]

No wonder *The Red Badge* made Crane a celebrity. To be sure, his star rose first in England, but the cult of masculinity was very much a transatlantic phenomenon: before America had Crane, Norris, and London, England had Stevenson and Kipling and a general assertion of literary "manliness" in reaction to such aesthetes as Oscar Wilde.[25] Yet there was something unsettling about *The Red Badge* all the same. While Crane's subject tied him to a writer like Kipling, he *wrote*, it seemed, like an aesthete. And readers could not be sure of the book's attitude toward its subject: Was it a celebration of the heroic myth, or was it an attack? I have already quoted the complaint of Civil War veteran, General A. C. McClurg, that *The Red Badge* is but "a mere work of diseased imagination . . . a mere riot of words," and his hostility stemmed from a deeper discontent. "The hero of the book," he protests, is "without a spark of patriotic feeling, or even soldierly ambition. . . . No thrill of patriotic devotion to cause or country ever moves his breast, and not even an emotion of manly courage. . . . Nowhere are seen the quiet, manly, self-respecting, and patriotic men, influenced by the highest sense of duty, who in reality fought our battles."[26]

Discussion of *The Red Badge of Courage* since the book's first appearance in 1895 has returned again and again to two basic questions. How could Stephen Crane, who had never seen a battle, portray one so "realistically"? And what exactly *is* his attitude toward the myth of military heroism, toward Henry's conviction at the close that "he was a man"? The first of these questions is a bit silly, at least when pursued at length, but we can understand why Crane's inexperience of war seemed important; to those disturbed by his ambiguous attitude toward men in battle his inexperience provided an easy out: he didn't know what he was talking about. Thus McClurg could dismiss *The Red Badge* because it was "the work of a young man of twenty-three or twenty-four years of age," one born too late to have witnessed the struggles he claimed to describe.[27] McClurg's reputation was hardly based on literary acuity, and as a veteran and an officer he had a personal ax to grind, but his opinion was shared, for instance, by no less a professional critic than William Dean Howells. In *The Red Badge of Courage*, Howells wrote in 1902, Crane "took leave of [the] simple aesthetics" of his slum fiction "and lost himself in a whirl of wild guesses at the fact from the ground of insufficient witness"—and thus "made the failure which formed the break between his first and second manner." Apparently it was all right to treat aloofly the "tragically squalid life" of the Bowery, but men in battle (for this writer who spent the Civil War in Venice) were different; they were to be treated only with complete and unquestioning respect. There is surely no other way to account for Howells's strange claim that the "aesthetics" of *Maggie* are more "simple" than those of *The Red Badge*.[28] In any case, the issue of Crane's inexperience of war was quite closely related to—and even a kind of stand-in for—the issue of his attitude toward his subject, toward the myth of masculine courage.

Crane would certainly seem to have sought, during his short life, to live out the masculine myth, far more so, for example, than such an overt proponent of this myth as Frank Norris—even though Howells, in 1902, would contrast Norris's manly "strength and courage" with Crane's "physical slightness," "delicacy," and "'electrical nerves.'"[29] For instance, if sports are part of the myth, we should remember that Crane was an accomplished athlete during his single year in college and considered becoming a professional baseball player, while Norris, although he idolized athletes in college, was never one himself. And while Crane's reckless courage as a war correspondent, when he finally did get to experience battle in Cuba, was notorious, Norris's forays into war correspondence—in South Africa in 1895 and in Cuba in 1898 (where he met Crane briefly)—were inept failures.[30] Nevertheless, people who need this sort of myth tend to be precisely those who lack the experience on which it is supposedly based, and the fact that Crane seemed to act out Norris's fantasy hardly means that he endorsed it; indeed, it seems more reasonable to suppose that it was in part impatience with this sort of fantasy, *as fantasy*, that drove Crane to find out what war was "really" like. There is no evidence to suggest that when Crane went to Cuba he was seeking to fulfill some kind of masculine fantasy; he was instead apparently fleeing the social and psychological difficulties of life in England with his supposed wife, Cora, former proprietress of the Hotel de Dream in Sarasota, Florida, and many of those on the scene in Cuba concluded that he was trying to get himself killed. These are complex motives, far more complex than anything implicit in the 1890s fantasy of manly heroism, and they finally tell us little about how Crane, as a man, regarded the cult of the "strenuous life."[31] To understand Crane's attitude toward the myth of masculine heroism, then, we must turn to *The Red Badge of Courage* itself—which is, one guesses, what Crane would have wished, for whatever else he cared about he certainly cared about writing.

There are two crucial technical differences between the irony of *The Red Badge* and the irony of *Maggie*. First of all, *The Red Badge* is confined to a single point of view; we see almost everything from the perspective of Henry Fleming, and it is to his thoughts alone, among the novel's characters, that we have access.[32] Second, in *The Red Badge* something apparently happens: Henry, "the youth," seems to grow from cowardice to manhood, and even if we read the ending ironically, seeing Henry's belief in his growth as self-delusion, *The Red Badge* still derives a developmental structure from what we might call, in this case, a parodic psychological action—and this is not the case with *Maggie*. Nevertheless, the operation of stylistic irony in *The Red Badge* is in most respects very similar to its operation in *Maggie:* it still depends on a contrast of discordant styles and perspectives; only now these are arranged as a disjoined sequence in a single mind instead of being distributed among a variety of different characters. And what is still very much at issue is the relationship between established styles and authentic experience—or the scarcity and fragility of authentic experience in a world dominated *by* established styles.

In *The Red Badge* as in *Maggie*, language precedes experience and largely determines perception; Crane's soldiers approach war absorbed in storied fantasies.[33] As the book opens, the tall soldier, later identified as Jim Conklin, comes running back to camp "swelled with a tale" (5); Henry, we soon learn, has "in visions . . . seen himself in many struggles" and "imagined peoples secure in the shadow of his eagle-eyed prowess"; and if this language smacks of literary cliché we should not be surprised, since Henry has been attracted to war in the first place by "tales of great movements" (7). At the outset, in any case, the language in which he conceives his fantasy of war sounds exactly like the language in which Frank Norris would soon conceive his fantasy of naturalism—the difference being that what is unintentionally parodic in Norris seems to be deliberately so in Crane. Moreover, while Henry is seeking an experience to match his fantasy, experience proves recalcitrant. For the "beautiful scene" of his farewell to his mother "he had prepared," we are told, "certain sentences which he thought could be used with touching effect," but he doesn't get to use them (8), and in the same way his experience of war keeps undercutting his preconceptions. Like Norris, Henry conceives of "the marching world" as a virile alternative to the ordinary and domestic, but his first battle keeps presenting him with images of domesticity: one officer displays "the furious anger of a spoiled child," while another resembles "a man who has come from bed to go to a fire" (28); when soldiers arrange cartridge boxes, it is "as if seven hundred new bonnets were being tried on" (29); a dead soldier lies "in the position of a tired man resting" (32); a youthful officer jerks his horse "with an abandon of temper he might display in a placid barnyard" (37).

Henry—unlike Pete, for instance, or Maggie's mother—is from the first unsure of the validity of his preconceptions, and this is an important difference; it explains why growth, in *The Red Badge of Courage*, is a possibility. And by the end of his adventure, Henry feels sure that he has closed the ironic gap between the rhetoric of preconception and the recalcitrant truth of experience: "He could look back upon the brass and bombast of his earlier gospels," we are told, "and see them truly" (109). Yet we wonder if this is a genuine resolution or only another surge of rhetorical self-assurance; when the narrator writes of Henry that "he was a man," we wonder if we are meant to accept this valuation, to take it seriously. In the book's final sentence we are told that "over the river a golden ray of sun came through the hosts of leaden rain clouds" (109), and once again we are uncertain: Is this a valid symbol of hope and change, in a book in which images of nature's sympathy have appeared again and again as rationalizations? Or are we to read the sentence ironically, as a parodic send-up of romantic conventions and an undercutting of Henry's alleged growth to true manhood? Critical debate over these questions has been, to say the least, voluminous.[34]

What is more to the point here, however, is that this debate is directly relevant to the issue of Crane's supposed relationship to American naturalism, since the values behind the myth of masculine heroism are identical with the ideas Frank Norris would soon be proclaiming in his critical writings. Does *The Red Badge* endorse these values, then, or does it, as General McClurg thought, ridicule them? Ultimately, it seems to me, the very nature of Crane's irony makes this question unanswerable, and quite possibly meaningless. The hallmark of the irony in *The Red Badge* as in *Maggie* is the refusal to authorize any single language or set of images, any single version of experience, as being "truer" than any other, and to ask how we are *supposed* to take the ending of *The Red Badge* is to ask for the very sort of certainty Crane's irony consistently subverts. Even if we are sure that we are in the presence of parody, of a self-conscious deployment of style *as* style, we have not necessarily identified the *purpose* of the seeming parody. At the close, then, we can be certain only of a contrast of perspectives. On the one hand, Henry clearly has performed actions which would conventionally be associated with "courage"; we might even want to call his experience of these actions "genuine," as distinguished from his earlier *fantasies* of military heroism. We certainly recognize that in the midst of the action, with his preconceptions at least momentarily shattered, Henry is extraordinarily open to sensory experience, and the clarity of his perception is recorded in some of Crane's most powerful writing:

It seemed to the youth that he saw everything. Each blade of the green grass was bold and clear. He thought that he was aware of every change in the thin, transparent vapor that floated idly in sheets. The brown or gray trunks of the trees showed each roughness of their surfaces. And the men of the regiment, with their starting eyes and sweating faces, running madly, or falling, as if thrown headlong, to queer, heaped-up corpses—all were comprehended. His mind took a mechanical but firm impression, so that afterward everything was pictured and explained to him, save why he himself was there. (86–87)

There is surely nothing parodic in the style of such a passage.

On the other hand, though, the rhetoric in which Henry *remembers* his experience at the close—after the fact, when he does begin to explain "why he himself was there"—is quite clearly parodic, like the rhetoric in which he has anticipated this experience, at least in the sense that we recognize it *as* self-conscious rhetoric. Its conventionality does not prove that Henry's experience was false, whatever that would mean; a completely ironic reading of the last chapter, in such terms, requires as much of an assertion of authority as does a completely serious reading. The distance of the narrator from the protagonist at the close is not the distance of a judge; in fact it is Henry who feels compelled to leap to judgment, to provide his experience with a large meaning, to formulate an explanation of "why he himself was there," and it is on this compulsion, rather than Henry's experience in battle, that the final parodic tone (if that is what it is) seems to comment. For readers to seek the same sort of meaning Henry is seeking is finally only to compound the problem. Crane's mode is at heart comic, but his vision is stark and unsettling, even frightening; understanding the need for authority and certainty, he again and again dramatizes its inevitable frustration. His best-known novels and stories, even as they propose questions, relentlessly discredit answers—at least answers purporting to be *the* answer.

In *Maggie*, Crane inhabits the conventional narrative structure of naturalism in order, as it were, to hollow it out from the inside; in *The Red Badge of Courage*, he appropriates, and then parodically enervates, the central *action* implicit in naturalist thinking. Here the supposed contrast between the study and the street is replaced by the paradigmatic movement, to use Norris's terms, from "the world of little things" to "the places where things are real," from the realm of "teacup tragedies" to "the forefront of the marching world."[35] But Crane leaves the outcome of this movement, and the authenticity of the terms on which it is based, ambiguous, and what bothered General McClurg—and, one guesses, William Dean Howells—was that this ambiguity has the effect of a repudiation at least of the popular *myth* of military heroism, the myth that attributes a privileged "reality" to brutal or aggressive masculinity. This myth appealed to men who, for whatever reasons of their own, regarded ambiguity and its attendant anxieties with hostility; indeed the myth functioned above all as a way of *evading* anxiety. In *The Red Badge of Courage*, Crane brings the anxiety back to the surface. At the heart of Norris's naturalism, I argued in Chapter 4, is a *fantasy* of "reality," and this is exactly the kind of fantasy on which Crane turns his irony, again and again. We recall that to Maggie and the rest of the audience at the theater, the stage's empty pastiche of experience is "transcendental realism." When Crane wrote *Maggie* the future author of *McTeague* and *The Octopus* was still a student at Berkeley, but this comment about accepting fantasy as "transcendental realism" is a fair token, one suspects, of what Crane would have made of the naturalism of Frank Norris.

6

Fine Styles of Sympathy

THEODORE DREISER'S *SISTER CARRIE*

"If we are to talk of bookishness, it is Dreiser who is bookish; he is precisely literary in the bad sense; he is full of flowers of rhetoric and shines with paste gems; at hundreds of points his diction is not only genteel but fancy. . . . Colloquialism held no real charm for him and his natural tendency is always toward the 'fine.'"

Lionel Trilling, "Reality in America" (1946)

"We talked about style. Yes, style!—the use of words minutely and technically employed. And I am bound to say that no one with whom I have ever talked about the employment of words—with the possible exception of Joseph Conrad—no one knew more about them than my friend."

Ford Madox Ford, *It Was the Nightingale* (1934)

It surely seems significant—if only, perhaps, in a fortuitous way—that Frank Norris, working in 1899 as a reader for Doubleday, should have discovered Theodore Dreiser's *Sister Carrie* (1900) and enthusiastically recommended that it be published.[1] Of course, when Dreiser wrote *Sister Carrie* he had read nothing by Norris, and Norris's national campaign for naturalism had not yet begun; but *Sister Carrie* would still appear to have a good deal in common with naturalism as Norris conceived it—and almost nothing in common with the so-called naturalism of Stephen Crane. It is a commonplace, for instance, that Dreiser's style is, like Norris's, often clumsy and crudely inflated and that his writing, unlike Crane's, is utterly without verbal irony. *Sister Carrie*, appearing at the very end of the 1890s, might be seen as the culmination of the literary naturalism of that decade; or, what is

149

more to the point, it might be seen as a final attempt to come to terms with the decade's problematic *idea* of naturalism. It is in this connection that I wish to consider it. ·

Dreiser and American Naturalism

When Dreiser writes on the first page of his 1922 memoir, *A Book about Myself*, that Chicago's "realistic atmosphere" derived from its suggestion of "romance," one is perhaps reminded of Frank Norris's habitual equation of "romance" and the "real." Dreiser's apparent kinship with Norris is also suggested by what he said in defense of *Sister Carrie* in a newspaper interview, when the novel was reissued in 1907:

Well, the critics have not really understood what I was trying to do. Here is a book that is close to life. It is intended not as a piece of literary craftsmanship, but as a picture of conditions done as simply and effectively as the English language will permit. To sit up and criticise me for saying "vest," instead of waistcoat, to talk about my splitting the infinitive and using vulgar commonplaces here and there, when the tragedy of a man's life is being displayed, is silly.

This sounds more than a little like the Norris to whom "life" was always more important than "literature" or "style," and the same stance has been taken by many of those who have praised and defended Dreiser. For instance, H. L. Mencken, in his long 1917 essay on the then-controversial novelist, notes many examples of stylistic ineptitude but finally argues that they are virtues: "One cannot imagine that stark, stenographic dialogue," he writes, "adorned with the tinsel of pretty words." Or there is Sinclair Lewis's famous response to criticism of Dreiser's style in his 1930 Nobel Prize acceptance speech: "I am not exactly sure what this mystic quality 'style' may be, but I find the word so often in the writings of minor critics that I suppose it must exist."[2] Anyone wishing to follow the antiliterary bias of realist or naturalist thinking in America into the twentieth century would do well to begin with the early defenses of Theodore Dreiser.

Most attacks on Dreiser, especially those published at the height of the controversy over *The "Genius"* in 1915, have concerned themselves with his subject matter or with his supposed immorality.[3] But in 1946, in "Reality in America," Lionel Trilling took issue with the central naturalist case for Dreiser's style, for his awkward writing; he challenged the assumption that Dreiser prefers the "stark" and "stenographic" to "the tinsel of pretty words." "It has been taken for granted," Trilling writes, "that the ungainliness of Dreiser's style is the only possible objection to be made to it, and that whoever finds in it any fault wants a prettified genteel style (and is objecting to the ungainliness of reality itself)." Yet, he insists, "if we are to talk of bookishness, it is Dreiser who is bookish; he is precisely literary in the bad sense; he is full of flowers of rhetoric and shines with paste gems; at hundreds of points his diction is not only genteel but fancy." "Colloquialism," Trilling adds, "held no real charm for him and his natural tendency is always toward the 'fine.'"[4] Whether or not one agrees with Trilling (and I will be returning to his description of Dreiser's style shortly), the fact remains that exactly the same terms could be used to describe the discrepancy between the announced intentions and the actual style of Frank Norris.

Yet, when all is said and done, Dreiser is no Norris, not even a greater Norris; the qualities that might seem to link them are mostly superficial and misleading, and to understand how and why this is so is to understand the complexity of Dreiser's relationship to the idea of American naturalism as Norris promoted it. First of all, we must recognize that in one crucial respect Dreiser's writing may be a good deal *more* "naturalistic" than Norris's—not in Norris's sense of the word but in terms of what many critics have meant by "naturalism." From the dentistry in *McTeague* to the commodity speculation in *The Pit*, Norris's concern for factual detail and specific process is, I argued in Chapter 4, at best perfunctory, tangential to his obsession with abstract "forces." Detail and process are, by contrast, the very essence of Dreiser: he loads his novels with specific information, ponderous accounts of just how things work, just how they are done. Whatever its literary value, *Sister Carrie* is a gold mine for historians interested in such things as the department store in the 1890s, or the popular theater, or the precise manners of the traveling salesman, and there is nothing like this in Norris. An aspiring wheat rancher, armed only with *The Octopus*, would soon lose his crop, and to find a copy of *McTeague* in a dentist's waiting room would be scarcely more encouraging than finding a copy of Poe's "Berenice."

Dreiser was at least as addicted as Norris to the popular scientism of his day: for every meditation on "force" in Norris there is in Dreiser a corresponding meditation on "chemisms" or some such. It is sometimes hard to read these meditations without a chuckle— Dreiser's science seems a crude amalgam of conventional clichés—but we must nonetheless admit that Dreiser cares about the substance of such meditations in a way that Norris does not. As Ellen Moers has painstakingly demonstrated, Dreiser read what was available to him— especially, before *Sister Carrie*, Herbert Spencer—attentively and, what is more important, with curiosity.[5] It is this quality of curiosity that utterly distinguishes his "scientific" digressions from Norris's: Dreiser turned to science as he turned to everything else, not because it was "real," in Norris's crude sense, but because it was *interesting*. Science, in his writing, is less an authority-conferring idea than a fascinating process, and to admit that his fascination often led him into conventional cliché, and that he did not understand scientific ideas in any concrete or technical sense, still does not link him to the Norris of abstract forces and "resistless" pressures.

Dreiser was of course not immune to his contemporaries' obsession with amoral and generally masculine "force." Frank Cowperwood, the businessman-hero of *The Financier* (1912) and *The Titan* (1914), makes Curtis Jadwin, in Norris's *The Pit*, seem kind-hearted and indecisive; and Dreiser writes in *A Book about Myself* that in the 1890s "my eyes were constantly fixed on people in positions far above my own. Those who interested me most were bankers, millionaires, artists, executives, leaders, the real rulers of the world." But the inclusion of artists in this list reveals, as we will see, another crucial difference between Dreiser and Norris: unlike Norris and Howells, Dreiser did not automatically dissociate the "literary" from "the world of men's activities." Moreover, there is in Dreiser's fiction little of the adulation of masculine violence that distinguishes, for instance, Norris and Jack London. In his 1917 essay, Mencken writes of Dreiser that "there is vastly more intuition in him than intellectualism; his talent is essentially feminine, as Conrad's is masculine; his ideas always seem to be deduced from his feelings"—and while Mencken's sexual stereotyping is characteristically crude in the manner of his age, his sense that Dreiser was not stereotypically "masculine" is nevertheless significant. Dreiser himself, in his 1922 memoir, insists that in the '90s he was far from living up to the masculine ideal:

> As to courage, when I examined myself in that direction I fancied that I had none at all. Would I slip out if a dangerous brawl were brewing anywhere? Certainly. . . . Could I stand up and defend myself against a man of my own height and weight? I doubted it, particularly if he were well-trained. . . . There was no hope for me among decently courageous men. Could I play tennis, baseball, football? No; not successfully. Assuredly I was a weakling of the worst kind.[6]

The charm here is that Dreiser does not take to bodybuilding like Theodore Roosevelt, nor to compensatory rhetoric like Frank Norris, nor even to authority-deflating irony like Stephen Crane; he simply reports how he felt, what he was; these are but additional objects of his curiosity and interest. We should remember, too, that Dreiser was a journalist in 1898, when war broke out with Spain, but unlike Crane and Norris and so many other newspapermen of his generation, he had no interest in going to Cuba. It is also surely significant, in this connection, that the protagonists of his first two novels, the characters from whom these novels take their titles, are women.

That Dreiser had no real need or use for the group of compensatory ideas and assumptions that constituted literary naturalism for a writer like Norris should not surprise us. The late-nineteenth-century cult of masculinity was in part a symptom of upper- or upper-middle class anxiety that privilege led to a sapping of virility, and the problems of privilege hardly played a role in Dreiser's early years. It is certainly true that he worried about his virility in the 1890s—as he later frankly confessed and as his subsequent sexual career clearly reveals—but his particular anxieties had little in common with those of an elite whose lowest reaches even were inaccessible to him. Nor could Norris's fantasy of the "reality" of the sordid have meant much to a writer who grew up in the very environment of ethnic urban poverty about which Norris fantasized—and who wanted more than anything to get out, to get into precisely the world Norris thought effeminate and "unreal." Norris's distinction between "life" and "literature," between "reality" and "art," while it links him to a good deal of American thinking about realism and naturalism, was finally irrelevant to the author of *Sister Carrie*. "Art" for Dreiser *was* "life," in the sense that it provided his ticket into the privileged environment for which he, like Carrie Meeber, longed; this is why he includes artists along with bankers, millionaires, and executives in his list of "the real rulers of the world." By the 1890s, he reports in *A Book about Myself*, "I was eager to know all about music, painting, sculpture, literature, and to be in those places where life is at its best." "The mere word *art*," he writes, "although I had no real understanding of it, was fascinating to me." Especially significant is his account of how he reacted to the first suggestion that he write a novel or a play:

A book or a play! I sat up. To be considered a writer, a dramatist—even a possible dramatist—raised me in my own estimation. . . .
    Plays or books, or both, were the direct entrance to every joy which the heart could desire. Something of the rumored wonder and charm of the lives of successful playwrights came to me, their studios, their summer homes and the like.

He tells us that a friend named Dick had a fantasy of marrying money. "Here at last, then," he writes of his new literary ambitions, "was the equivalent of Dick's wealthy girl!"[7] The conventional defense of Dreiser as a supposed naturalist—the claim that he wrote crudely because "style" is antithetical (and inferior) to "reality"—may tell us more about Dreiser's defenders than about Dreiser himself. The ambitious poor boy who turned to journalism and then to literature relied on no such distinctions; his dream of "art" was identical with his dream of "reality."

The conventional line on Dreiser, the line taken by such anti-"literary" supporters as Mencken, is not the only position from which admirers have praised his achievement. Indeed, some of Dreiser's most eloquent admirers have been not anti-"literary" realists or naturalists but self-conscious modernists. For instance, Ford Madox Ford—in his 1934 memoir, *It Was the Nightingale*—tells a wonderful story about having lunch in 1923 with someone he identifies only as "a gentleman whom I will call the doyen of American letters." "We talked," he says, "about style. Yes, style!—the use of words minutely and technically employed. And I am bound to say that no one with whom I have ever talked about the employment of words—with the possible exception of Joseph Conrad—no one knew more about them than my friend." This lunch, in Ford's account, lasts three hours, and the talk continues as the men walk to a trolley. Here the friend turns and says to Ford: "You know I've read all your books and I like them very much." To which Ford replies, at last identifying his companion: "Well you know, Dreiser, I've read all *your* books and I like them very much." Given the near unanimity of both friendly and hostile critics about the crudeness and sloppiness of Dreiser's writing, it is simply extraordinary that a writer like Ford could think of no one—except maybe Joseph Conrad, who had been a close friend of Stephen Crane and who was associated with Henry James—who knew more about "style."[8]

In an essay published three years after *It Was the Nightingale*, Ford tries to explain the power of Dreiser's apparently sloppy prose. "Dreiser," he writes, "obviously is untidy . . . but he had to be untidy in order to be big. He wants you to read immense wads of pages; you could not do it if they were my peach-stone carvings."[9] Ford here reverts to the standard line on Dreiser, the idea that he was a clumsy genius, not finally to be explained by a maker of "peach-stone carvings," and we have been assured again and again that Dreiser was a natural, writing from inspiration without really understanding what he was doing—an image that hardly squares with Ford's earlier report of Dreiser's knowledge of "the use of words minutely and technically employed."[10] Yet Ford does not revert completely to the conventional image of Dreiser; he still wonders, in the 1937 essay, if the novelist's apparent sloppiness might be "due to . . . the fact that Dreiser knc what he was about and was trying after effects hitherto unessayed." While we can have no way of knowing with any certainty if "Dreisei knew what he was about," we certainly can investigate the specific "effects" achieved by his style, and we can explore the relationship of the stylistic achievement of *Sister Carrie* to the ideology of American naturalism in the 1890s—that naturalism which has so often been supposed to have culminated in Dreiser's first novel. We can also ask how Dreiser's style could elicit such varied and contradictory responses from intelligent readers—how it could seem "stark" and "stenographic" to Mencken, "bookish" and "genteel" to Trilling, and, to Ford, the work of a writer who knew more than almost anyone about "the use of words minutely and technically employed," who was perhaps "trying after effects hitherto unessayed."

Condescension and Identification

Sister Carrie begins—it is one of the most famous beginnings in American fiction—with its heroine on a train, bound for Chicago. At times we see things from her point of view and more or less in her terms: "What, pray, is a few hours—a few hundred miles? She looked at the little slip bearing her sister's address and wondered." But we are made overwhelmingly aware, from the outset, of the quite distinct perspective, voice, and authority of the obtrusively omniscient narrator. In the third sentence he tells us of Carrie what she would scarcely think of herself, that she was "full of the illusions of ignorance and youth," and in the third paragraph we are given the first of those general historical or philosophical essays that recur throughout the novel:

When a girl leaves her home at eighteen, she does one of two things. Either she falls into saving hands and becomes better, or she rapidly assumes the cosmopolitan standard of virtue and becomes worse. Of an intermediate balance, under the circumstances, there is no possibility. (1)[12]

No one could imagine that this generalization reports Carrie's own thoughts as she approaches the city. From this narrator's lofty perspective, Carrie's experience matters not because of its individuality or immediacy but because it illustrates general assertions about what happens "when a girl leaves home at eighteen"; for this narrator, Carrie's story is essentially a case study.

Already on the first page, then, we see the narrative polarity that prevails through the whole novel. To Carrie, for instance, the salesman Drouet, whom she meets on the train, is a glamorous intimation of the splendors she anticipates; but to the narrator he is mainly a specimen, "a type of the travelling canvasser," and we are immediately provided with an essay on this type—"lest," as the narrator writes, "this order of individual should permanently pass" (3). While the department store is to Carrie a region of wonder, it is to the narrator the occasion for an essay on this institution—which, he writes, was "at that time . . . in its earliest form of successful operation" (16). Toward the end of *Sister Carrie*, the story of Hurstwood's decline is presented in moving detail, largely from Hurstwood's point of view:

He wondered how all these other lodging-house people around him got along. Perhaps they begged—unquestionably they did. Many was the dime he had given to such as they in his day. He had seen other men asking for money in the streets. Maybe he could get some that way. There was horror in this thought. (337)

Such writing, mirroring the poignantly disjointed rhythms of Hurstwood's own thinking, anticipates stream of consciousness in the manner of Ernest Hemingway, and Hemingway would write nothing more effective. But this passage is preceded by a long explanatory essay, of the sort Hemingway would never have written, on the similarity of "a man's fortune or material progress" to "his bodily growth"—an essay that offers Hurstwood's impending decline as an illustration of an inevitable, universal process, and climaxes with an infamous discussion of the importance of chemicals, "anastates" and "katastates," to mental and physical well-being (239–40). In *Sister Carrie* there are apparently two narrative voices: an "immediate" voice whose style mimics the thoughts, feelings, and values of his characters, and an "omniscient" voice whose interest is less in these characters than in the historical facts and general ideas they exemplify.[13]

This narrative contrast is central to the case for viewing *Sister Carrie*, in formal terms, as a specimen of literary naturalism. As June Howard notes, Dreiser's omniscient narrators, like those in many texts conventionally regarded as works of naturalism, "constantly reveal to the reader what his characters do not know about themselves." Commenting on the engineer Ames—whom Carrie meets in New York, who is "by far the most educated character portrayed in *Sister Carrie*" and whose "class and . . . consciousness mark him as belonging to a realm of freedom rather than forces"—Howard writes that his "understanding is exceeded only by the narrator's. Mankind as a whole is expected to reach such understanding through generations of evolution, but as he loftily pronounces on the progress of human civilization the narrator seems to speak from a place where it has already been achieved."[14] This aloof narrator is also responsible for what so many readers have seen as the stylistic crudeness of *Sister Carrie*. "The mystic cords of affection!" he interjects as Hurstwood succumbs to Carrie's spell, "How they bind us all" (187); to an account of Carrie's disappointment on learning that an attractive young man is leaving right after a theater party he adds: "Oh, the half-hours, the minutes of the world; what miseries and griefs are crowded into them!" (238) This is the sort of writing Lionel Trilling has in mind when he complains of Dreiser's "bookishness," when he says that Dreiser is "precisely literary in the bad sense," that "at hundreds of points his diction is not only genteel but fancy."

The apparent problem of Dreiser's style is at bottom a problem of point of view: the omniscient narrator, the narrator who supposedly understands the characters as they cannot understand themselves, nevertheless speaks to us in a language seemingly as limited as the language and sensibilities of these characters. To explain Mrs. Hurstwood's dissatisfaction with her daughter's opportunities in Chicago, we are told that "there was an earlier exodus this year of people who were anybody to the watering places and Europe" (143), and we need not be troubled here by such clichés as "people who were anybody" and "the watering places and Europe" because this is precisely the sort of language that would be used by a woman like Mrs. Hurstwood—from whose perspective we are at this point seeing things. But we *are* likely to be troubled when we are told earlier that the Hurstwoods' furnishings include "a number of small bronzes gathered from heaven knows where" (63); for while "heaven knows where" is also the sort of cliché Mrs. Hurstwood would use, here it is pretty clearly not she but the narrator who is using it. Our reaction at such moments is likely to be something like embarrassment: we don't know what to make of a supposedly aloof and omniscient narrator whose language is in fact often indistinguishable from the limited, pretentiously clichéd language of the characters to whom he strives so conspicuously to condescend.

The narrator's "heaven knows where" is hardly a serious lapse, but it is typical of what happens again and again in *Sister Carrie*, especially in the narrator's extended philosophical ruminations. A much discussed example is the brief essay on the meaning of Carrie's "fall" at the beginning of chapter 10:

For all the liberal analysis of Spencer and our modern naturalistic philosophers, we have but an infantile perception of morals. There is more in the subject than mere conformity to things of earth alone. It is more involved than we, as yet, perceive. Answer, first, why the heart thrills; explain wherefore some plaintive note goes wandering about the world, undying; make clear the rose's subtle alchemy evolving its ruddy lamp in light and rain. In the essence of these facts lie the first principles of morals.

"Oh," thought Drouet, "how delicious is my conquest."

"Ah," thought Carrie, with mournful misgivings, "what is it I have lost?"

Before this world-old proposition we stand, serious, interested, confused; endeavouring to evolve the true theory of morals—the true answer to what is right. (68–69)

In spite of the reference to "Spencer and our modern naturalistic philosophers," and the possibly Darwinian allusions of "evolving" and "evolve," this is not a "naturalist" appeal to the authority of science but an assertion of science's inadequacy; and what is most notable here is the *expression* of this idea—which is as conventionally and meretriciously decorated as the Hurstwoods' residence. Such phrases as "the heart thrills" and "wherefore some plaintive note goes wandering about the world, undying," as well as the poetic inversions and imperatives, reek of what the *characters* would think of as "refinement," of romantic gentility filtered down through second-rate poetry and popular ballads. But this is meant to be the voice of the aloof *narrator,* and in the face of such prettified writing we may find it difficult to accept him at his own implicit self-valuation.

There has often been a fair amount of class and ethnic snobbery in complaints about the meretriciousness of Dreiser's style, particularly in complaints lodged during the first half of the twentieth century; there has been an assumption that one could after all expect nothing else from this uneducated child of immigrants. F. O. Matthiessen, seeking to defend Dreiser from such complaints, insists that he "could not have been a [Booth] Tarkington if he had tried," and that this disability was ultimately an advantage because this "immigrant's son from the wrong side of tracks . . . broke through the genteel tradition . . . by drawing on a store of experience outside the scope of the easily well-to-do—experience which formed the solid basis of his subsequent thought."[15] One problem with this sort of defense, however, is that it misrepresents (as we have already seen) the aloof narrator's actual style, whose seeming defects stem not from being "solid" but from being "genteel." Moreover, Dreiser is himself guilty, however unsuccessfully, of striving for the very snobbery from which Matthiessen wishes to protect him, since class condescension is built into the essential narrative structure he seems to adopt from conventional naturalist fictions. It is precisely the famous metaphorical "tracks" that divide the narrator and the reader from the characters, placing the characters on the "wrong" or "other" side—or so the narrator seeks to assure us. In this light, anything that seems unwittingly to separate him from us, by calling attention to *his* limitations, would appear to be fatal, revealing that he is only pretending to live in "our" neighborhood, on "our" side of the tracks. Walter Michaels writes that "Carrie's taste in art, like her definition of money, is 'popular' and thus profoundly at odds with the realism demanded by Howells."[16] What is even more important, as Michaels clearly recognizes, is that the same thing is apparently true of *Dreiser's* taste—or at least of the taste of the narrative voice that addresses us, with seeming omniscient authority, throughout *Sister Carrie*.

Sandy Petrey argues that the effect of the narrator's stylistic crudeness, although Dreiser surely did not intend this effect, is to instill in the reader a radical sense of narrative unreliability. The novel's "moral passages," Petrey writes, "stand as formal parodies of the language of sentimentality," and he considers this self-parody, however unintentional, to be thoroughly functional. "By severing the language of realism from the language of sentimentalism," he argues, "*Sister Carrie* presents reality and meaning as incommensurable," so that "the novel's stylistic contrast conveys one style's validity and the other's nullity."[17] One is certainly willing to agree that the effect of *Sister Carrie's* omniscient narrative style, whatever Dreiser's intention, is to discredit the narrator's apparent claim to exclusive authority, to the kind of authority conventionally associated with naturalist texts. Less persuasive, however, is the idea that this discrediting of narrative authority leads to an assurance of the validity of the novel's "language of realism," and it is even hard to know what, exactly, we would mean by referring to the "language of realism" in *Sister Carrie*. It is perfectly "realistic," for instance, to have Mrs. Hurstwood think about "people who were anybody" and "the watering places and Europe," although this is just the sort of conventionally genteel language that troubles us when it comes directly from the narrator. Moreover—and this is the most important point here—the apparent trouble with *Sister Carrie* is not that the language of the narrator is severed from the language of the characters but that it is apparently not sufficiently *distinct* from their language. The narrator writes, we feel, as his characters would write if they were in his position; he seems, for all his overt distance, to be in some covert way identified with them. And the assumption behind, for instance, Lionel Trilling's attack on Dreiser's style is that this identification is unfortunate: "paste gems" impress only those too ignorant to distinguish them from the genuine article.

What I would question, however, is Trilling's assumption that this kind of identification is in fact unfortunate. Might it not rather lie at the heart of Dreiser's powerful appeal?[18] Might not the apparent trouble with Dreiser's style be its most valuable resource? In any case, the ultimate effect of "omniscient" narration in *Sister Carrie*, however inadvertent this effect often seems, is to collapse the very distance on which the book's apparently naturalistic narrative structure is based. For instance, after an assignation with Hurstwood, Carrie returns to the flat she shares with Drouet, and we are told that "she undid her broad lace collar before the mirror and unfastened her pretty alligator belt which she had recently bought" (90). In the fiction of a writer like Crane, the use of "pretty" in this context would surely be ironic, focusing our critical attention on Carrie's narcissism, on her self-absorption in her reflected image and purchases, on the distance between her valuation of this belt and our own. But it is impossible to tell whether there is irony in Dreiser's use of the word; indeed, it is difficult to determine whose valuation it is meant to register, Carrie's or the narrator's.

We might also look, in this connection, at another much discussed passage, the first description of Fitzgerald and Moy's saloon, where Hurstwood is employed as manager. Drouet frequents it, we are told, because "to him [it] represented in part high life—a fair sample of what the whole must be" (32).

> This was really a gorgeous saloon from the Chicago standpoint. . . . The floors were of brightly coloured tiles, the walls a composition of rich, dark, polished wood, which reflected the light, and coloured stucco-work, which gave the place a very sumptuous appearance. The long bar was a blaze of lights, polished wood-work, coloured and cut glassware, and many fancy bottles. It was a truly swell saloon, with rich screens, fancy wines, and a line of bar goods unsurpassed in the country. (33)

In the presence of "gorgeous," "sumptuous," "fancy" (twice), "a truly swell saloon," and that salesman's appreciation of "a line of bar goods unsurpassed in the country," we might wish to attribute this description wholly to Drouet's point of view—a point of view which we, in the aloofness we share with the narrator, may be encouraged to judge ironically. But it is again hard to be sure of the distinction between the perspectives of the narrator and the character: the initial distancing of "from the Chicago standpoint" seems to be soon forgotten. The narrator is in effect as enthralled with the scene as Drouet is and so, for the moment, are we; the very words and phrases which might distance us serve, paradoxically, to draw us into a sensibility which would "really" consider this a "gorgeous," a "truly swell" saloon.

It is instructive to compare this description of Fitzgerald and Moy's to the account of the saloon over which Pete presides in Crane's *Maggie*:

The interior of the place was papered over in olive and bronze tints of imitation leather. A shining bar of counterfeit massiveness extended down the side of the room. Behind it a great mahogany-appearing sideboard reached the ceiling. Upon its shelves rested pyramids of shimmering glasses that were never disturbed. Mirrors set in the face of the sideboard multiplied them. . . . The elementary senses of it all seemed to be opulence and geometrical accuracy.[19]

"*Imitation* leather," "*counterfeit* massiveness," "mahogany-*appearing*": the judgment behind these phrases, and behind the information that the "shimmering" glasses have no function, establishes a clear position outside and above the limited perspective that could consider this bar *truly* "shining" and "shimmering," a realm of *genuine* "opulence and geometrical accuracy." The mockery of pretentious artifice here, even while it recognizes the reality of such artifice and proposes no more genuine alternative to it, nevertheless keeps us at a distance. The effect of Dreiser's description, by contrast, stems from an effacement of ironic distance—and ultimately from an effacement of the distinctions that make such distance possible.

Equally instructive are the different ways Crane and Dreiser treat theater and theatrical display in *Maggie* and *Sister Carrie*. Maggie and her companions, we recall, regard theatrical artifice as "transcendental realism"; "viewing it," we are told, "they hugged themselves in ecstatic pity of their imagined or real condition."[20] Once again, the elevation of phrases like "transcendental realism" and "ecstatic pity," even while it registers the true feelings of the characters, keeps us outside their minds; we understand their self-delusion in ways that they do not. Theater is also a form of illusion in *Sister Carrie*, but here, as Philip Fisher has noted, "acting draws its moral meaning not from a world of true and false but from a dynamic society where all are rising and falling"; Dreiser refuses "to contrast acting with sincerity, . . . to oppose the representation of what one is not to authentic self-representation."[21] While we might wonder how much even Crane's irony depends on a standard of "authentic self-representation," it is certainly true that in *Sister Carrie* distinctions between authentic and inauthentic, between true and false—and the kinds of ironic distance Crane constructs in *Maggie*—simply melt away.[22] We thus are told of Carrie's absorption in theater, for instance, that she "lived as much in these things as in the realities which made up her daily life"; she is moved by an actress because "her dresses had been all that art could suggest, her sufferings had been so real." At the theater Carrie longs "to give expression to the feelings which she, in the place of the character represented, would feel" (228–29),[23] and here Dreiser, far from standing above his heroine, is allowing her in effect to define the principle of his own art; for he too seeks to give expression to the feelings which he, in the place of the character represented, would feel. The essence of such art, in spite (or because) of Carrie's performative self-consciousness, is the absence of the ironic aloofness implicit in the narrative structure of *Sister Carrie* but repeatedly belied by the actual style—the eager, sometimes clumsily earnest (and seemingly inadvertent) sympathy—of the omniscient narrator.

To say that Dreiser's power derives from the effacement of irony might make him sound like Norris, but in this respect as in so many others they are most notably *dis*similar. Norris's interjected essays inevitably strike us as unwittingly ironic, and they distance the narration so completely from the characters that they often seem to bear absolutely no relation to what is happening in the books in which they occur. These essays are imposed from the outside. Dreiser begins, again and again, on the outside, but he always moves inward—even and maybe especially when he seems to *mean* to keep his distance—toward an affective stylistic identification with the sensibilities of his characters. He does not impose his obsessions on them; instead, he mimics their sufferings and aspirations, even ventriloquizes their inarticulateness, and if this is sloppiness it is sloppiness that mostly works. It may be that this effect is achieved unintentionally; we know that Dreiser wrote *Sister Carrie* rapidly and, according to his later accounts of the novel's composition, almost instinctively. Still, if the writing was instinctive, Dreiser's instincts led him to a complex intermingling of normally antithetical perspectives, and this intermingling represented (and still represents) something new and important in American fiction.

Dreiser is capable of real (and apparently intentional) mastery of point of view, and nowhere is this mastery clearer than in the beautiful account of Hurstwood's suicide:

> It seemed as if he thought a while, for now he arose and turned the gas out, standing calmly in the blackness, hidden from view. After a few moments, in which he reviewed nothing, he turned the gas on again, but applied no match. Even then he stood there, hidden wholly in that kindness which is night, while the uprising fumes filled the room. When the odour reached his nostrils, he quit his attitude and fumbled for the bed.
>
> "What's the use?" he said, weakly, as he stretched himself to rest. (367)

Among the sources of this passage's power, surely, is the oddly indeterminate perspective that is sustained throughout: we are external observers, only knowing, for instance, that "*it seemed as if* he thought for a while"; we infer Hurstwood's emotions from his gestures, even, strangely and magically, when he is "hidden from view," "hidden wholly in that kindness which is night"; yet the whole paragraph, even the strange spectatorial distance, is suffused with Hurstwood's feeling, with his reticent anguish. It is as if Hurstwood were somehow with *us*, regarding himself, and as if in regarding Hurstwood we were also regarding ourselves, experiencing the feelings which we, in the place of the character represented, would feel. No wonder Ford Madox Ford found in Dreiser "effects hitherto unessayed"; nor need we be surprised, finally, that Ford knew no one, with the possible exception of Conrad, who knew more about "style."

Following Hurstwood's death, Dreiser's mastery of point of view seems to collapse, suddenly and utterly. The final pages of the novel return to Carrie, now successful but discontented, gazing out of her hotel window, reflecting wistfully on the emptiness of what she has achieved, and this conclusion returns as well—and notoriously—to the sentimental clichés of the omniscient narrative voice. It is full of poetic inversions: "Friends there were, as the world takes it. . . . For these she had once craved. Applause there was, and publicity" (368). There is a persistent movement toward essayistic generalization: "Thus in life there is ever the intellectual and the emotional nature— the mind that reasons, and the mind that feels" (368). As has so often been the case, Carrie seems to matter to the narrator mainly as she exemplifies his generalizations: "Sitting alone, she was now an illustration of the devious ways by which one who feels, rather than reasons, may be led in the pursuit of beauty" (369). And in the final paragraph all the stylistic stops are pulled out:

Oh, Carrie, Carrie! Oh, blind strivings of the human heart! Onward, onward, it saith, and where beauty leads, there it follows. Whether it be the tinkle of a lone sheep bell o'er some quiet landscape, or the glimmer of beauty in sylvan places, or the show of soul in some passing eye, the heart knows and makes answer, following. It is when the feet weary and hope seems vain that the heart aches and the longings arise. Know, then, that for you is neither surfeit nor content. In your rocking-chair, by your window, shall you dream such happiness as you may never feel. (369)

This conclusion would seem to bear out everything Lionel Trilling says about Dreiser's "bookishness," and many readers have wished that *Sister Carrie* had ended instead with the more conventionally novelistic or modernist account of Hurstwood's suicide—which is how the 1981 Pennsylvania edition, following the surviving typescript of the novel, *does* end.[24]

Nevertheless, I would argue that this conclusion in fact works, however inadvertently, quite effectively, since its crudeness once again manages to identify the supposedly omniscient narrator with the sensibility of his character. Carrie longs for "essential things," but "time" proves each "representation false," an illusion of "tinsel and shine" (368). What remains is the longing, and it is as much the narrator's as Carrie's; for he is no more able than his heroine to believe in a separate order of "essential things" that would render *his* representations truer than hers. F. O. Matthiessen argues that the story of Carrie's spiritual aspiration fails of realization because "Dreiser's realm of 'the spirit,' in rejecting conventional standards, is so loosely defined and moreover so cluttered with clichés that it is hard to respond any longer to his sense of liberation in it," but more recent critics have tended to see in this very looseness the essence of Dreiser's insight and achievement. Thus Walter Michaels writes that "where Howells identifies character with autonomy, Dreiser . . . identifies it with desire," so that "the distinction between what one is and what one wants tends to disappear." Or as Philip Fisher puts much the same idea, Dreiser bases "his entire sense of the self on the dramatic possibilities inherent in a dynamic society," so that "acting involves primarily in Dreiser not deception but practice, not insincerity but installment payments on the world of possibility."[25] Carrie's longing finally expresses Dreiser's, and the novel's conclusion, through the very "tinsel and shine" of its narrative style, reverberates above all with the sympathetic power of this longing.

The naturalism to which Frank Norris and others declared allegiance in the 1890s was riddled with contradictions. As ideology, Norris's naturalism, like Howells's realism, expressed a fantasy of transparent access to the "real"—of representation so radically unmediated by "style" and by what Howells called "literary consciousness" that it would scarcely even *be* representation. Formally, however, texts produced in the name of naturalism, or claimed on its behalf, have tended to filter the "reality" of their materials through aloof narrative consciousnesses and styles that translate it into radically different terms, opening a chasm between "reality" as being and "reality" as understanding. The actual stylistic mark of naturalism, then, is not transparency but a contest between competing styles and perspectives, between transparency *and* mediation. In "How 'Bigger' Was Born," his essay on the writing of *Native Son* (1940), Richard Wright attests to the endurance of this tradition as he describes his attempts to come to terms with the division at the heart of naturalist narrative. "I'd find it impossible to say what I wanted to say," he writes, "without stepping in and speaking outright on my own; but when doing this I always made an effort to retain the mood of the story, explaining everything only in terms of Bigger's life and, if possible, in the rhythms of Bigger's thought (even though the words would be mine)."[26] In *Sister Carrie*, I have been arguing, Dreiser achieves something like the transparency for which Howells and Norris longed, and he is able to do so, apparently, because he ignores Howells's and Norris's assumptions about the location of the "real," about the distinction between "reality" and "style." Dreiser seems far less concerned than Wright to tie his narrator to the "moods" and "rhythms" of his characters' points of view; he is always happy to intervene in his own words. But these words turn out to be at least as appropriate to the characters as to the narrator, and they thus bridge the chasm at the heart of realist thinking and of so many narratives conventionally considered to be examples of literary naturalism.

Howells may have recognized how little his assumptions meant to Dreiser. "You know," he is supposed to have said when the two met by chance at the office of *Harper's Monthly*, "I don't like Sister Carrie"; and the support he had given to so many of the new writers was never extended to Dreiser.[27] We should recall the final sentence of the essay on Tolstoy that concludes Howells's 1895 memoir, *My Literary Passions:* "The supreme art in literature had its highest effect in making me set art forever below humanity."[28] These are the terms in which Dreiser has repeatedly been described, the terms in which his alleged lack of style has been defended, and they almost seem pertinent. Yet there is something authoritarian and hierarchical in Howells's insistence on *"supreme* art," *"highest* effect," "forever *below,"* and this sort of insistence is finally irrelevant to Dreiser. He does not, to be sure, reverse Howells's formulation; he simply ignores it. Dreiser is not a naturalist in Norris's sense, nor is he an ironist like Crane; he is a ventriloquist, like his heroine, imitating a whole series of available styles in order to invest them all with at least the simulation of sympathetic emotion. Dreiser did not set "art" below "humanity"; in his own way, rather, and partly because this distinction was not included in his cultural baggage, he in effect reconciled them. If he fulfilled the ideal of American naturalism he was apparently able to do so, paradoxically, because he was immune to naturalist thinking.

PART THREE

A "Woman's Place" in American Realism

SARAH ORNE JEWETT

In 1883, Mary E. Wilkins (she would add the Freeman when she married in 1902) published a strikingly odd story, "A Symphony in Lavender," in *Harper's Bazar*.[1] It is narrated by a city woman, who describes a visit to a friend in a country village. Across from the friend's house lives an aging spinster who devotes all her energy to her flower garden. Although Miss Caroline Munson is a recluse, the narrator is nevertheless able rather easily to strike up an acquaintance with her, and eventually Miss Munson tells the visitor her story. At the age of twenty-two, she says, she had a dream in which she met a young man with a "handsome dark face" (44), who asked for one of the flowers she was carrying in a basket. But as she reached for a lily, a dove landed on her shoulder; then, as Miss Munson was overcome by "a sort of fascination . . . which would not let me take my eyes from him," the stranger's face seemed to change, to become "at once beautiful and repulsive"—and she fled, as she puts it, with "a great horror of something, I did not know what, in my heart" (45). A year later, she uncannily encountered the same young man again, now in the flesh, on the main street of her village. They were introduced, and she fell in love with him—although "from the first," she says, "there was . . . a kind of horror of him along with love" (46). The young man at last proposed, but again, as in the dream, his face seemed to change, and Miss Munson once more felt an inexplicable revulsion: "the same horror came over me." She rejected him in "sudden repulsion," and he left. And she adds that she has never seen him again in all the intervening years. Then, in a truly peculiar twist, the narrator tells us (what she did not tell Miss Munson): that she thinks she knows the man Miss Munson rejected (they live in the same city) and that "if he were the one—well, I think Miss Munson was right" (47), although we are never told *why* she thinks so.

This is not a very successful story, as Wilkins herself apparently recognized.[2] Its form is also rather uncharacteristic of Wilkins's normal practice: the device of the sympathetic urban narrator visiting the country and learning the stories of its eccentric inhabitants was more typical of Sarah Orne Jewett (a writer by whom Wilkins was strongly influenced); one thinks, for instance, of Jewett's *Deephaven*, which had been published in 1877. "A Symphony in Lavender" seems to be a fairly straightforward, even heavily allegorical, account of sexual revulsion and frigidity.[3] Such a reading fails to account, however, for the curious kinship between the narrator and Miss Munson, for the surprising ease with which the narrator gains access to this rural recluse, for the narrator's acquaintance with Miss Munson's suitor and her approval of the decision to reject him. We should also attend to another strange detail of this strange story. In both the dream and the actual meeting, the young man carries an easel under his arm; he is a professional artist. This fact seems to have no overt function in Miss Munson's tale, but it may suggest something that is going on beneath the surface. Caroline Munson does not simply reject a man; she rejects a male *artist*; and what she regards with both fascination and horror may have as much to do with the man's artistic power as with his sexuality.

Caroline Munson has rejected this urban male artist in order to cultivate her "feminine" flower garden in rural seclusion, and this gesture makes her a convenient emblem of the so-called local color fiction of the 1880s and 1890s—a tradition of which Mary Wilkins was herself one of the most successful practitioners and one whose most important figures were mainly women. Local color writing has conventionally been categorized, by literary historians, as a subset of American realism, and I will have a good deal to say about this supposed connection in Chapter 7. What I would stress here is simply that, if Miss Munson's renunciation is in some sense an emblem of local color fiction, the meaning of this emblem is profoundly ambiguous. "Now I want to know," Miss Munson declares to her listener after finishing her story, "if you think that my dream was really sent to me as a warning, or that I fancied it all, and wrecked—no, I won't say wrecked—dulled the happiness of my whole life for a nervous whim?" (47). Is local color writing, as many critics have argued, a symptom of neurotic self-isolation in rural backwaters, an expression of "nervous whim"? Or is it—as more recent critics have insisted, and as the narrator's unexplained kinship with Miss Munson might suggest—a fulfilling, authentic, even perhaps distinctively "feminist" form of artistic expression? Did Miss Munson, in other words, make a mistake, or did she make the right—or at least the best—choice?

It may be, though, that Caroline Munson's choice—or the idea that she had a choice—is to a large extent illusory. In handing over or withholding her lily she could choose between handing over or withholding herself, but the young man never offered to hand over his easel, and this fact may point to the deepest problem for an American woman writer wishing to produce serious fiction in the context of the heavily "masculine" discourse of realist thinking. The situation is portrayed even more starkly in a later and less obscure Wilkins story, "A Poetess," collected in *A New England Nun and Other Stories* in 1891. The title character, Betsey Dole (whose last name suggests her utter lack of independence), writes "lines" and looks "like the very genius of gentle, old-fashioned, sentimental poetry." To her deep delight, one of her obituary effusions, on a dead child, is printed and circulated by the child's mother. But Betsey soon learns that the local minister thinks the poem "*jest as poor as it could be*," and the information literally kills her: she burns all her "lines" and retires to her room to die. On her deathbed she asks the minister, who has published verse in magazines, to write an obituary poem about her. "I've been thinkin'," she tells him, "that—mebbe my—dyin' was goin' to make me—a good subject for—poetry, if I never wrote none."[4] "A Poetess" is clearly satirical rather than autobiographical; Betsey Dole is meant to be ridiculous in the manner, for instance, of Emmeline Grangerford in *Huckleberry Finn*. Nevertheless, her punishment (or self-punishment) is far too extreme to evoke anything like humor, and it is as if Betsey is punished (humiliated and then killed) not for writing badly but for writing at all, for usurping the minister's male prerogative.[5] A woman might appropriately be the subject of poetry; she could give up herself as she would give up a flower. But she was not herself to publish, to compete with men in the marketplace; she was not, herself, to be the artist with the easel under his arm.

Many American women writers confronted this situation in the last quarter of the nineteenth century—women who, unlike such popular predecessors as Susan Warner and Harriet Beecher Stowe, were more concerned with achieving distinction as "serious" artists than with securing wide moral influence. I have chosen, in Chapter 7, to confine myself to the career and writings of one of these women, Sarah Orne Jewett, because her early career was so closely connected to the sponsorship of William Dean Howells and because she has had a more consistently secure (if usually "minor") place in discussions of nineteenth-century American "realism" than any of her contemporaries. I do not mean, by confining myself to Jewett, to dismiss any of these contemporaries or any of her immediate successors. As I noted in my introduction, this book is not meant to "cover" American fiction in the 1880s and 1890s but to provide a series of related case studies on the influence of realist thinking—and on resistance *to* this thinking. In my opinion, the question of the relevance (or irrelevance) of this thinking to a woman writer with serious ambitions can best be served, at least in the context of this study, by looking at one case in detail. As I also noted in my Introduction, I certainly hope my discussion of Jewett will provoke readers to think about other women writers of this period—such as Kate Chopin, Edith Wharton, and Willa Cather—in some of my terms.

7

Local Color and Realism
SARAH ORNE JEWETT

"I am getting quite ambitious and really feel that writing is my work—my business perhaps; and it is so much better than making a mere amusement of it as I used."
Sarah Orne Jewett to Horace Scudder (1873)

"Sometimes, the business part of writing grows very noxious to me, and I wonder if in heaven our best thoughts—poet's thoughts, especially—will not be flowers, somehow, or some sort of beautiful live things that stand about and grow, and don't have to be chaffered over and bought and sold."
Jewett to Annie Fields (1889)

Ever since the 1890s, Sarah Orne Jewett has been accorded a fairly consistent place in the American literary canon—although even her most enthusiastic partisans have felt compelled to insist that this place is very small. Thus Henry James, in a 1915 essay, describes the "minor compass" of Jewett's art and praises (if that is the right word) "her beautiful little quantum of achievement"; Willa Cather writes in a 1936 memoir that Jewett "was content to be slight, if she could be true"; Warner Berthoff, in a 1959 essay on *The Country of the Pointed Firs*, concludes that the book, "with a secure and unrivaled place in the main line of American literary expression," is "a small work but an unimprovable one."[1] Yet the consistency and endurance of Jewett's literary reputation, however hedged by diminutives, make her almost unique among American women fiction writers of the nineteenth century. And her place in what Berthoff calls "the main line of American literary expression" has not simply depended on critical taste, at least not overtly; it

175

also has been secured by the persistent location of her works within the categories of official American literary history. As a central figure in the supposed tradition of "local color" fiction, of "regionalism," Jewett has conventionally been categorized as an American realist.[2]

Jewett's Place in American Realism

Associating Jewett with realism makes a good deal of sense. "Don't try to write *about* people and things," her father early urged her, "tell them just as they are!"—a piece of advice his daughter cherished, and one that certainly sounds like the *credo* of a realist. In a similar vein, Jewett herself would advise Willa Cather, in a well known letter of 1908: "You must write to the human heart, the great consciousness that all humanity goes to make up. Otherwise what might be strength in a writer is only crudeness, and what might be insight is only observation; sentiment falls to sentimentality—you can write about life, but never life itself."[3] Moreover Jewett's first influential mentor in the public literary world was the very William Dean Howells who would lead the battle for literary realism in the 1880s and 1890s: in 1869, as assistant editor of the *Atlantic Monthly*, Howells accepted the first of the many stories Jewett would publish in that magazine, and his encouragement continued for the rest of her career. Jewett was also one of the writers who led Howells to proclaim, in 1897, that in America "the sketches and studies by the women seem faithfuler and more realistic than those of the men," and he later praised her "incomparable sketches" for their "free movement, unfettered by the limits of plot, and keeping only to the reality."[4]

Still, there are problems with classifying Jewett as a Howellsian realist—problems raised by her subject matter, by her style, and perhaps above all (in spite of Howells's praise for women's stories) by her gender, her status as a *woman* writer. Howells, we recall, sought to dissociate realism from "preening and prettifying, after the fashion of literary men"—to associate it, instead, with "the world of men's activities."[5] In this respect, American local color fiction of the 1880s and 1890s—especially the New England local color fiction produced by such women as Jewett, Mary Wilkins Freeman, Rose Terry Cooke, and others—is the very antithesis of Howellsian realism. For if realism sought to ally itself with "the world of men's activities," the characteristic world of New England local color fiction is distinguished above all by the absence of men and of masculine activity. The young and fit have fled this world for a reality which is always elsewhere, in the West or in the city, while those who remain, mostly women, maintain old proprieties and rituals whose function, like the men, seems long since to have vanished. Ann Douglas, in the title of an important essay, has called this women's local color tradition a "literature of impoverishment," and the realism with which its world is portrayed only serves to underscore that what is absent from it is precisely the sort of "reality" to which writers like Howells wished to turn.[6]

Jewett's achievement, or at least the way it has come to be understood, also stands apart from the strange but habitual denigration of "style" by writers like Howells and Norris. "Who cares for fine style!" Norris declared. "Tell your yarn and go to the devil. We don't want literature, we want life." Jewett's reputation, by contrast, has had everything to do with attention to style. "Style has not been such a common phenomenon in America that its possessor can ever be ignored," writes F. O. Matthiessen at the end of his 1929 book on the author of *The Country of the Pointed Firs;* "Sarah Jewett," he continues, "realized its full importance." Or as Willa Cather puts it in her 1936 memoir: "[A]mong fifty thousand books you will find very few writers who ever achieved a style at all. The distinctive thing about Miss Jewett is that she had an individual voice. . . . If you can . . . go to a quiet spot and take up a volume of Miss Jewett, you will find the voice still there, with a quality which any ear trained in literature must recognize."[7] Cather's insistence on the rare quality of "style," and her grounding proper appreciation of Jewett on training "in literature," could not more clearly distinguish her sense of Jewett's achievement from the ideas of such realists or naturalists as Howells and Norris.

At the heart of this distinction, clearly, are ingrained assumptions about gender, assumptions at the heart of realist thinking, assumptions that in effect prohibited women from full participation in the realist program. Some of the implications of these assumptions can be seen in an astonishing essay by Frank Norris, "Why Women Should Write the Best Novels"—"and," so its title as a 1901 magazine article adds, "Why They Don't." Women, according to Norris, should write the best novels because they have leisure and a literary rather than a business education. Even more important, he insists, is what he sees as a fundamental difference of temperament separating women from men:

The average man is a rectangular, square-cut, matter-of-fact, sober-minded animal who does not receive impressions easily, who is not troubled with emotions and has no overmastering desire to communicate his sensations to anybody. But the average woman is just the reverse of all these. She is impressionable, emotional, and communicative. And impressionableness, emotionality, and communicativeness are three very important qualities of mind that make for novel writing.

Why, then, do women *not* write the best novels? First of all, says
Norris, trotting out his favorite aphorism, because "life is more important than literature"; and women, he writes, have little knowledge
of "life itself," of "the crude, the raw, the vulgar"—which of course
constitute, for Norris, "real life." Women are also, he insists, physi-
ologically and temperamentally incapable of serious literary exertion;
he thus points to "the make-up of the woman," to the supposed "fact
that protracted labour of the mind tells upon a woman quicker than
upon a man." A man, he writes, "may grind on steadily for an almost
indefinite period, when a woman at the same task would begin, after a
certain point, to 'feel her nerves,' to chafe, to fret, to try to do too
much, to polish too highly, to develop more perfectly. Then come
fatigue, harassing doubts, more nerves, a touch of hysteria occasionally, exhaustion, and in the end complete discouragement and a final
abandonment of the enterprise."[8]

Such ideas are blatantly, perhaps even laughably, compensatory, but
for this very reason they served an important purpose for male writers
who worried that being "literary" might compromise their masculinity. These ideas have also no doubt played a role in the formation of
Sarah Orne Jewett's somewhat peculiar literary reputation. She certainly did care for style, but one suspects the critical attention that has
been paid to this concern (hardly a surprising concern, one would like
to think, for a writer) has owed more than a little to the fact that
Jewett was a woman. According to realist orthodoxy, after all, "style"
is "feminine." And what about the bizarre but persistent critical interest in the *size* of Jewett's place in the canon? We should remember
Norris's essay of 1896 (the year Jewett's *Country of the Pointed Firs* was
published) on the father of French naturalism: "To be noted of M.
Zola," he writes, "we must leave the rank and the file, either turn to
the forefront of the marching world, or fall by the roadway. . . . The
world of M. Zola is a world of big things; the enormous, the formidable, the terrible, is [*sic*.] what counts; no teacup tragedies here."[9] If the
masculine ("marching") world of Zola is "a world of big things," as
distinguished from the feminized world of "teacup tragedies," then *of
course* the place accorded a woman writer in the main line of American
literary expression would be bound to be small, a kind of respite from
"the enormous, the formidable, the terrible." "Your voice," Howells
wrote to Jewett in 1891, "is like a thrush's in the din of all the literary
noises that stun us so."[10] This kind of thinking, moreover, has been as
characteristic of women as of men; Cather, we recall, recommends
that the reader who wants to appreciate Jewett's distinctive voice
should "go to a quiet spot" before taking up one of her volumes.

The heavily gendered assumptions at the heart of American realist thinking have surely had a lot to do with what official literary history has made of Jewett and other so-called local color writers, but there may be a more interesting way to approach the relation of American realism to Jewett's work. Instead of asking what American realism made of Jewett, we might ask what Jewett made of American realism—of the ideas of Howells and others about the "reality" of "men's activities." While Jewett did not expound on Howells's ideas in letters and prefaces, in aesthetic manifestos, we still might ask what attitudes are expressed or implied in her fiction. One way of answering this question would be to say that Jewett, in her fiction, quite deliberately and completely turns Howellsian realism on its head, reversing or undercutting its deepest ambitions and assumptions. I will ultimately be disagreeing with this answer, or at least qualifying it to a significant degree, but it certainly has a strong and plausible appeal. The programs of Howells and Norris endorse a movement from the less to the more "real," from the feminine world of "teacup tragedies" to "the marching world," "the world of men's activities." Jewett's fiction—notably, for instance, *The Country of the Pointed Firs*—seems to reverse this movement while retaining the valuation. For her it appears to be a movement *out* of "the world of men's activities," a withdrawal into a rural world of women's communities, that leads into a more intense "reality."

Maine Person and Boston Professional

Sarah Orne Jewett was born in South Berwick, Maine, in 1849, and this small coastal town remained her home for the rest of her life; she died there, in the house in which she had been raised, in 1909.[11] She published her first story at nineteen and her first book, *Deephaven*, at twenty-eight; she wrote stories for children, three novels—*A Country Doctor* (1884), *A Marsh Island* (1885), and *The Tory Lover* (1901)—and eleven collections of stories and sketches. Her fiction deals with a fairly wide variety of subjects and settings—for instance, urban businessmen (and businesswomen), Irish and French Canadian immigrants, and the American Revolution—but she is now known almost entirely for her Maine local color writing, especially *The Country of the Pointed Firs* (1896). By the early 1880s, Jewett's literary success had led to the forming of firm and lasting professional and social ties far beyond South Berwick. The most notable of these was with Annie Fields, widow (after 1881) of Boston publisher James T. Fields. Annie Fields's home on Charles Street was the social center for literary Boston—as many Bostonians proudly noted, it was their equivalent of the Parisian *salon*—and here Jewett, for the rest of her life, spent her winters, just as Fields regularly visited Berwick in the summers. The two women also frequently traveled together, to Europe, the West Indies, and elsewhere.[12] So Sarah Orne Jewett, lifelong resident of South Berwick, chronicler and champion of rural simplicity, of pastoral withdrawal, was also very much a citizen of the world, a woman of cosmopolitan—or at least Bostonian—culture. The trajectory of her career was thus rather different from the movement that is supposed to be celebrated in so much of her best-known fiction.

"I count myself entirely a Maine person and not a (transplanted) Boston citizen," Jewett wrote in 1895, "even though I may spend many weeks of the winter within the limits of Ward Nine." What matters most about this statement is that she felt the need to make it at all; for she clearly recognized that she was in fact, both by residence and by temperament, two different people, a "Maine person" and a "(transplanted) Boston citizen," a lover of rural isolation and an active literary professional, and this sense of personal and vocational division is reflected in the passages I have chosen as epigraphs to this chapter. "Sometimes," Jewett writes in an 1889 letter to Annie Fields, "the business part of writing grows very noxious to me, and I wonder if in heaven our best thoughts—poet's thoughts, especially—will not be flowers, somehow, or some sort of beautiful live things that stand about and grow, and don't have to be chaffered over and bought and sold." Sixteen years earlier, however, at the beginning of her professional career, she had written to Horace Scudder, at the *Atlantic:* "I am getting quite ambitious and really feel that writing is my work—my business perhaps; and it is so much better than making a mere amusement of it as I used."[13] The effort to reconcile the identities of Maine person and worldly professional, to reconcile the quite distinct values they represented, informs almost all of Jewett's best writing.

In *Deephaven*—a group of interrelated *Atlantic* sketches collected in book form in 1877, at the urging of William Dean Howells—the narrator, Helen Denis, spends a summer in a Maine costal town with her friend, Kate Lancaster, whose aunt's death has left a large house available to them. These young women are genteel Bostonians, and from first to last they are outsiders in this rural world. Helen finds the stasis and isolation of Deephaven profoundly attractive; this retreat seems to offer what has been missing from her own worldly experience. "Deephaven," she writes, "never recovered from the effects of the embargo of 1807, and a sand-bar has been steadily filling the mouth of the harbor"; "there was no excitement about anything; there were no manufactories; nobody seemed in the least hurry" (70, 98).[14]

"It seemed," Helen writes, "as if all the clocks in Deephaven, and all the people with them, had stopped years ago, and the people had been doing over and over what they had been busy about during the last week of their unambitious progress. . . . There were no young people whom we knew" (74). "Do you notice," Kate whispers to her friend, "how many more old women there are than old men?" (76). These details might seem more ominous than gratifying, but Kate and Helen ignore such hints, at least at the outset; they have fled Boston, if only temporarily, for something "truer," and this motive determines their perception of their new surroundings.

Helen's idealization of Deephaven often becomes positively rhapsodic. "It is wonderful," she writes,

the romance and tragedy and adventure which one may find in a quiet old-fashioned country town, though to heartily enjoy the every-day life one must care to study life and character, and must find pleasure in thought and observation of simple things, and have an instinctive, delicious interest in what to other eyes is unflavored dulness. (65–66)

In this credo for local color writing the emphasis is on the vicarious experience of the spectator rather than the reality of rural life, the actual experience of country people; phrases like "heartily enjoy" and "delicious interest" only underline the distance between observers and observed. And Jewett's awareness of this distance is revealed clearly when Helen's rhapsody is immediately undercut by the account a Mrs. Dockum gives of a local woman known as "Widow Jim":

"Good neighbor, does according to her means always. Dreadful tough time of it with her husband, shif'less and drunk all his time. Noticed that dent in the side of her forehead, I s'pose? That's where he liked to have killed her; slung a stone bottle at her."

"*What!*" said Kate and I, very much shocked. (66)

Their shock is understandable, and very much to the point. For Widow Jim, the actual Maine person, life in "quiet old-fashioned" Deephaven has hardly been a matter of "hearty" enjoyment, of "pleasure" or "delicious interest."

As the book proceeds, it becomes increasingly clear that the terms in which Helen and Kate see this village are quite irrelevant to the actual experience of its inhabitants. And Helen and Kate become increasingly aware of, and uncomfortable with, their own false position as privileged observers. Visiting a circus in the company of a local woman, they see the fat lady, on exhibit as "the Kentucky giantess," who turns out to be an old acquaintance of their companion. "Kate and I," Helen writes, "felt ashamed of ourselves for being there. No matter if she had consented to be carried round for a show, it must have been horrible to be stared at and joked about day after day" (138). Soon after, traveling in the back country, they meet an unemployed boat builder, driven from work by the collapse of local shipping, whose only hope is a son who has escaped to the city, the "real" world, to make his fortune. Such actual tragedy is neither romantic nor delicious, and when Kate and Helen later learn that the man and his wife have died and that their children are to be separated among various more or less grudging relatives, they decline an invitation to attend the funeral. "We had no right there," Helen explains, "and it would seem as if we were merely curious, and we were afraid our presence would make people ill at ease. . . . It would be an intrusion" (215). Such moments threaten to undermine the pastoral premise underlying their entire summer visit.

As this visit comes to an end, Kate and Helen begin to feel that they have in a sense become part of the town. They "half dreaded," Helen writes, the thought of returning to Boston; "we were surprised to find how little we cared for it, and how well one can get on without many things which are thought indispensable" (241); and they even entertain the thought of settling in permanently. But this fantasy only reveals, once again, the uncomfortable truth of their false position. "I wonder," Kate muses, "if we should grow lazy if we stayed here all the year round; village life is not stimulating, and there would not be much to do in winter" (243). Helen's reply could stand as a kind of epigraph for the whole book:

> "I suppose if we really belonged in Deephaven we should think it a hard fate, and not enjoy it half so much as we have this summer. . . . Our idea of happiness would be making long visits in Boston; and we should be heart-broken when we had to come away and leave our lunch-parties, and symphony concerts, and calls, and fairs, the reading-club and the children's hospital." (244)

They might also, one could add, starve like the unemployed boat builder and his wife or have dents in the sides of their foreheads like Widow Jim. *Deephaven* is by no means as grim as my summary may suggest, and it largely endorses its narrator's love for the old ways of this rural backwater. But Helen's narrative still resonates with the ironic understanding that, while Deephaven fulfills her own fantasy of the "reality" of country life, those who really belong in Deephaven mainly want to get out, to escape to the city. One might compare all of this to the cross-class comedy of Henry James's *Princess Casamassima*, with its aristocrats and working-class characters eagerly exploring each others' haunts. "We used to pity the young girls so much," Helen writes. "It was plain that those who knew how much easier and pleasanter our lives were could not help envying us" (191).

A similar irony informs a comic Jewett story of 1889, "Going to Shrewsbury." The genteel narrator, on a train, meets a Mrs. Peet, "a perturbed old countrywoman, laden with a large basket and a heavy bundle tied up in an old-fashioned bundle-handkerchief." Mrs. Peet, we learn, has had to leave her country farmhouse and is going to the city of Shrewsbury to throw herself on the uncertain charity of her urban relatives, and the narrator finds "the atmosphere of her loneliness, uncertainty, and sorrow . . . touching"; tears come to her eyes as she thinks of the old woman's loss of her rural home. Mrs. Peet, however, views things quite differently: "You see," she says, "'t won't be so tough on me as if I hadn't always felt it lurking within me to go off some day or 'nother an' see how other folks did things." Yet as Mrs. Peet gets off the train the narrator still feels pity: "The sight of that worn, thin figure," she writes, "adventuring alone across the platform gave my heart a sharp pang as the train carried me away." At the close, the joke is on this sentimental perspective: Mrs. Peet's nieces turn out to have accepted her with open arms, and they share the narrator's sentimental ideal of rural happiness, but Mrs. Peet will have none of it. The nieces even wished, a companion tells the narrator, "to buy the farm here, and come back to live, but [Mrs. Peet] wouldn't hear of it, and thought they would miss too many privileges. She has been going to concerts and lectures."[15]

Many of Jewett's best stories deal with country people who long, like Mrs. Peet, "to go off some day or 'nother an' see how other folks [do] things." Like the servant Martha, in "Martha's Lady" (1897), who consoles herself through years of drab rural existence by remembering a woman who had been kind to her before marrying and moving to London, they measure their own lives against a fantasy of the freedom the "real" world might offer them. And quite a few of Jewett's country characters actually manage to escape, at least briefly. In "The Flight of Betsey Lane" (1893), the title character sneaks away from the Byfleet village poorhouse to visit the 1876 Centennial celebrations in Philadelphia. In "The Hiltons' Holiday" (1893), a farmer takes his daughters on their first trip to town. "I want 'em to know the world," he tells his wife, "an' not stay right here on the farm like a couple o' bushes" (292)—and his comparison of rural stasis to the condition of "bushes" might even recall Jewett's comparison of "poet's thoughts" (as contrasted with "the business part of writing") to "live things that stand about and grow." Yet in both of these stories escape is only temporary, as much a vacation as Helen's and Kate's summer excursion, albeit in the opposite direction. Betsey Lane, having seen the Centennial, immediately returns. "I never see a place more friendly than Pheladelphy," she explains to her friends; "but 't ain't natural to a Byfleet person to be always walkin' on a level." The Hilton girls are more profoundly changed by their experience: "[S]omehow," we are told, "the children looked different; it seemed to their mother as if . . . they belonged to the town now as much as to the country." Nevertheless, they do come back. "The great day was over," the story ends, certifying their return, "and they shut the door."[16]

My overall point here is that Jewett in fact treats the values that supposedly constitute her connection to the tradition of local color fiction, and that might lead us to find in her fiction a reversal of the emphases of realist thinking, with a fair amount of irony and critical scrutiny. She does not dismiss these values, but she recognizes both their complexity and their artificiality. *Deephaven* and stories like "The Flight of Betsey Lane" reveal that the "Maine person" is, in fact, a worldly *construction*, a pastoral convention, quite distinct from the identity, for instance, of those "who really belonged in Deephaven." After all, Helen and Kate's sentimental journey is enabled by precisely the mobility that is for the most part denied to the country people they idealize for, among other things, their *im*mobility. Jewett also recognizes and dramatizes, again and again, a desire in her country people that expresses itself in a movement quite contrary to the withdrawal from "the world of men's activities," from "the world of big things," with which women's local color writing has normally been associated.

There is a quality of slightness, of emotional disengagement, in many of Jewett's stories: even when they depend upon the tension between tedium and escape, between resignation and rebellion, they tend not to probe it very deeply. Stories like "Going to Shrewsbury" and "The Flight of Betsey Lane" turn such tension into light comedy, and while the tone of "The Hiltons' Holiday" is more deeply resonant—it is in fact a very lovely story—here too the emotional complexity of the characters' ambivalent urges is kept at arm's length. But the theme is engaged far more deeply and (one guesses) personally in the two most interesting works of fiction Jewett produced between *Deephaven* and *The Country of the Pointed Firs:* her first novel, *A Country Doctor* (1884), and the title story of *A White Heron and Other Stories* (1886). Both deal with young girls who have an opportunity to escape their rural surroundings in one way or another. And in both of them the theme of escape, or of contemplated escape, becomes inextricably enmeshed in issues of gender, the same issues that gird the underpinnings of realist thinking.[17]

Jewett intended *A Country Doctor* as a tribute to her physician father, with whom she had traveled on his far-flung rounds as a child, and who had died in 1878. He is portrayed in the novel as a childless widower, Dr. Leslie, with a rural practice in a village named, significantly, Oldfields. "There was that about him," we learn of Dr. Leslie, "which gave certainty, not only of his sagacity and skill, but of his true manhood, his mastery of himself" (33).[18] This fictional portrait of a beloved father is admiring and affectionate, but what gives *A Country Doctor* its special interest is Jewett's fantasized portrayal of herself, more or less, as Nan Prince, the doctor's ward, who grows up to become a doctor herself—as Jewett, with her father's encouragement, grew up to become a professional writer. Nan Prince's mother, we learn, had been raised on a local farm; she went off to the Lowell mills and then, instead of coming home, drifted to the city of Dunport, where she married, as they say, above her station. Her husband died, she quarreled with his surviving sister and took to drink, and at the beginning of the book she comes back to Oldfields to die and to leave her baby in the care of the girl's grandmother. "She was a strange character," says Dr. Leslie, "a handsome creature, with a touch of foolish ambition, and soon grew impatient with the routine of home life" (98). The terms of judgment could scarcely be more explicit: "ambition," at least in a woman, is "foolish"; she should confine herself to "the routine of home life."

At the mother's deathbed, Dr. Leslie promises to serve as guardian for the child, and when the grandmother dies, Nan moves into his home. Her inclinations, even as a child, seem to link her to her mother and to set her in direct opposition to the values by which Dr. Leslie judged that mother: impatient of domesticity, she becomes ambitious to practice medicine when she grows up. Oddly enough, given his views on women and "the routine of home life," Dr. Leslie supports this ambition. "I see plainly," he tells a neighbor,

"that Nan is not the sort of girl who will be likely to marry . . . ; and if I make sure by and by, the law of her nature is that she must live alone and work alone, I shall help her to keep it instead of break it, by providing something else than the business of housekeeping and what is called a woman's natural work, for her activity and capacity to spend itself upon." (137)

With such encouragement, Nan does go on to study medicine. Then, in a gesture that sets the plot of *A Country Doctor* in motion, she is reconciled with her dead father's wealthy sister, Anna Prince, and on a visit to this aunt in Dunport she is pressured to forsake her career and marry a local young man. But Nan resists this pressure, and Dr. Leslie approves; to him, at the close, Nan seems "one of the earlier proofs and examples of a certain noble advance and new vantage-ground of civilization," one of those women "who, sometimes honored and sometimes persecuted, have been drawn away from home life by a devotion to public and social usefulness" (332). Having renounced marriage (as Jewett herself never married), Nan returns to Oldfields to take over her aging guardian's practice.

Nan's career certainly seems to overthrow contemporary assumptions about "a woman's natural work." Like her mother she follows her ambition, but unlike her mother she prospers. And Nan's sense of vocation is supported by some pointed allusions: "Listen, Aunt Nancy!" she declares, echoing one of the more famous lines in the New Testament, "I must be about my business" (308). Embracing the image of professionalism, of "business," Nan rejects precisely the values we might suppose the "Maine person" in Jewett to have cherished. After Nan's first visit to Boston, in Dr. Leslie's company, we are told that

she had ceased to belong only to the village she had left; in these days she became a citizen of the world at large. Her horizon had suddenly become larger, and she might have discovered more than one range of mountains which must be crossed as the years led her forward steadily, one by one.[19] (153–54)

As she follows her path into "the world at large," Nan also takes on an explicitly "masculine" power (her last name, after all, *is* "Prince"), as the romantic plot turns increasingly into a kind of gender contest. Her Dunport suitor is shocked when she coolly resets a farmer's dislocated shoulder: "[H]e felt weak and womanish," we are told, "and somehow wished it had been he who could play the doctor" (266). He reacts to Nan's refusal of his offer of marriage in similar terms, terms that reveal the extent to which Jewett apparently regarded marriage as an assertion of arbitrary male authority: "All his manliness was at stake," the narrator reports, "and his natural rights would be degraded and lost, if he could not show his power to be greater than her own" (295). In the event, of course, it is Nan who demonstrates superior power; she rejects this suitor who seems to regard her mainly as a potential trophy, and in a symbolic moment near the end of the book Dr. Leslie—praised earlier for "his true manhood, his mastery of himself"—transfers this mastery to his ward. When she returns from Dunport, he meets her at the railroad station, she climbs into his carriage, and as they head for home we are told that "he gave the reins to Nan and leaned back in the carriage" (340).

A Country Doctor, Jewett's most nearly autobiographical work of fiction, seems to assert women's fitness for supposedly "masculine" activities in no uncertain terms; and it also seems by implication to claim for Jewett herself, as a writer, full power to engage in the "masculine" enterprise of literary realism—to take her place in what Howells would call "the world of men's activities." Yet we must recognize the many ways in which Nan's quite overtly "masculine" self-assertion, and Jewett's endorsement of such self-assertion, are ultimately limited and qualified in the novel. For one thing, Nan's male role model, Dr. Leslie, is not really a figure of "the world at large"; he has in fact withdrawn from this world, and any power he hands over to his ward operates only in a rather constricted sphere. A man of learning and sophistication, he long ago returned to Oldfields, we are told, "somewhat unwillingly"; but even after the deaths of his young wife and child, years before the beginning of the novel, "he felt less and less inclination to break the old ties and transplant himself to some more prominent position in the medical world"—even though he has gained "great repute among his professional brethren" (94).[20] Like Sarah Orne Jewett, Dr. Leslie has chosen the identity of "Maine person" over that of "(transplanted) Boston citizen."

And Nan's "ambition," strangely enough, brings *her* back to Oldfields too. It is crucial to recognize the effect of Jewett's plot, particularly of her having Nan visit Dunport, on the novel's full meaning. By associating marriage with the city of Dunport and worldly Aunt Nancy rather than with the old fashioned values of Oldfields, Jewett in effect inverts the terms of the dilemma facing her heroine. One would think that in order to rebel completely Nan would have to reject both marriage *and* Oldfields for ambition and the world. Jewett, however, sets things up in such a way that "the world" retains its association with a threatening and forbidden "masculine" power, so that Nan asserts herself, in the end, by conforming, and explores the expanding horizon by staying at home. Only thus, apparently, can Nan avoid the obscure disaster that overtook her "foolish" mother. As a young girl, Nan has strangely mixed motives: if she longs to be "famous in her chosen profession," she also wishes to fulfill this longing as "the valued partner of Dr. Leslie"; "she would help him so much," we are told, "that he would wonder how he ever had been able to manage his wide-spread practice alone" (87). We should pay close attention to the force of phrases like "valued partner" and "help him so much" here; Nan's ambition is to be realized, apparently, not in individual self-assertion but in a domestic "partnership," something like a marriage, in which the woman fulfills herself by giving "help" to the man.

In reimagining her life with her father, Jewett hardly went so far as to produce a fantasy of incest, although the removal of all other family members (Jewett in fact had two sisters, and her mother outlived her father) is suggestive. What matters, rather, is that this pseudomarriage, and even Nan's professional success, ultimately function to provide a *refuge* from "the world at large." The novel's final compromise between the radically antithetical imperatives of Nan's world—a compromise imaged in the rural, domestic relationship of Nan and her guardian—is achieved not by resolving the issue between escape and return, between ambition and conformity, but by obscuring and confusing this issue. At the outset, Oldfields is the repository of traditional values, particularly traditional ideas of a woman's proper role, but once these ideas have been shifted to the outside world, once they have been displaced to the city, to "the world of men's activities," Nan is left free to defy tradition, as it were, by embracing it. The paradoxical result, for Nan, is that she must pursue her "masculine" ambition as a form of traditional (if also professional) domesticity, in a realm withdrawn from the "real" world. "The world at large" is finally, for her, exactly what it was for her mother, a forbidden realm. So too, apparently, could Jewett be—as she wrote to Horace Scudder in 1873—"quite ambitious," and pursue literature as "work," as a "business," if she could identify herself as a "Maine person" and write mostly about places like the village in which Nan ends up practicing medicine.

Sylvia, the nine-year-old protagonist of "A White Heron," in many ways recalls Nan Prince; indeed, the 1886 story functions in some respects as a kind of stylized or allegorized revision of the 1884 novel.[21] A character in *A Country Doctor* remarks of Nan as a child that "she belongs with wild creatur's, I do believe,—just the same natur'" (61), and Sylvia too, as her name would suggest, finds her chief companionship in the woods and fields around her isolated rural home. Also like Nan, Sylvia was not born in the country; she spent her first eight years in "a crowded manufacturing town" (162).[22] She was then selected by her grandmother, Mrs. Tilley, to help on the old woman's farm. Mrs. Tilley is something of a local color archetype: her husband has died, and her two children have long ago left for the outside world; her daughter, Sylvia's mother, lives in the city, and her son, of whom she has heard nothing in years, is either dead or living in California. Sylvia, unlike Nan, has no ambition to escape her rural routine. When she entered her grandmother's house for the first time she whispered to herself "that this was a beautiful place to live in" (163), and her main memory of the "noisy town" is of a "great red-faced boy who used to chase and frighten her" (162).

Yet Sylvia, in spite of her contentedness, is (again like Nan) offered a chance of escape, or at least a chance to forge a connection with "the world," and her response to this opportunity is the subject of her story. As she wanders in the woods, thinking of the "red-faced boy," she is "horror-stricken to hear a clear whistle"—"not a bird's whistle, which would have been a sort of friendliness, but a boy's whistle, determined, and somewhat aggressive." Its source is a "tall young man, who carried a gun over his shoulder," an ornithologist seeking a white heron to add to his collection (163). Reluctantly, Sylvia takes him to her grandmother's, where he stays the night, announcing that he will pay ten dollars if Sylvia will guide him, next day, to the heron's secret nest. Sylvia is shocked by this young man: "[S]he could not understand," we are told, "why he killed the very birds he seemed to like so much." Yet she is also attracted by him: "[S]he had never seen anybody so charming and delightful; the woman's heart, asleep in the child, was vaguely thrilled by a dream of love" (166). So Sylvia is torn, and the narrator seems to be quite explicit about what is at issue: "Alas, if the great wave of human interest which flooded for the first time this dull little life should sweep away the satisfactions of an existence heart to heart with nature and the dumb life of the forest!" (168). Once again the issue is drawn between "the world at large," what Frank Norris called "the world of big things," and the rural isolation of local color fiction.

Next morning, Sylvia steals away before dawn to the edge of the woods and climbs "a great pine-tree . . . , the last of its generation" (167). From this vantage point she sees the sunrise, described in one of the most beautiful passages Jewett ever wrote, and for the first time in her life—rather astonishingly, since it is only a few miles from her grandmother's house—she sees the ocean, gleaming beyond the salt marshes. This moment corresponds quite precisely to Nan Prince's vision of the expanding horizon after her first visit to Boston. Then Sylvia sees the white heron: "a white spot of him like a single floating feather comes up from the dead hemlock. . . . She knows his secret now" (170). But when she returns to the farmhouse, we are told that "Sylvia cannot speak; she cannot tell the heron's secret and give its life away"; she remains silent even though "she suffered a sharp pang as the guest went away disappointed later in the day, that could have served and followed him and loved him as a dog loves!" (171).

The mode of "A White Heron" is far more allegorical than is customary in Jewett's best-known fiction, and the meaning of the allegory seems pretty straightforward. Sylvia, like Nan, is offered a choice between her "dull little life" and "the great wave of human interest" aroused by the stranger. "Has she been nine years growing," asks the narrator, as Sylvia ponders whether to reveal her secret, "and now, when the great world for the first time puts out a hand to her, must she thrust it aside for a bird's sake?" (170–71). The answer to this rhetorical question is, of course, yes, and Sylvia's decision is apparently far less equivocal than Nan's. After all, she lacks the option of a professional career, so that she has only the stark alternatives of staying in the woods in silence or selling out the heron's secret. In the event she does fully renounce "the great world," the attraction of the "noisy town," and remains loyal to "the dumb life of the forest"; before the stranger's entreaties she remains, like this forest, "dumb" (170). Sylvia, this is to say, chooses nature, and her choice seems to be approved and endorsed by the narrator—not very surprisingly, perhaps, since Sylvia's choice seems so closely to resemble Jewett's own insistence on identifying herself as a "Maine person" rather than a "Boston citizen."

Yet the "nature" to which Sylvia remains loyal is strangely delimited, purged of many qualities we might normally regard as "natural." Sex, for instance, is here displaced, as it was in *A Country Doctor,* from the realm of nature to the city—where it mainly expresses itself as sadistic violence, imaged in the red face of the little boy, or in the urban intruder's "determined" and "aggressive" whistle and in the gun he carries on his shoulder. This sort of masculine aggression is excluded from Sylvia's woods; it is surely significant, for example, that Mrs. Tilley's son, who escaped to California after defying his father, "was a great hand to go gunning" (164). In place of such violence, Sylvia's ideal nature is dominated by passive *relics* of phallic authority: by the "great pine-tree . . . , the last of its generation," and by the solitary and silent heron, who nests in a "dead hemlock." Jewett, moreover, is fully aware of the artificiality of the nature Sylvia chooses. The girl is shocked that the ornithologist kills birds, but when she first arrives at her grandmother's house and whispers that "this was a beautiful place to live in," she overlooks the significance of the fact that Mrs. Tilley's cat is "fat with young robins" (162). The "nature" for which Sylvia has so much protective respect has no such respect for itself.

What Sylvia chooses, finally, is the defining landscape of local color fiction, a rural hermitage in which she will be safe from the incursions of the masculine "great world."[23] The story, however, keeps under-mining the narrator's overt celebration of this decision. I do not mean to imply that Sylvia makes a mistake; the "red-faced boy" *did* chase her, and not only is the handsome stranger armed, he thinks he can purchase her allegiance; even in her daydream of loving him, Sylvia recognizes that to follow him would be to "serve" him, to love him "as a dog loves." In the era of "manly" realism and the "strenuous life," an era in which Teddy Roosevelt was also invading the wilderness to bag specimens of his prowess, the "great world" was perhaps not a safe place for women, at least for women with a sense of their own auton-omy; so Sylvia preserves her autonomy by renouncing "the great wave of human interest" that has flooded her "dull little life." She and her grandmother will live on, but it is clear that they will experience what the narrator calls "the satisfactions of an existence heart to heart with nature" with, in fact, a good deal of regret. Long after the stranger's departure, Sylvia still hears "the echo of his whistle haunting the pasture path" (171), while Mrs. Tilley has already reflected on her son's departure, wistfully: "There, I don't blame him, I'd ha' seen the world myself if it had been so I could" (164). The point is that it never *was* so that she could.

"This is my birthday," Jewett wrote to a friend in 1897, "and I am always nine years old";[24] and this is also, as many readers have noted, Sylvia's age in "A White Heron." It would be a great mistake, of course, to read the story in any strict sense as veiled autobiography—Jewett was hardly a "lonely country child" (171) living in impover-ished isolation—but Sylvia does seem an apt and deliberate emblem of Jewett's literary persona, of the "Maine person." Sylvia's refusal of the stranger's offer of $10.00 for the heron's story, and her oneness with "dumb" nature, anticipate Jewett's 1889 complaint to Annie Fields about "the business part of writing" and her hope that in heaven "poet's thoughts" might be "flowers, somehow, or some sort of beauti-ful live things that stand about and grow, and don't have to be chaf-fered over and bought and sold." Jewett also saw this story as itself being exempt from, or at least in a special way inappropriate to, the chaffering of the literary marketplace. "What shall I do with my 'White Heron' now she is written?" she wrote to Annie Fields after finishing the story (and the personification of "she" is surely signifi-cant). "She isn't a very good magazine story, but I love her, and I mean to keep her for the beginning of my next book."[25]

What makes "A White Heron" particularly interesting in this con-text is the complexity of its *attitude* toward Sylvia's choice, toward the form of literary identity that seems to be embodied in her choice. This is no rhapsodic celebration of what Helen Denis, in *Deephaven,* calls the "delicious interest" of simple country life; the story as a whole significantly qualifies the narrator's valuation of "the satisfactions of an existence heart to heart with nature," satisfactions central to local color writing's supposed inversion of the gender assumptions of realist thinking. Autonomy, for Sylvia, is secured not through growth but through regression into a perpetual childhood, into oneness with a permanently desexualized nature. The story in this sense revises the conclusion of *A Country Doctor* by fully literalizing the implications of Nan's remaining in Dr. Leslie's house, of her coming into professional maturity *as* his ward.[26]

Even more important to an understanding of "A White Heron" as a parable of literary identity or vocation is the fact that Sylvia achieves safety through *silence;* for what she declines, at the close, is perhaps above all a *literary* opportunity. The man from the city, she thinks, "can make them rich with money"; he is "well worth making happy, and he waits to hear the story she can tell," but she cannot tell it; "she must keep silence." (170) While Sylvia's silence is understandable, it is rather strange and chilling as an emblem of literary or artistic vocation, suggesting that to withdraw from what Howells called "the world of men's activities" might be to renounce expression altogether. "What is it," the narrator asks in the face of Sylvia's refusal, "that suddenly forbids her and makes her dumb?" (170) This question, which may in fact be a translation of Sylvia's own thoughts at her moment of crisis, is not directly answered, but we may already have gotten an answer of sorts at the very beginning of the story. Sylvia is introduced, in the opening paragraphs, "driving home her cow," an animal bent, like so many of Jewett's country characters, on resisting confinement. "It was her greatest pleasure," we are told of this cow, "to hide herself away among the high huckleberry bushes, and though she wore a loud bell she had made the discovery that if one stood perfectly still it would not ring" (161). The problem is that freedom achieved by such means, by standing so perfectly still as not to make a sound, is scarcely to be distinguished from confinement. It is a bit difficult, likewise, to distinguish Sylvia's victory over the noisy urban intruder, as she stuns herself into protective dumbness, from defeat.

Realism, Feminism, and the World of Dunnet Landing

The Country of the Pointed Firs seems to signal a return to the mode of *Deephaven.* Its narrator, a city resident like Helen Denis, summers in the Maine seacoast town of Dunnet Landing in order to escape "those petty excitements of every day that belong to cities" (96).[27] Yet while we learn far less about this narrator than we learn about Helen (we never even learn her name), what we do know tends mainly to distinguish her from her *Deephaven* predecessor. She is no young socialite but a mature woman, a professional writer who has come to Dunnet Landing to pursue her work. Also, her idealization of the simplicity and tranquil authenticity of her adopted village is apparently never undercut by the kinds of irony that repeatedly qualify Helen's enthusiasm. It is significant, finally, that she has been to Dunnet Landing before; the book's opening sketch is entitled "The Return," and this title is meant in more than the literal sense. Returning to Dunnet Landing, the narrator seems to be returning as well to certain primal qualities lost or atrophied in the rush of modern urban life. I noted earlier that women's local color fiction might be seen as turning realist thinking on its head by reversing its assumptions about the superiority of what Frank Norris called "the marching world," "the world of big things"—and by substituting for this realm a rural, communal world of women. However much this idea of local color fiction may be qualified or complicated in *Deephaven*, *A Country Doctor* and some of Jewett's stories, there is a great deal in *The Country of the Pointed Firs* to suggest that here, at least, the movement *out* of "the world of men's activities" leads fairly unambiguously into a more intense and genuine "reality." While there are problems with this way of reading Jewett's best-known book, problems to which I will be turning shortly, there is also much to recommend it.

Think, for instance, about the book's portrayal of male characters. Most of the men have died long ago, like Mrs. Todd's father and her husband, and the few male survivors of the old days are aptly represented by Captain Littlepage, who visits the narrator in the schoolhouse she has rented in order to pursue her writing, and whose diminutive name already undermines the emphasis of writers like Norris on masculine bigness. "It was a dog's life," he says of the old days at sea, "but it made men of those who followed it" (20)—the point being, of course, that these man-making days are long past. The town doctor seems to maintain true authority, functioning in effect as Almira Todd's professional colleague—in a way that recalls both Nan Prince's relationship with her guardian, Dr. Leslie, and Sarah Orne Jewett's relationship with her father—but the Dunnet Landing doctor never really appears in the book; he is only mentioned a few times in passing. More typical is the minister, Mr. Dimmick, with whom Mrs. Todd remembers having sailed to visit "poor Joanna" Todd on Shell-Heap Island. Against Mrs. Todd's protests he insisted on tying the

sheet to a cleat (the rope hurt his delicate hands), and when the wind
rose he jumped up in panic and cried for help. "I knocked him right
over into the bottom o' the bo't," she recalls, "getting by to catch hold
of the sheet an' untie it." "He wasn't but a little man," this large
woman continues; "I helped him right up after the squall passed, and
made a handsome apology to him, but he did act kind o' offended"
(70). Mrs. Todd also recalls that later, when Mr. Dimmick took an
accusatory tone with Joanna, "she didn't take no notice," instead
showing him some Indian remains, "same's if he was a boy" (75). Or
there is old Santin Bowden, who organizes the line of march at the
family reunion. A "soldierly little figure of a man," he is obsessed with
matters military. We soon learn, however, that he was rejected for
service in the Civil War—"he ain't a sound man," Mrs. Todd explains,
"and they wouldn't have him" (101)—and his dreams of military glory
are only an empty parody of martial masculinity. "His life's all in it,"
says Mrs. Todd, "but he will have these poor gloomy spells come over
him now an' then, an' then he has to drink" (102). And when Mrs.
Todd takes the narrator to visit Mrs. Blackett on Green Island, she has
a clear reason for preferring to make the trip in a small boat: "We
don't want to carry no men folks," she explains, "havin' to be considered every minute an' takin' up all our time" (32).

Two male characters in *The Country of the Pointed Firs*, the old
fisherman Elijah Tilley and Mrs. Todd's brother William, are exempted from this general dismissal—largely, it seems, because they
have in many respects become "feminine." Elijah Tilley, a widower for
the last eight years, is still unconsoled over the loss of his "poor dear."
In fair weather he fishes, but in winter he occupies himself with
knitting; "Mother," he explains, "learnt me once when I was a lad; she
was a beautiful knitter herself" (125). William Blackett, an aging
bachelor, has chosen to stay on Green Island with his mother. He is
almost pathologically shy, he is "son and daughter both" to Mrs.
Blackett (41), and when the narrator finally meets him she notes that
he looks "just like his mother" (44). According to Mrs. Todd, who
takes after her father, William is in spite of his maternal resemblance
even *less* "masculine" than Mrs. Blackett. "He ought," she says, "to
have made something o' himself, bein' a man an' so like mother; but
though he's been very steady to work, an' kept up the farm, an' done
his fishin' too right along, he never had mother's snap an' power o'
seein' things just as they be" (47).

When Captain Littlepage visits the narrator's schoolhouse, he tells
her a story he heard from a man named Gaffett, whom he met when
he was shipwrecked and stranded on the shores of Hudson's Bay with

winter setting in. Gaffett claimed to be the sole survivor of a polar expedition (recalling the Southern voyage in Poe's *Narrative of Arthur Gordon Pym*) which discovered "a strange sort of a country 'way up north beyond the ice, and strange folks living in it." From a distance the place looked like any other town, but it was inhabited by silent "blowing gray figures," "fog-shaped men" who vanished when approached "like a leaf the wind takes with it, or a piece of cobweb." The explorers believed this to be "a kind of waiting-place between this world an' the next" (24–26). The captain's story, with which he has become obsessed, is dismissed by his neighbors as the raving of an unbalanced mind, but this "waiting place" might strike one as a pertinent and somber analogue of Dunnet Landing itself, stranded in Northern isolation, populated mainly by relics of its own lost past. The narrator is quite aware of this potential analogy; later, when Mrs. Todd offers her a mug of root beer, she feels "as if my enchantress would now begin to look like the cobweb shapes of the arctic town" (31).

Still, what seems to matter most about Gaffett's "waiting-place" is that it is a community of fog-shaped *men*, an image of failed *male* power, and Dunnet Landing, by contrast, is a community of *women*, presided over by Almira Todd and her universally beloved mother. This is the reality Jewett seems to substitute for the compensatory masculinity of writers like Howells and Norris. Mrs. Todd appears to possess an almost magical power over nature; for instance, when she twitches the sheet on the way to Green Island, "as if she urged the wind like a horse," the elements oblige: "There came at once a fresh gust, and we seemed to have doubled our speed" (35). Immediately following the story of Gaffett's "waiting-place," the narrator's first sight of Green Island from the shore produces something like an effect of apotheosis:

It had been growing gray and cloudy, like the first evening of autumn, and a shadow had fallen on the darkening shore. Suddenly, as we looked, a gleam of golden sunshine struck the outer islands, and one of them shone out clear in the light, and revealed itself in a compelling way to our eyes. . . . The sunburst on that outermost island made it seem like a sudden revelation of the world beyond this which some believe to be so near.
    "That's where mother lives," said Mrs. Todd. (29–30)

It is only fitting that the *female* "world beyond this," the world "where mother lives," be *Green* Island, its fertility standing in contrast to the polar grayness of Gaffett's realm of fog-shaped men. So, too, the true center of authority at the Bowden family reunion is not Sant Bowden—whose military posturing nicely deflates, for instance, such things as Frank Norris's fantasy of the "marching world"—but Mrs. Blackett. As Mrs. Todd puts it, shortly after the crowd has been described as resembling "bees . . . swarming in the lilac bushes": "Mother's always the queen" (98). In this matriarchal world, it would seem, the men can only be drones.

The most interesting recent discussions of *The Country of the Pointed Firs*, overtly feminist in their intentions, have rejected the notion of the impoverishment of the book's female characters, stressing instead its celebration of women's experience and women's communities, and even its cultivation of distinctively female styles and modes of narrative.[28] For instance, Marjorie Pryse, drawing on Adrienne Rich's *Of Woman Born*, writes that the "lost world" of Jewett's book "is not the world of shipping, but a world in which women were once united with their mothers and inherited their mothers' powers." Jewett, she argues, "does not share the literary historians' fiction of a New England in decline," and "the apparent loss of male paradise in the American literary imagination in the years following the American Civil War simply serves as a contrast to the fecundity and depth of imagination in Jewett and her female contemporaries." Thus "the world of Dunnet Landing is," for Pryse, "above all else, a world in which women learn to belong again. . . . *Pointed Firs* reminds us that there still exists a country—and a world—where the vision of women is not only vital, but can be shared." In a similar vein Elizabeth Ammons, drawing on Carol Gilligan's *In a Different Voice*, finds behind Jewett's rejection of masculine, linear plot an alternative structure relying on "essentially female psychic patterns," patterns of "web" and "descent." The experience expressed in *The Country of the Pointed Firs*, Ammons writes, is "not grounded in separation and aggression but in connection, in feelings of intimate relatedness to others."[29]

Readings like these, rejecting the idea that women's local color writing is inherently impoverished, help us recognize aspects of *The Country of the Pointed Firs* that had earlier seemed, at best, indistinct and blurred.[30] They also attribute to the book something it has surely never before been seen as having: a polemical or even political intention, and it is this idea of the book's polemical intention that I want to investigate. Just what sort of feminist point, it seems appropriate to ask, is being attributed to *The Country of the Pointed Firs;* just what sort of power is Jewett supposed to be claiming for her powerful women characters? Or, to raise a somewhat different question by returning to the issue with which I opened this chapter: to what extent do these new readings of *The Country of the Pointed Firs* overcome the way Jewett has been placed and marginalized in the main line of an Ameri-

can literary history defined largely in terms of masculine (or masculin-
ist?) "realism"? And here, paradoxically, one is compelled to recognize
that these new readings may tend less to overcome this marginaliza-
tion than to perpetuate it.

In his 1959 essay on *The Country of the Pointed Firs*, Warner Berthoff contends that Jewett's women, women deserted by men, exemplify "distorted, repressed, unfulfilled or transformed sexuality," and
that for these women "the only choice, the sacrifice required for
survival, is to give up a woman's proper life and cover the default of
the men."[31] It is hard to share Berthoff's assumptions about what is
normal or proper for women, or to imagine that Jewett shared them;
she, after all, never married and never wished to, and the major
emotional relationships of her life were with other women—most
notably, from the early 1880s on, with Annie Fields. But it may be
equally hard to find any other clear position on "woman's proper life"
in *The Country of the Pointed Firs*. Again and again the reader confronts
disparities between what the women of Dunnet Landing seem to
represent and the actual circumstances of their lives.

Marjorie Pryse writes of the "fecundity and depth of imagination in
Jewett and her female contemporaries," and images of fecundity are
repeatedly associated, in *The Country of the Pointed Firs*, with Almira
Todd, with her mother, and with Mrs. Blackett's refuge on Green Island.[32] But on what literal reality, we should ask, are images like this
based? Mrs. Blackett may be the "queen," but she has long ago passed
the years of childbearing, and her daughter had no children nor, apparently, did Elijah Tilley and his "poor dear." Fecundity, in the world of
Dunnet Landing, is conveyed wholly through images and metaphors—Pryse is exactly right to refer to fecundity "of imagination"—
and these are images, as well, of plants and flowers. There are no
visible signs here of human or even animal reproduction; such things,
in a world where such "children" as William and Almira have reached
advanced middle age, are as much in the past as the days of shipping.
There are young children at the Bowden family reunion, but their
presence is registered only as a brief intrusion. Mrs. Todd's "great grief
and silence," we are told in chapter 10, stand in marked contrast to the
"noisy world" (49). In this context the "chattering crowd of noisy children" at the reunion (99) is linked not with Dunnet Landing but (in
the same way that heterosexual desire is displaced from country to city
in *A Country Doctor* and "A White Heron") with the outside world—
just as the narrator finds even Dunnet Landing, when she returns from
her visit to Green Island, "large and noisy and oppressive" (55).

Both Pryse and Ammons observe that the women in *The Country of*

the Pointed Firs, unlike the male characters, are associated with belonging, with community, and there can be no doubt of the truth and
importance of this observation—which indicates, too, an important
distinction between the values of *The Country of the Pointed Firs* and
the more individualistic feminism of *A Country Doctor*.[33] But this
point, too, can be exaggerated. What makes the Bowden family reunion memorable, after all, is the fact of its being a rare occurrence, an
annual respite from what is mainly a life of isolation and solitude. Mrs.
Blackett, although she has an innate gift of hospitality, lives almost
alone on a remote island, and her daughter Almira, surely the book's
principal representative of its women's community, also—and in some
essential way—lives alone. "There was something lonely and solitary
about her great determined shape," the narrator writes in chapter 10;
"she might have been Antigone alone on the Theban plain" (49); and
in the final chapter, as Mrs. Todd walks away before the narrator's
departure, her distant figure looks "mateless and appealing, with
something about it that was strangely self-possessed and mysterious"
(131). Here again, actual circumstances seem to be at odds with symbolic "women's values."

Berthoff writes that Captain Littlepage's story is "in some ways . . .
the boldest and most decisive passage in the book, for it secures that
reference to the life of male action and encounter without which the
narrator's sympathy for backwater Dunnet would seem myopic, sentimental."[34] It is a little difficult to see what is supposed to be bold or
decisive about this tale of intangible fog creatures, except for the fact
that it is told by men and about men, and maybe this is the point, so
that we see again the careful distinction of Jewett's "backwater" world
from the masculine mainstream of American realism, from "the life of
male action and encounter"—like Howells's distinction of Jewett's
thrush-like voice from "the din of all the literary noises that stun us
so." Here, though, we should recognize that the new feminist readings
of *The Country of the Pointed Firs*, while they disagree with Berthoff's
valuation, generally retain the terms of his distinction. Thus Ammons,
for instance, writes that *The Country of the Pointed Firs* "turns its back
on the competitive world of men, literally leaving cantankerous Boston miles behind, and explores the quiet affectional realm of
women."[35] Berthoff and Ammons agree, albeit with different emphases and agendas, that the culture of women exists somehow outside the
competitive culture of men, and this similarity should probably not
surprise us. Jewett herself, after all, distinguishes Almira Todd's "grief
and silence" (which might recall Sylvia's dumb refusal at the end of "A
White Heron") from the "noisy world."

But while the underlying similarity between Berthoff's "backwater" and Ammons's "quiet affectional realm" should not surprise us, perhaps it ought to trouble us a bit. To focus exclusively on what we might call the communal or separatist feminism of *The Country of the Pointed Firs* seems inevitably to perpetuate the gendered terms of realist thinking. Such a focus obscures, too, a rather different sort of feminism also at work in the book, a feminism in fact rather similar to that of *A Country Doctor*, a set of values that might help explain the disparity between what the women of Dunnet Landing seem to represent and the actual circumstances of their lives. Following her account of the trip to Green Island, for example, the narrator turns to the visit she and Mrs. Todd received from Mrs. Fosdick, a visit whose centerpiece is the story of Mrs. Todd's cousin by marriage, "poor Joanna." Years before the narrator's sojourn in Dunnet Landing, Joanna Todd was jilted by her fiancé, and she moved out to Shell-heap Island to live and die alone; she was, as Mrs. Todd puts it, "done with the world" (76). Joanna's retreat from "the world" bears an intriguing resemblance to the narrator's own retreat from the city to Dunnet Landing (as well as to the general movement associated with women's local color fiction), and Mrs. Todd seems to recognize this resemblance; among the presents she leaves for the narrator at the end of the book is the coral pin that Nathan Todd, years before, had bought for Joanna. Joanna's withdrawal, it should be clear, is less an expression of personal sorrow than an act of protest, even defiance. "I've done the only thing I could do," she told Almira, "and I've made my choice. . . . I was in great wrath and trouble, and my thoughts was so wicked towards God that I can't expect ever to be forgiven" (76). She did not, this is to say, seek forgiveness; she remained true to her anger. According to Mrs. Fosdick, Joanna "thought she wasn't fit to live with anybody, and wanted to be free" (65); Joanna's story leads the narrator to reflect "upon a state of society which admitted such personal freedom and a voluntary hermitage" (69). This may seem a severely restricted sort of freedom, but that is of course the point: Joanna makes her "choice," ironically but inevitably, by doing "the only thing I could do."

"In a wider sphere," the narrator writes of Mrs. Fosdick, "one might have called her a woman of the world . . . , but Mrs. Todd's wisdom was an intimation of truth itself" (59). Almira Todd, for the worldly and apparently world-weary narrator, is the antithesis of "the world"; she is a kind of primal essence. We might wonder, though, if this sort of valorization bears any relation to the way Mrs. Todd sees herself, and we ought to pay attention to what we learn about the story of her life. When the narrator tells Mrs. Blackett that "it was impossible not to wish to stay on forever at Green Island," Mrs Blackett agrees but adds that Almira would have been "very restless" if she had stayed, since she "wanted more scope" (52). So Almira, as a child, was sent to Dunnet Landing to stay with an aunt and go to school—presumably to the very same schoolhouse the narrator is now renting as a place to pursue the solitary and worldly career of literature. And even the apparently sentimental tale of Almira's hopeless love for "one who was far above her" (7), in some ways similar to the story of Joanna's jilting, may matter less as a love story than as another example of Mrs. Todd's restlessness, of her desire for scope, for "the world," a desire she shares with so many of Jewett's characters, including Nan Prince and little Sylvia. What has happened in Almira Todd's story, clearly, is that this desire has been frustrated.

The Country of the Pointed Firs, Marjorie Pryse insists, "portrays a world in which women are alone but not tragic."[36] It is certainly true that the absence of men from this world is not presented as a tragedy for Jewett's women, but Mrs. Todd does remind the narrator of "Antigone alone on the Theban plain," and there surely *is* something tragic about the absence for these women of the kinds of freedom and mobility that have enabled the men to *become* absent. In the social bustle of the Bowden reunion, the narrator comes to recognize that "sometimes when Mrs. Todd had seemed limited and heavily domestic, she had simply grown sluggish for lack of proper surroundings"; "it was not the first time," she continues, "that I was full of wonder at the waste of human ability in this world. . . . More than one face among the Bowdens showed that only opportunity and stimulus were lacking,—a narrow set of circumstances had caged a fine able character and held it captive" (105–7). The narrator's recognition that Almira Todd has been "caged" by narrow circumstances, that her worldly ambitions have been frustrated, does not undercut our sense of Mrs. Todd's primal power, nor does it ironize the affirmation of the ideal of women's community represented by Mrs. Todd and her mother. But it does reveal that a price has been paid for the isolation of these qualities in places like Dunnet Landing.

What this isolation suggests about the relationship of *The Country of the Pointed Firs* to realist thinking is, in the last analysis, somewhat complicated. In the most obvious sense, realist thinking would seem simply irrelevant to Jewett; she surely had no need to downplay style and the literary in order to present herself as a "real" man, and the portraits of the minister Dimmick and Sant Bowden reveal an amused scorn for men with such needs. It is thus tempting, and perhaps inevitably so, to see Jewett as presenting a radical alternative to what

Howells called "the world of men's activities," an alternative secured through removal, through withdrawal from the world; and such withdrawal—from the city to Dunnet Landing, or from Dunnet Landing to Green Island and the Bowden reunion—does constitute the main action of *The Country of the Pointed Firs*. Yet the stories of Almira Todd and Joanna (and, perhaps, the androgyny of the latter's name, combining "Joe" and "Anna") seem to suggest a counterimpulse, albeit a frustrated one: a desire to move *out* of the world of Dunnet Landing and *into* "the world of men's activities," an urge that lies behind so many of Jewett's stories of country life. Should we see here, then, a kind of secret, frustrated connection to the ideological underpinnings of Howellsian realism?

The answer to this question is no—for reasons revealed, for instance, in a story told by Mrs. Fosdick. The chapter in which she first appears is entitled "A Strange Sail," and Mrs. Fosdick is consistently associated with the supposedly masculine realm of sea travel, with mobility rather than the quiet community of women. Soon after her arrival, she describes having gone to sea with her whole family when she was eight years old. She wore her brother's clothes, since her own had inadvertently been left at home. As soon as the ship reached a port, her mother went ashore to purchase proper "feminine" attire, but they did not reach port for some time. "So I had quite a spell o' freedom," Mrs. Fosdick concludes.

"Mother made my new skirt long because I was growing, and I poked about the deck after that, real discouraged, feeling the hem at my heels every minute, and as if youth was past and gone. I liked the trousers best; I used to climb the riggin' with 'em and frighten mother till she said an' vowed she'd never take me to sea again" (61).

We should pay careful attention to the meaning of cross-dressing in this brief story. Mrs. Fosdick's fondness for trousers had nothing to do with wanting to be masculine, or wanting to be *with* men. What she regrets, rather, is her loss of freedom, and this is a masculine quality only in the sense that in her world it is denied to women.

Mrs. Fosdick's regret over her loss of freedom may help explain her fascination with the story of "poor Joanna," but she is by no means consumed with regret, and soon after telling the story of her sea voyage, this seasoned traveler is commenting on the sociable pleasures of "old acquaintance"—since, as she puts it, "conversation's got to have some roots in the past" (61). The truth is that Jewett's women in *The Country of the Pointed Firs* are at the same time rooted *and* restless, enriched *and* impoverished, sustained by domestic routine *and* frus-

trated by it. While they experience a genuine sense of communal shar-
ing they also, in Mrs. Fosdick's wonderful domestic image, feel the
hem at their heels every minute. In contrast to the view of a reader like
Warner Berthoff, Jewett's own view of her characters is not at all
pathological; she does not, from the perspective of what I have been
calling realist thinking, regard the lives of her solitary women as *abnor-
mal*. But she does recognize the limitations that hem these lives in:
limitations imposed by, among other things, the norms—the assumptions about "reality," and about the gendered allocation of different
"realities"—that underlay the literary ideas of men like Howells and
Norris. *The Country of the Pointed Firs* does not finally force either/or
distinctions, and it may be this quality, above all, that separates the
book from the discourse of American realism, with its rigid bifurcation
of "literature" and "life," "teacup tragedies" and "the world of men's
activities." We should resist the impulse to reimpose these bifurcations
on *The Country of the Pointed Firs*, even in the interest of finding in it
an *inversion* of realist values. The book itself is capable of affirming its
community of women without conspiring in the assumption that
women should inevitably be hemmed and marginalized. And its elegiac
celebration of the world of Dunnet Landing still contains at least an
undercurrent of protest against a climate in which women like Joanna
must make their choices by doing the only thing they can do.

In 1901 Jewett published her third and last novel, *The Tory Lover*, a
historical romance of the American Revolution featuring eighteenth-
century South Berwick and John Paul Jones. A year later, on her
fifty-third birthday, she was seriously injured when she was thrown
from a carriage, and this accident brought her career to an end; during
the remaining seven years before her death in 1909 she never recovered sufficiently from her injuries to return to the work of writing. In
a sense, however, her career had already effectively ended in 1896,
with the publication of *The Country of the Pointed Firs*. "You must
throw everything and everybody aside at times," Jewett wrote in 1889,
after rereading Harriet Beecher Stowe's *Pearl of Orr's Island*, "but a
woman made like Mrs. Stowe cannot bring herself to that cold selfish-
ness of the moment for one's work's sake."[37] By the time she turned to
writing *The Tory Lover*, Jewett would seem to have lost touch with this
sense of literary purpose. The book is now almost unreadable, at least
for admirers of Jewett's other work; if "the distinctive thing" about
Jewett was, as Willa Cather puts it, "that she had an individual voice,"
that voice is very nearly inaudible amid the stilted conventionalities of
this attempt to cash in on the late-1890s vogue of historical fiction.[38]

In fact, the idea for the book was not Jewett's but Charles Dudley Warner's, and she initially felt "great reluctance," as she put it in an 1899 letter to Horace Scudder, "before the thought of turning aside into a new road." "I can see the wide difference between it and the *Pointed Firs*," she wrote to a friend in 1901, while the novel was being serialized in the *Atlantic*. "One can't get the same immediate hold." "I suppose," she adds a bit wistfully, "I had to do it."[39]

There can be no doubt that *The Country of the Pointed Firs* is Jewett's masterpiece. But in terms of the development of her career—in terms of her evolving sense of her vocation as a woman writer in what one of her most important mentors, William Dean Howells, proclaimed to be the age of realism—the book would appear to have been something of a dead end, and it is surely significant that Jewett's best work after 1896 consists of four Dunnet Landing stories that return to the narrator, setting, and characters of *The Country of the Pointed Firs*.[40] "Contented ain't all in this world," says the father in "The Hiltons' Holiday," explaining his reasons for taking his daughters on their first trip to town; "hopper-toads may have that quality an' spend all their time a-blinkin'. I don't know's bein' contented is all there is to look for in a child. Ambition's somethin' to me."[41] The narrator of *The Country of the Pointed Firs* is at peace, and also scarcely present as a distinct person, because she seems to have drained herself of the ambition that drives, or at least haunts, Nan Prince and Sylvia and so many of Jewett's characters. This quality gets projected instead, and in ways to which the narrator often seems even deliberately inattentive, into the stories of Almira Todd and "poor Joanna." Although this narrator is, in fact, a professional writer, we learn very little about her literary career; this is another aspect of her personality that remains indistinct, something else she seems to be trying to leave behind. It is also significant that the more absorbed the narrator becomes in the women's communities of Dunnet Landing and Green Island, the less time she seems to spend in her rented schoolhouse, pursuing her profession. We are to assume, of course, that the book we are reading, the story the narrator is telling us, is the product of her literary labor. But writing itself is not part of this story.

"It is not often given in a noisy world," the narrator muses as she thinks of Almira Todd, "to come to the places of great grief and silence" (49). Such silence, the essential quality of Dunnet Landing, is finally not an inspiration for literary vocation but an alternative to it, or a respite from it—like little Sylvia's silence before the stranger's offer in "A White Heron." *The Country of the Pointed Firs* seems to work out the implications of Sylvia's refusal, or of the conclusion of

Nan Prince's story, by forcing ambition even further underground. Increasingly, over the course of her career, Jewett dismissed the rationales that motivated writers like Howells and Norris; and her implicit criticisms of these rationales, of their "masculine" bluster, can be quite telling. But once she had left the ambition projected into the story of Nan Prince behind her, she would appear to have left herself with no clear rationale or counterrationale to put in its place, and after *The Country of the Pointed Firs* there was no obvious direction for her career to go, no way to regain, as she put it in 1901, "the same immediate hold." There were "enough young people" at the Bowden family reunion, the narrator acknowledges, but she adds that such occasions are mainly valued by the old—since "for the young . . . the time of separation has not come" (109). The elegiac tone of *The Country of the Pointed Firs*, one suspects, mourns not just the passing of a rural way of life but also the passing of a literary career into an ultimate separation from "the business part of writing," from being "chaffered over and bought and sold."

NOTES

Introduction

1. "On a Book Entitled *Lolita*," in *The Annotated Lolita*, ed. Alfred Appel, Jr. (New York: McGraw-Hill, 1970), 314.

2. *The Ferment of Realism: American Literature, 1884–1919* (New York: Free Press, 1965), 1.

3. The widespread currency of generalizations about the rise of "realism" is indicated by the frequency with which the term has appeared in the titles and subtitles of books and chapters dealing with post–Civil War American literature, for instance (in addition to Berthoff's *Ferment of Realism*): Vernon Louis Parrington, *The Beginnings of Critical Realism in America*, vol. 3 of *Main Currents in American Thought* (New York: Harcourt, Brace, 1930); Everett Carter, *Howells and the Age of Realism* (Philadelphia: Lippincott, 1954); Donald Pizer, *Realism and Naturalism in Nineteenth-Century American Literature* (Carbondale: Southern Illinois University Press, 1966); Harold H. Kolb, Jr., *The Illusion of Life: American Realism as a Literary Form* (Charlottesville: University Press of Virginia, 1969); Edwin H. Cady, *The Light of Common Day: Realism in American Fiction* (Bloomington: Indiana University Press, 1971); chap. 6, "Fictions of the Real," in Alan Trachtenberg, *The Incorporation of America: Culture and Society in the Gilded Age* (New York: Hill and Wang, 1982); Alfred Habegger, *Gender, Fantasy, and Realism in American Literature* (New York: Columbia University Press, 1982); Eric J. Sundquist, ed., *American Realism: New Essays* (Baltimore: Johns Hopkins University Press, 1982); and his chapter, "Realism and Regionalism," in *Columbia Literary History of the United States*, ed. Emory Elliott (New York: Columbia University Press, 1988), 501–24; Amy Kaplan, *The Social Construction of American Realism* (Chicago: University of Chicago Press, 1988); and Daniel H. Borus, *Writing Realism: Howells, James, and Norris in the Mass Market* (Chapel Hill: University of North Carolina Press, 1989). The first part of Kaplan's in-

troduction (1–8) contains an excellent survey of the changing definitions and understandings of "realism" in American literary history.

4. *The Ferment of Realism*, 1–3. Henry James, Berthoff is careful to note, "stands as the signal exception to these . . . remarks" (2). Harold Kolb, while he ultimately undertakes to define "realism as a literary form," begins his study with a thorough survey of the problems inherent in the term as it was used by nineteenth-century American "realists" (*The Illusion of Life*, 11–35). An earlier and extremely important criticism of the vagueness of American thinking about "realism," directed primarily against Vernon Parrington, is Lionel Trilling's "Reality in America" (1940, 1946), reprinted in *The Liberal Imagination* (New York: Scribner's, 1950), 3–21.

5. *The Ferment of Realism*, 3, 4. Compare, for example, Alfred Kazin's assertion that "while in Europe realism and naturalism grew out of the positivism of Continental thought and the conviction that one literary movement had subsided and another was needed, realism in America grew out of the bewilderment, and thrived on the simple grimness, of a generation suddenly brought face to face with the pervasive materialism of industrial capitalism. . . . Realism in America, whatever it owed to contemporary skepticism and the influence of Darwinism, poured sullenly out of agrarian bitterness, the class hatreds of the eighties and nineties, the bleakness of small-town life, the mockery of the nouveaux riches, and the bitterness in the great new proletarian cities" (*On Native Grounds: An Interpretation of Modern American Prose Literature* [Garden City, N.Y.: Doubleday, 1956], 12–13). A similar emphasis on literary response to social change provides the organizing principle of Jay Martin's *Harvests of Change: American Literature, 1865–1914* (Englewood Cliffs, N.J.: Prentice-Hall, 1967), but Martin has little interest in characterizing this response as a species of "realism." A more recent and more concretely historical variant of the responsive school stresses writers' responses, in the years following the Civil War, to specific changes in the means and conditions of literary production; see, for instance, Daniel Borus's *Writing Realism*; and Christopher P. Wilson, *The Labor of Words: Literary Professionalism in the Progressive Era* (Athens: University of Georgia Press, 1985).

6. An important, if controversial, exception to this generalization is Michael Fried, *Realism, Writing, Disfiguration: On Thomas Eakins and Stephen Crane* (Chicago: University of Chicago Press, 1987). Dismissing "the traditional argument from reality" for the details of Eakins's *The Gross Clinic*, for instance, Fried nevertheless insists on the painting's "nearly overwhelming realism *of effect*" (64, my emphasis), and he argues that irruptions of the "scene of writing" in Crane, of suppressed awareness of the materiality of the literary text as a thing made rather than a transcription of "reality," threatens "to abort the realization of the 'impressionist' project as classically conceived" (120).

7. Eric Sundquist, for instance, in his preface to *American Realism: New Essays* (1982), describes the American "realists" as "a group of writers who virtually had no program but rather responded eclectically, and with increasing imaginative urgency, to the startling acceleration into being of a complex

industrial society following the Civil War" (viii). Similarly, in his chapter on "Realism and Regionalism" in the *Columbia Literary History of the United States* (1988), Sundquist defines "realism from the 1870s through the early 1900s" as "a developing series of responses to the transformation of land into capital, of raw materials into products, of agrarian values into urban values, and of private experience into public property"; he writes that "the energetic transformations of the period serve to unite writers whose subjects and styles seem divergent but who all claimed to practice the new realism" and that "no one strategy of 'realism' seemed adequate to portray the effects of capitalism across the spectrum of American life" (501, 503, 520).

8. Howard, *Form and History in American Literary Naturalism* (Chapel Hill: University of North Carolina Press, 1985), 70; Walter Benn Michaels, *The Gold Standard and the Logic of Naturalism: American Literature at the Turn of the Century* (Berkeley: University of California Press, 1987), 27; Kaplan, *The Social Construction of American Realism*, 9. Another important member of this "school" of interpreting American realist or naturalist texts is Philip Fisher; see his essay, "Appearing and Disappearing in Public: Social Space in Late-Nineteenth-Century Literature and Culture," in Sacvan Bercovitch, ed., *Reconstructing American Literary History* (Cambridge, Mass.: Harvard University Press, 1986), 155–88; and chap. 3 (on Theodore Dreiser) of his *Hard Facts: Setting and Form in the American Novel* (New York: Oxford University Press, 1987), 128–78.

9. Howard has a rather straightforward reason for identifying her subject as "naturalism" rather than "realism": the writers in whom she is particularly interested—Frank Norris, Jack London, and Theodore Dreiser—have long been described as "naturalists." But Michaels dispenses with "realism" and the problems that accompany the term for more fundamental reasons. "I use the term *naturalism* rather than the more general term *realism*," he explains, "not to help breathe new life into the old debate over what naturalism is and how exactly it differs from realism; indeed, I hope to avoid that debate entirely and, if possible, some of the fundamental assumptions that govern it. Insofar as naturalism has been continually (and plausibly) defined as a variant of realism, it has been caught up in endless theorizing about the nature and very possibility of realistic representation: do texts refer to social reality? if they do, do they merely reflect it or do they criticize it? and if they do not, do they try to escape it, or do they imagine utopian alternatives to it? . . . [T]hese questions seem to me to posit a space outside the culture in order then to interrogate the relations between that space (here defined as literary) and the culture. But the spaces I have tried to explore are all very much within the culture, and so the project of interrogation makes no sense; the only relation literature as such has to culture as such is that it is part of it" (*The Gold Standard and the Logic of Naturalism*, 26–27).

10. See Erich Auerbach, *Mimesis: The Representation of Reality in Western Literature*, trans. Willard R. Trask (Princeton: Princeton University Press, 1953); Georg Lukács, *Studies in European Realism*, trans. Edith Bone (New York: Grosset and Dunlap, 1964); E. H. Gombrich, *Art and Illusion: A Study in the Psychology of Pictorial Representation* (Princeton: Princeton University Press, 1961).

11. *The Gold Standard and the Logic of Naturalism*, 178, 27.

12. In this respect, my standpoint is closer to Kaplan's than to that of Michaels. "If realism is a fiction," Kaplan writes, "we can root this fiction in its historical context to examine its ideological force." "Why," she then asks, choosing authors as the site of this contextualizing, "does the fiction of the referent become a powerful rallying cry for some, a point of contention for others, and an assumption taken for granted by still other writers at the particular historical juncture of the 1880s and 1890s?" (*The Social Construction of American Realism*, 8).

Part One

1. See, for instance, Leon Edel, *Henry James, The Master: 1901–1916* (Philadelphia: J. B. Lippincott, 1972), 36–39.

2. For example, in the *Columbia Literary History of the United States* (ed. Emory Elliot [New York: Columbia University Press, 1988]), in the section devoted to the period 1865–1910, Twain and James both get separate chapters (along with Emily Dickinson and Henry Adams), with Twain getting nineteen pages and James getting twenty-one. The main discussion of Howells, however, is part of a larger chapter on "Realism and Regionalism," and here he gets only *five* pages.

3. Richard H. Brodhead, *The School of Hawthorne* (New York: Oxford University Press, 1986), 147.

Chapter One

1. Howells records this remark in *Literary Friends and Acquaintance* (hereinafter cited as *LFA*), ed. David F. Hiatt and Edwin H. Cady (Bloomington: Indiana University Press, 1968), 36. For biographical information I have relied especially on Edwin H. Cady's two volume life of Howells: *The Road to Realism* and *The Realist at War* (Syracuse: Syracuse University Press, 1956, 1958); on Kenneth Lynn, *William Dean Howells: An American Life* (New York: Harcourt Brace Jovanovitch, 1971); and on John W. Crowley, *The Black Heart's Truth: The Early Career of William Dean Howells* (Chapel Hill: University of North Carolina Press, 1985).

2. Howells published the "Editor's Study" from January 1886 to March 1892. The idea of collecting selections from the column to form *Criticism and Fiction* was not that of Howells but of his publisher. Howells put the book together hastily and, apparently, somewhat reluctantly (see Cady, *The Road to Realism*, 49).

3. For surveys of attacks on Howells, and of the "realism war" generally, see especially Herbert Edwards, "Howells and the Controversy over Realism in American Fiction," *American Literature* 3 (1931): 237–48, and chap. 2, "The Realism War," in Cady, *The Realist at War*, 28–55.

4. *Criticism and Fiction* (hereinafter cited as *C&F*), in *Criticism and Fiction and Other Essays by W. D. Howells*, ed. Clara Maburg Kirk and Rudolf Kirk (New York: New York University Press, 1959), 62. Perhaps more indicative of the limitation of "realist" subject matter in *Criticism and Fiction* is the nervous handling in essay 24 of "the question of how much or how little the American novel ought to deal with certain facts of life which are not usually talked of before young people, especially young ladies" (*C&F*, 69–70).

5. Reprinted in George Perkins, ed., *The Theory of the American Novel* (New York: Rinehart, 1970), 302.

6. Scudder, "Mr. Howells's Literary Creed," *Atlantic Monthly* 18 (1891): 569; Matthews, "Recent Essays in Fiction," *Cosmopolitan* (November 1891): 125, 126. One might compare the assertion with which René Wellek concludes his 1960 essay, "The Concept of Realism in Literary Scholarship": "The theory of realism is ultimately bad aesthetics because all art is 'making' and is a world in itself of illusion and symbolic forms" (reprinted in Wellek, *Concepts of Criticism*, ed. Stephen G. Nichols, Jr. [New Haven: Yale University Press, 1963], 255).

7. *LFA*, 101; for Poe's attack see "The Poetic Principle," in *The Complete Works of Edgar Allan Poe*, ed. James A Harrison (New York: Thomas Y. Crowell, 1902), 14:272; "Emile Zola," in *William Dean Howells: Representative Selections* (hereinafter cited as *RS*), ed. Clara Marburg Kirk and Rudolf Kirk (New York: Hill and Wang, 1961), 381; *C&F*, 15.

8. In 1878, for instance, Howells wrote to Charles Eliot Norton, who had sent a circular offering a subscription to a set of "Turner pictures": "I know they will be very useful to the artistic branches of the family, and I shall look up at them from the inferior levels of literature, and do my best to have some ideas about them." Or, as he wrote to Howard Pyle in 1891: "I can feel only the literary quality of pictures" (*Life in Letters of William Dean Howells* [hereinafter cited as *Life in Letters*], ed. Mildred Howells [Garden City, N.Y.: Doubleday, Doran, 1928], 1:254, 2:14). As Cady summarizes this matter, Howells "seems never to have achieved much grasp of the 'painterly' qualities of pictures" (*The Road to Realism*, 106).

9. *C&F*, 15.

10. *My Literary Passions* (hereinafter cited as *MLP*) (New York: Harper and Brothers, 1895), 256, 258; *Life in Letters*, 1:361; *LFA*, 266; *MLP*, 48–49; *C&F*, 26.

11. See Richard Cary, ed., *Sarah Orne Jewett Letters* (Waterville, Maine: Colby College Press, 1967), 16. "I read 'Madame Bovary' all last evening . . . ," Jewett wrote to Annie Fields in 1890. "It is quite wonderful how great a book Flaubert makes of it. People talk about dwelling upon trivialities and commonplaces in life, but a master writer gives everything weight" (Annie Fields, ed., *Letters of Sarah Orne Jewett* [Boston: Houghton Mifflin, 1911], 82–82).

12. "William Dean Howells" (*Harper's Weekly* [June 1886], reprinted in James, *Literary Criticism: Essays on Literature, American Writers, English Writers*, ed. Leon Edel (New York: Library of America, 1984), 505.

13. "What is Realism?" (1948), in *Contexts of Criticism* (Cambridge, Mass.: Harvard University Press, 1958), 71.

14. *The Ferment of Realism: American Literature, 1884–1919* (New York: Free Press, 1965), 3.

15. Perkins, ed., *The Theory of the American Novel*, 302, 307, 302.

16. *C&F,* 26.

17. Trilling, "William Dean Howells and the Roots of Modern Taste," in *The Opposing Self* (New York: Viking, 1965), 79; James, *Hawthorne,* in *Literary Criticism: Essays on Literature,* ed. Edel, 342; Howells, *The Landlord at Lion's Head* (New York: New American Library, 1964), 204; James, *Hawthorne,* 342.

18. Trilling, *The Opposing Self,* 79; Cady, *The Road to Realism,* 114.

19. Washington Irving, *Biographies and Miscellanies,* ed. Pierre M. Irving (New York: Putnam, 1866), 367; Hawthorne, *The Scarlet Letter* (Columbus: Ohio State University Press, 1962), 10.

20. *The Development of American Romance: The Sacrifice of Relation* (Chicago: University of Chicago Press, 1980), esp. 29–36.

21. *Tales of a Traveller* (New York: Putnam, 1865), 232–33, 309.

22. Lynn, *William Dean Howells: An American Life,* 48, 51; Parker, "William Dean Howells: Realism and Feminism," in *Uses of Literature: Harvard English Studies 4* ed. Monroe Engel (Cambridge, Mass.: Harvard University Press, 1973), 148–49. The gender implications of Howells's childhood "morbidness" are also discussed by Alfred Habegger in *Gender, Fantasy, and Realism in American Literature* (New York: Columbia University Press, 1982); and by John W. Crowley in *The Black Heart's Truth* and particularly in his essay, "Howells's Obscure Hurt," originally published in 1975 and collected (in an expanded form) in Crowley's *The Mask of Fiction: Essays on W. D. Howells* (Amherst: University of Massachusetts Press, 1989), 17–34.

23. *The Rise of Silas Lapham,* ed. George Arms (New York: Rinehart, 1964), 60; *Letters Home* (New York: Harper and Brothers, 1903), 125. (Kenneth Lynn quotes the passage from *Letters Home* in *William Dean Howells: An American Life,* 283.)

24. *MLP,* 121, 141, 14, 18.

25. Howells, *MLP,* 165–66; Cady, *The Road to Realism,* 70.

26. *LFA,* 39.

27. *The Profession of Authorship in America, 1800–1870,* ed. Matthew J. Bruccoli (Columbus: Ohio State University Press, 1968), 116, 120, 122, 126, 134, 135.

28. *LFA,* 169, 143, 197, 189. Lowell wrote to Howells in 1869 that "if women only knew how much woman there is in me, they would forgive all my heresies on the woman-question"—a somewhat dubious proposition but nonetheless interesting for its opening confession or assertion. Rather more curious, and curiously reminiscent of the description of reacting to "the look of the type" in Howells's account of his early reading in *My Literary Passions,* is Howells's description of visiting Lowell, in a 1903 letter to Charles Eliot Norton: "I used to falter at his gate, and walk up the path to his door with

the same anxious palpitations I felt when I dared to call upon the girl I was first in love with; it was a real passion" (*Life in Letters*, 1:172; 2:153).

29. *LFA*, 125. Howells describes New York, by contrast, as "a community which seems never to have had a conscious relation to letters" (*LFA*, 75).

30. Edwin Cady argues that it is in fact rather difficult to pinpoint "any definitive 'move to New York'" (*The Realist at War*, 93), and it is certainly true that Howells never wholly renounced his ties to Boston. Still, the 1885 decision to take on the "Editor's Study" seems definitive enough at least to indicate an important transformation in Howells's sense of his vocation, or of the sort of community in which this vocation might most effectively be pursued.

31. Lynn, *William Dean Howells: An American Life*, 283; Simpson, "The Treason of William Dean Howells," in *The Man of Letters in New England and the South: Essays on the History of the Literary Vocation in America* (Baton Rouge: Louisiana State University Press, 1973), 92.

32. *LFA*, 148, 155, 195.

33. "Mr. Howells's Literary Creed," *Atlantic Monthly*, 68 (1891): 566–69. Also see Cady, *The Realist at War*, 50–51.

34. Trilling, *The Opposing Self*, 79.

35. Compare John W. Crowley's observation that "realism is the answer to Howells's gender anxiety" (an anxiety Crowley relates to Howells's having avoided combat in the Civil War), an answer Howells hoped might provide "a 'manly' alternative to a code of masculinity based on military prowess" ("Howells's Obscure Hurt," 28). For a quite different argument about the relationship between realism and male gender anxiety, one with little or no interest in Howells's critical writings about realism, see Habegger's *Gender, Fantasy, and Realism in American Literature*.

36. *C&F*, 51, 11, 87; *LFA*, 101.

37. On the realists' populist political ambitions, see esp. chap. 6, "The Lure of Classlessness: The Antipolitics of Realism," in Daniel Borus's *Writing Realism* (Chapel Hill: University of North Carolina Press, 1989), 139–82.

38. Howells, "Emile Zola," in *RS*, 382; Whitman, *Leaves of Grass*, ed Sculley Bradley and Harold W. Blodgett (New York: Norton, 1973), 731. The linking of Howells and Whitman may seem a bit forced, but it is worth noting that *Criticism and Fiction* elicited from John Burroughs, a pro-Whitman critic to whom Howells as editor of the *Atlantic* had been anathema, an approving review entitled "Mr. Howells's Agreements with Whitman" (see Cady, *The Realist at War*, 50).

39. *C&F*, 15, 20.

40. *C&F*, 72, 73.

41. *LFA*, 266, 264, 265; *MLP*, 250, 258.

42. Thomas Jefferson to Nathaniel Burwell, March 14, 1818, in *The Works of Thomas Jefferson*, ed. Paul Leicester Ford (New York: Putnam, 1899), 10:104–5. On hostility toward fiction and imagination in eighteenth-century and early nineteenth-century America, see William Charvat, *The Origins of American Critical Thought, 1810–1835* (Philadelphia: University of

212 Notes to Pages 35–40

Pennsylvania Press, 1936); Michael Davitt Bell, *The Development of American Romance*, 9–14; and especially Terence Martin, *The Instructed Vision: Scottish Common Sense Philosophy and the Origins of American Fiction* (Bloomington: University of Indiana Press, 1961).

43. *The Problem of Boston: Some Readings in Cultural History* (New York: Norton, 1966), 27, 35, 164, 186. Green's reluctance to see the "problem" of Boston as in fact the *purpose* of its "encouragement" of literature seems to stem from a reluctance to admit what is suggested by his own evidence: namely, that "encouragement" of the arts can function, and often does function, as a means of social control, rendering the image of the ideal community where art is taken seriously, in America at any rate, too often a dangerous delusion—at least for artists. On his last page, in any case, Green is still able to write that "when [Romanticism] was rejected, even the extraordinarily favourable attitude of society . . . could not bring writers to the point of successful creation" (*ibid.*, 200). What he will not quite admit is that "the extraordinarily favourable attitude of society" apparently *forbade* the cultivation of "Romanticism," that it was a quite deliberate system of punishments and rewards, and that what it punished, most of all, was what Green calls "Romanticism" and what I would call, in the context of this chapter, a belief in the power of art *as art*—a belief in the reality of the artist on his or her own terms.

44. This is, for instance, William Charvat's conclusion about what happened to Longfellow in the later stages of his career (see *The Profession of Authorship in America*, 140–54).

45. *Life in Letters*, 2:138, 256.

46. On some of the literary ramifications of this solidification, mainly in England and the United States, see Eve Kosofsky Sedgwick's *Between Men: English Literature and Male Homosocial Desire* (New York: Columbia University Press, 1985); and her *Epistemology of the Closet* (Berkeley: University of California Press, 1990). An earlier version of the latter volume's chapter on Henry James was published in 1986, as "The Beast in the Closet: James and the Writing of Homosexual Panic," in *Sex, Politics, and Science in the Nineteenth-Century Novel*, ed. Ruth Bernard Yeazell (Baltimore: Johns Hopkins University Press, 1986 [Selected Papers from the English Institute, 1983–84]), 148–86.

47. Nobel Prize Acceptance Speech, in Perkins, *Theory of the American Novel*, 307.

48. Perry Miller and Thomas H. Johnson, eds., *The Puritans* (New York: Harper and Row, 1963), 679, 672.

Chapter Two

1. Brooks, *The Ordeal of Mark Twain* (New York: E. P. Dutton, 1920), 31, 208, 218; DeVoto, *Mark Twain's America and Mark Twain at Work* (Boston: Houghton-Mifflin, 1967), 101. The locus classicus of the stand-off between proponents of the humorous and serious versions of Mark Twain is the famous debate about the ending of *Huckleberry Finn*, beginning with Ernest Hemingway's declaration

that "if you read it you must stop where the Nigger Jim is stolen from the boys. The rest is just cheating" (*Green Hills of Africa* [New York: Scribner's, 1935]. 22). Serious readings that defend the ending include, for instance, Lionel Trilling, *"Huckleberry Finn"* (1948), in *The Liberal Imagination* (New York: Scribner's, 1950), 104–17, and T. S. Eliot's 1950 introduction to an edition of the novel, reprinted in Claude M. Simpson, ed., *Twentieth Century Interpretations of Huckleberry Finn* (Englewood Cliffs, N.J.: Prentice-Hall, 1968), 107–8. The best-known example of a serious reading that *attacks* the ending is Leo Marx, "Mr. Eliot, Mr. Trilling, and *Huckleberry Finn*," *American Scholar* 22 (1953): 423–40. James Cox, to continue the available permutations and combinations, *defends* the ending, as part of his *attack* on serious readings of the book, in *Mark Twain: The Fate of Humor* (Princeton: Princeton University Press, 1966), 175–82. For a general discussion of this debate, see John Reichert, *Making Sense of Literature* (Chicago: University of Chicago Press, 1977), 191–203.

2. For a notable dissent from this view, see Alfred Habegger, *Gender, Fantasy, and Realism in American Literature* (New York: Columbia University Press, 1982), 103–4. "Not only does [*Huckleberry Finn*] not deal with contemporary society," Habegger argues, "it presents a view of antebellum life . . . that is highly colored. . . . In none of Mark Twain's 'novels' was he 'objective' or 'contemporary.' No doubt a debunking factuality was one of the tricks of his trade, but I doubt whether his trade was realism" (104).

3. *Criticism and Fiction and Other Essays by W. D. Howells*, ed. Clara Marburg Kirk and Rudolf Kirk (New York: New York University Press, 1959), 51.

4. DeVoto, *Mark Twain's America*, 91, 257; Dreiser, "Mark the Double Twain," *English Journal* 24 (1935): 622, 623.

5. At times, for instance, DeVoto simply seems to equate "realism" with Western "Americanism" as opposed to Eastern "intellectualism." Twain, he writes in this vein, "was untutored; his only discipline was reality." Or we might note DeVoto's Howells-like dismissal of "literary criticism" on the grounds that "that department of beautiful thinking is too insulated from reality for my taste" (*Mark Twain's America*, 194, xii). For a more recent example of the tendency to apply the term "realism" to whatever qualities a reader happens to find in Twain, one might note Harold H. Kolb, Jr.'s *The Illusion of Life: American Realism as a Literary Form* (Charlottesville: University Press of Virginia, 1969). Twain, Kolb writes, shared with James and Howells "the instinct for the antiomniscient point of view" (68), which is no doubt true, but which hardly therefore distinguishes Twain, as a realist, from such supposed romancers as, for instance, Charles Brockden Brown, Edgar Allan Poe, or Herman Melville. Nor, to cite one more example, does the fact that Twain's characters, as Kolb puts it, "tend to have mixed motives and confused consciences" (110) seem in any obvious way to distinguish Twain as a realist.

6. "How to Tell a Story" (*Youth's Companion*, 1894) reprinted in *Great Short Works of Mark Twain*, ed. Justin Kaplan (New York: Harper, 1967), 182–87; "What Paul Bourget Thinks of Us" (*North American Review*, 1895), in *How to Tell a Story and Other Essays* (Hartford: American Publishing Company, 1900),

141–64; "Fenimore Cooper's Literary Offenses" (*North American Review*, 1895), reprinted in Kaplan, ed., *Great Short Works*, 169–81; "William Dean Howells," *Harper's Magazine* 113 (1906): 221–25. For a portion of the Cooper essay deleted from the published version, see Bernard DeVoto, "Fenimore Cooper's Further Literary Offenses," *New England Quarterly* 19 (1946): 291–301.

7. *Mark Twain–Howells Letters: The Correspondence of Samuel L. Clemens and William Dean Howells, 1872–1910* (hereinafter cited as *THL*), ed. Henry Nash Smith and William M. Gibson (Cambridge, Mass.: Harvard University Press, 1960), 396; letter to Matthews quoted in Albert Bigelow Paine, *Mark Twain: A Biography* (New York: Harper, 1912), 1197.

8. *THL*, 245, 427, 633.

9. Kaplan, ed., *Great Short Works*, 169–71.

10. *THL*, 534.

11. Howells understood and appreciated this insight. "What people cannot see," he complained in his reply to Twain's letter, "is that I analyze as little as possible, but go on talking the analytic school—which I am suppose[d] to belong to; and I want to thank you for using your eyes" (*THL*, 535–36).

12. Everett Carter, summarizing "Fenimore Cooper's Literary Offenses," writes that "the rules governing literary art, Twain made it clear, should be the rules of the realist" (*Howells and the Age of Realism* [Philadelphia: Lippincott, 1954], 72). Richard Chase, however, writes of the essay that it "is not an attempt to demolish romance and substitute realism. On the contrary, despite its negative approach, Mark Twain's essay is intended to show how romance must be written. He is lecturing Cooper on the 'rules governing literary art in the domain of romantic fiction.' He is pleading not for realism as such but for realism as the only way of effectively assimilating the miraculous" (*The American Novel and Its Tradition* [Garden City, N.Y.: Doubleday, 1957], 147–48).

13. *THL*, 613.

14. "Realism," Howells writes in *Criticism and Fiction*, "is nothing more and nothing less than the truthful treatment of material, and Jane Austen was the first and the last of the English novelists to treat material with entire truthfulness" (Kirk and Kirk, eds., *Criticism and Fiction and Other Essays*, 38). Twain's attacks on Jane Austen are legion; especially picturesque is the comment in a 1909 letter to Howells: "Jane is entirely impossible. It seems a great pity they allowed her to die a natural death" (*THL*, 841).

15. The fullest source of information about Twain's childhood and adolescence is still Albert Bigelow Paine's authorized 1912 biography, *Mark Twain: A Biography*. Justin Kaplan's *Mr. Clemens and Mark Twain: A Biography* (New York: Simon and Schuster, 1966) is authoritative on Twain's professional career, but it skips over the first thirty-one years of his life.

16. *Mark Twain: A Biography*, 65.

17. *The Ordeal of Mark Twain*, 12.

18. There was the drunk in the town jail, for instance. With his own money Sam Clemens bought him a box of matches—with which the drunk then acci-

dentally set fire to the jail, thereby burning himself alive. As Paine summarizes Mark Twain's recollection of the incident: "For weeks the boy was tortured, awake and in his dreams, by the thought that if he had not carried the man the matches the tragedy could not have happened" (*Mark Twain: A Biography*, 65).

19. In fact, it was not Sam but Orion, his older brother, who was abandoned during the departure for Hannibal, and only very briefly; his absence from the wagon was discovered when the vehicle had gone only a few feet. Some time later, Sam's father did absent-mindedly leave Sam behind when he left Hannibal to join the rest of the family at Quarry Farm. Sam spent all of Sunday alone in the house, before being retrieved by an uncle (see Paine, *Mark Twain: A Biography*, 24–25, 30).

20. Ibid., 48–49.

21. *The Ordeal of Mark Twain*, 31, 28.

22. Paine's testimony on this subject is consistent. During the period of Clemens's first printer's apprenticeship (1847–50), he writes, "[I]t is not believed that Sam had any writing ambitions of his own. His chief desire was to be an all-round journeyman printer." In the letters home preserved from 1863, the year in which Clemens, in Nevada, adopted his now-famous pseudonym, "there is no mention of his new title and its success. In fact, the writer rarely speaks of his work at all, and is more inclined to tell of the mining shares he has accumulated, their present and prospective value." Even in 1869, Paine writes, following the success of *The Innocents Abroad*, "Mark Twain still did not regard himself as a literary man. He had no literary plans for the future; he scarcely looked forward to the publication of another book. He considered himself a journalist" (*Mark Twain: A Biography*, 78, 222, 385). One should also remember that the kind of writing to which Twain turned, "masculine" dialect humor, was utterly distinct from what he and his contemporaries thought of as "literature." On this matter, see Habegger, *Gender, Fantasy, and Realism in American Literature*, 115–56.

23. Kirk and Kirk, eds., *Criticism and Fiction and Other Essays*, 87.

24. All parenthetical page references to *Huckleberry Finn* are to *Adventures of Huckleberry Finn: An Authoritative Text, Backgrounds and Sources, Criticism*, ed. Sculley Bradley, Richmond Croom Beatty, E. Hudson Long, and Thomas Cooley (New York: Norton, 1977; 2d ed.).

25. See especially, in this regard, Kenneth S. Lynn, *Mark Twain and Southwestern Humor* (Boston: Little, Brown, 1960); and Henry Nash Smith, *Mark Twain: The Development of a Writer* (Cambridge, Mass.: Harvard University Press, 1962).

26. *Mark Twain: The Fate of Humor*, 172, 44, 179.

27. Ibid., 16.

28. *Mark Twain: A Biography*, 48–49.

29. *Mark Twain: The Fate of Humor*, 12, 47.

30. *Death in the Afternoon* (New York: Scribner's, 1932), 2.

31. *A Hazard of New Fortunes* (New York: New American Library, 1965), 65.

32. One thinks particularly, here, of the education of the Eastern poet,

Presley, in Frank Norris's *The Octopus* (1901), and of the melodramatic growth to "real" manhood of the effete socialite, Ross Wilbur, in Norris's *Moran of the Lady Letty* (1898). As this last example suggests, the paradigmatic realist plot shades over rapidly into the tale of atavistic, "Darwinian" regression (from effete civilization to instinctively "real" brutality) produced again and again by so-called American naturalists: for instance, Norris's *McTeague* (1899) and *Vandover and the Brute* (1914, posthumous) and Jack London's *The Call of the Wild* (1903) and *The Sea Wolf* (1904).

33. *Harper's Monthly* 80 (January 1890): 320.

34. All parenthetical page references to *A Connecticut Yankee* are to *A Connecticut Yankee in King Arthur's Court: An Authoritative Text, Backgrounds and Sources, Composition and Publication, Criticism*, ed. Alison R. Ensor (New York: W. W. Norton, 1982).

35. "Introduction," *A Connecticut Yankee in King Arthur's Court*, ed. Bernard L. Stein, vol. 9 of *The Works of Mark Twain* (Berkeley: University of California Press, 1979), 4. "My family is American," reads Grant's first sentence, "and has been for generations, in all its branches, direct and collateral" (*Personal Memoirs of U. S. Grant* [New York: Charles L. Webster and Co, 1894], 15).

36. "Have a battle between a modern army," reads a notebook entry of early 1885, "with gatling guns—(automatic) 600 shots a minute, <with one pulling of the trigger,> torpedos, balloons, 100-ton cannon, iron-clad fleet &c & Prince de Joinville's Middle Age Crusaders" (*Notebooks and Journals*, 3:86). The New York *Sun's* account of Twain's November 1886 reading from the first three or four chapters of his work in progress, before the Military Services Institute, after which he described parts of the story yet to be written, includes the information that the Boss (called, at this point, Sir Robert Smith) "took a contract from King Arthur to kill off, at one of the great tournaments, fifteen kings and many acres of hostile armored knights. When, lance in rest they charge by squadrons upon him, he behind the protection of a barbed wire fence charged with electricity mowed them down with Gatling guns that he had made for the occasion" (reprinted in Stein, ed., *A Connecticut Yankee*, 501–2).

37. *Criticism and Fiction and Other Essays by W. D. Howells*, ed. Clara Marburg Kirk and Rudolf Kirk (New York: New York University Press, 1959), 26, 87.

38. *Life on the Mississippi* (New York: Hill and Wang, 1957), 216, 242–43.

39. *Battle Pieces and Aspects of the War* (1866), reprinted in *Collected Poems of Herman Melville* (Chicago: Hendricks House, 1947), 40. The same vision of historical transformation animates the narrative framework of Melville's last work, *Billy Budd*, in which an apparently garrulous old tale-teller recalls "the time before steamships," a time whose record of naval heroism stands as a "poetic reproach" to the modern age of ironclads and "martial utilitarians" (*Billy Budd Sailor [An Inside Narrative]*, ed. Harrison Hayford and Merton M. Sealts, Jr. [Chicago: University of Chicago Press, 1962], 43, 57). Although *Billy Budd* was not published until 1924, it was written in the late 1880s, at roughly the same time that Mark Twain was working on *A Connecticut Yankee*.

40. *Mark Twain: The Fate of Humor*, 218. See, too, Daniel Aaron, *The Unwritten War: American Writers and the Civil War* (New York: Oxford University Press, 1975), 140–45.

41. *Mark Twain: The Fate of Humor*, 224.

42. *Mark Twain's Notebooks & Journals, Volume III (1883–1891)*, ed. Robert Pack Browning, Michael B. Frank and Lin Salamo (Berkeley: University of California Press, 1979), 78. In 1889 Twain inserted a note to this entry, explaining that in the fall of 1884, while he was touring with George Washington Cable, "Cable got a Morte d'Arthur & gave it me to read. I began to make notes in my head for a book" (*ibid.*, 79).

43. *Mark Twain to Mrs. Fairbanks*, ed. Dixon Wecter (San Marino, Calif.: Huntington Library, 1949), 257.

44. The passage may even be explicitly echoed in the ending of Raymond Chandler's *The Big Sleep:* "I stopped at a bar and had a couple of double Scotches. They didn't do me any good. All they did was make me think of Silver-Wig, and I never saw her again" (*The Big Sleep* [New York: Random House, 1976], 216).

45. *My Literary Passions* (New York: Harper and Brothers, 1895), 250.

46. It was just before he began work on *A Connecticut Yankee* that Twain wrote "A Private History of a Campaign That Failed" (published in December 1885), his fictionalized account of his brief service in (and flight from) the Confederate army. Daniel Aaron writes of Howells that "perhaps his literary credo . . . enabled him ultimately to excuse his own withdrawal from the War" (*The Unwritten War*, 132). Compare John W. Crowley's suggestion that realism offered an "answer to Howells's gender anxiety: by providing a 'manly' alternative to a code of masculinity based on military prowess"—even if Howells was ultimately "never inwardly confident that 'fulfilling the duties of a good citizen' was equivalent to 'dying for one's country'" (*The Mask of Fiction: Essays on W. D. Howells* [Amherst: University of Massachusetts Press, 1989], 29, 34). I am also indebted here to an unpublished essay by my colleague John Limon: "Missing in Action: Realism and the Civil War."

47. See Ensor, ed., *A Connecticut Yankee*, 16. Clarence's femininity also may be signaled by a perhaps unintentional verbal echo: Morgan le Fay, Hank writes at the end of chap. 19, was "as fresh and young as a Vassar pullet" (99); Clarence's real name, we have learned earlier, is "Amyas le Poulet" (68).

48. Hank's last name, of course, links him to one of his book's principal women characters, Morgan le Fay, and when we learn that one of Morgan le Fay's prisoners was confined because "he had said she had red hair" (95), we should note that Samuel Clemens, before his hair turned white, was also a redhead. But Morgan le Fay—who is immune to sentiment, and in whose castle indelicate stories are told by both men and women—is significantly lacking in "feminine" qualities. It may also be significant, in this connection, that when Merlin infiltrates Hank's final fortress he does so disguised as a woman.

49. *The Works of Thomas Jefferson* (New York: Putnam, 1899), 10:104–5.

50. An excellent example of this tendency is the end of the Morgan le Fay

episode, when Morgan, having no idea of the meaning of the word, volunteers to "photograph" the freed captives—with an ax. This is basically a replay of the "ransom" joke from the Tom Sawyer's gang episode in *Huckleberry Finn*, but Hank feels obliged, before the joke, to give us a brief essay about "that kind of people who will never let on that they don't know the meaning of a new big word," who, "the more ignorant they are, the more pitifully certain they are to pretend you haven't shot over their heads"—and then, after the joke, to explain that Morgan "had no more idea than a horse, of how to photograph a procession; but being in doubt, it was just like her to try to do it with an axe" (96–97). We also might recall Twain's frequent recourse, in his praise for the accuracy or fidelity of Howells's writing, to the metaphor of photography.

Chapter Three

1. For information about James's life and career I have mainly relied on Leon Edel's five-volume biography, *Henry James* (Philadelphia: J. B. Lippincott, 1953–72): *The Untried Years: 1843–1870, The Conquest of London: 1870–1881, The Middle Years: 1882–1895, The Treacherous Years: 1895–1901*, and *The Master: 1901–1916*.

2. Edel, *The Middle Years*, 124; Brodhead, "James, Realism, and the Politics of Style," *The School of Hawthorne* (New York: Oxford University Press, 1986), 141. For other discussions of these middle years as a deliberate experiment in realism or naturalism see, for instance, Warner Berthoff, *The Ferment of Realism: American Literature, 1884–1919* (New York: Free Press, 1965), 103–26, and Lyall H. Powers, *Henry James and the Naturalist Movement* (East Lansing: Michigan State University Press, 1971).

3. "William Dean Howells" (*Harper's Weekly* [June 1886]), reprinted in James, *Literary Criticism: Essays on Literature, American Writers, English Writers*, ed. Leon Edel (New York: Library of America, 1984) [cited from here on as *Essays in Literature*], 497–506.

4. See *The Complete Works of Edgar Allan Poe*, ed. James A. Harrison (New York: Thomas Y. Crowell, 1902), 13:153–54.

5. See, for instance, the collection edited by F. O. Matthiessen, *Henry James, Stories of Writers & Artists* (New York: New Directions, 1944).

6. *A Small Boy and Others* (New York: Charles Scribner's Sons, 1913), 8, 10, 25, 43; *Notes of a Son and Brother* (New York: Charles Scribner's Sons, 1914), 58.

7. See *Notes*, chap. 9 (290–319). William James (unlike the younger brothers, Wilky and Bob) also did not serve in the war, but strangely enough, as Daniel Aaron has noted, this fact is never mentioned in *Notes of a Son and Brother* (*The Unwritten War: American Writers and the Civil War* [New York: Oxford University Press, 1973], 108). Perhaps such an admission would have interfered with the allegorical role assigned to William in Henry's autobiographical artist-fable.

8. *Small Boy*, 290; *Notes*, 339–40; *The Middle Years* (New York: Charles Scribner's Sons, 1917), 58; *Notes*, 403.

9. *My Literary Passions* (New York: Harper and Brothers, 1895), 121, 165–66, 14.

10. *Small Boy*, 194–95; *Notes*, 344.

11. *Literary Friends and Acquaintance*, ed. David F. Hiatt and Edwin H. Cady (Bloomington: Indiana University Press, 1968), 39.

12. James, *Letters*, ed Leon Edel (Cambridge, Mass.: Harvard University Press, 1974–84), 1:272; *Letters*, 2:339; Edel, *The Conquest of London*, 78.

13. *Letters*, 2:262, 264.

14. *Essays on Literature*, 505; Henry James to William James, quoted in Edel, *The Untried Years*, 272.

15. *Essays on Literature*, 613, 194, 846, 404, 194, 1326, 1313, 1316. James's dismissal of photographic detail might remind us, by contrast, that one of Mark Twain's most characteristic compliments for his friend Howells was to compare his works to photographs (see *Mark Twain-Howells Letters: The Correspondence of Samuel L. Clemens and William Dean Howells, 1872–1910*, ed. Henry Nash Smith and William M. Gibson [Cambridge, Mass.: Harvard University Press, 1960]), 245, 427, 633).

16. *Essays on Literature*, 915–16; *Literary Criticism: French Writers, Other European Writers, the Prefaces to the New York Edition*, ed. Leon Edel (New York: Library of America, 1984) [cited from here on as *French Writers*]), 280, 279, 185.

17. *French Writers*, 1012, 290, 974, 978, 865–67,

18. Howells, *Criticism and Fiction and Other Essays by W. D. Howells*, Clara Marburg Kirk and Rudolf Kirk, eds. (New York: New York University Press, 1959), 72; James, *Essays on Literature*, 30–31.

19. See, for instance, Nina Baym, *Novels, Readers, and Reviewers: Responses to Fiction in Antebellum America* (Ithaca: Cornell University Press, 1984), esp. chap. 8 and 9.

20. *French Writers*, 37, 49, 53, 67; *Essays on Literature*, 1045, 1343, 46–47.

21. *French Writers*, 1014.

22. *Essays on Literature*, 46, 52; Howells, *Criticism and Fiction*, 14; *Essays on Literature*, 47–48, 56, 64; *William Dean Howells: Representative Selections*, ed. Clara Marburg Kirk and Rudolf Kirk (New York: Hill and Wang, 1961), 348.

23. *Essays on Literature*, 62; *French Writers*, 1075; *Essays on Literature*, 52–53; *Letters*, 4:770.

24. *Essays on Literature*, 45–46.

25. *Essays on Literature*, 46.

26. See Justin Kaplan, *Mr. Clemens and Mark Twain: A Biography* (New York: Simon and Shuster, 1966), 209–11. I may simply be stretching to find an elusive "missing link" between James and Twain in this allusion to California gambling, but it seems to me in any case inconceivable that James, himself an *Atlantic* author and a friend of Howells, with numerous other Boston connections in 1877, could have been wholly ignorant of the Whittier Dinner Speech—even if, by 1884, there might have remained only a vague memory associating California, in his mind, with fraud and poker.

27. *Essays on Literature*, 56.

28. *The School of Hawthorne*, 147, 165, 162–63.

29. On the conventional distinction between "literature" and "politics," see, for instance, Mark Seltzer's critique of the way James has been read "as the very exemplar of a novelist outside the circuit of power"—of the way "his novelistic and critical practice has been appropriated to support an absolute opposition between aesthetic and political claims" (*Henry James & the Art of Power* [Ithaca: Cornell University Press, 1984], 13). Seltzer also rejects, it should be noted, the particular association of the "political" with the "realistic." "James's art of representation," he writes, "always . . . involves a politics of representation, and one reason for suspecting this link between art and power is that James works so carefully to deny it" (16).

30. *The School of Hawthorne*, 142–43. Brodhead's sense of James's "disdain" for realism's legitimating mythology is central to his argument about this phase of James's career. "Practicing [the realists'] style in the absence of their convictions," he concludes, "can only produce two outcomes: a conversion of realism's recorded 'external conditions' into an inactive externality, as in . . . *The Bostonians;* or a connecting of self and circumstance that, as . . . in *The Princess . . .* , he can only feign to believe" (3).

31. *The Complete Notebooks of Henry James*, ed. Leon Edel and Lyall H. Powers (New York: Oxford University Press, 1987), 20. This prospectus for *The Bostonians* was copied from a letter to James's publisher, J. R. Osgood.

32. For a notoriously extreme view of the novel's sexual conflicts, see Lionel Trilling's "The Bostonians"—originally the introduction to a 1953 edition of the novel, reprinted in *The Opposing Self* (New York: Viking Press, 1955), 104–17. Trilling writes, for instance, that "in a struggle for general social justice there is a natural force and dignity; and in a violent revolutionary intention there is the immediate possibility of high tragedy," but that "the doctrinaire demand for the equality of the sexes may well seem to promise but a wry and constricted story, a tale of mere eccentricity"—and he describes the nineteenth-century "movement for female equality" as a political program with "an outright anti-erotic bias which exposed it to the imputation of crankishness and morbidity" (109–10). *The Bostonians*, this contemporary of Dr. Benjamin Spock writes in his well known final sentence, "is a story of the parental house divided against itself, . . . of the sacred mothers refusing their commission and the sacred fathers endangered" (117). For an important opposing view, directly attacking Trilling and other male critics of *The Bostonians*, see Judith Fetterley, *The Resisting Reader: A Feminist Approach to American Fiction* (Bloomington: Indiana University Press, 1978), 101–53. The novel, Fetterley writes, "is inspired by a sense of the tragic fate which awaits the sensitive and thoughtful woman in a patriarchal culture" (115); "in the fate of Olive and Verena one can read the central tenets of radical feminism: women will never be free to realize and become themselves until they are free of their need for men, until they know that their basic bonds are with each other, and until they learn to make a primary commitment to each other rather than to the men who would so basely ransom them" (152–53). For other recent treatments that view the gender politics of *The Bostonians* from a perspec-

tive notably different from Trilling's, see, for instance: Nina Auerbach, *Communities of Women: An Idea in Fiction* (Cambridge, Mass.: Harvard University Press, 1978), 117–41; Judith Wilt, "Desperately Seeking Verena: A Resistant Reading of *The Bostonians,*" *Feminist Studies* 13 (1987): 293–316; Susan L. Mizruchi, *The Power of Historical Knowledge: Narrating the Past in Hawthorne, James, and Dreiser* (Princeton: Princeton University Press, 1988), 135–81; Lynn Wardley, "Woman's Voice, Democracy's Body, and *The Bostonians,*" *ELH* 56 (1989): 639–65; and Claire Kahane, "Hysteria, Feminism, and the Case of *The Bostonians,*" in *Feminism and Psychoanalysis*, ed. Richard Feldstein and Judith Roof (Ithaca: Cornell University Press, 1989), 280–97. For a recent dissent from such readings, insisting (like Trilling) that James's position in *The Bostonians* is essentially *anti*-feminist, see Alfred Habegger, *Henry James and the "Woman Business"* (New York: Cambridge University Press, 1989), 182–229. Quite *unlike* Trilling, it should be noted, Habegger does not himself endorse the position he attributes to James.

33. All parenthetical page references to *The Bostonians* are to the Penguin Classics edition, ed. Charles R. Anderson (London: Penguin, 1984).

34. *The Opposing Self*, 113.

35. The anagram was originally even nearer. A list of names in a March 1884 notebook entry—a list that includes two others destined for *The Bostonians* ("Birdseye" and "Tarrant")—includes the first mention of the future surname of the novel's hero, but spelled as "Ransome," with the final "e" producing (if one allows the equivalence of the "s" and soft "c") a full anagram for "romance." One might also note that Basil's initials, B. R., are the same as those of the Hawthorne work generally considered to be James's precursor for *The Bostonians: The Blithedale Romance*—with the "R" again, however unconsciously, standing for "romance."

36. *The School of Hawthorne*, 154–55.

37. Kirk and Kirk, eds., *Criticism and Fiction and Other Essays by W. D. Howells*, 87, 51.

38. We might note here, as a different but not necessarily antithetical way of developing this line of interpretation, Nina Auerbach's hypothetical reading of the ambiguous ending of the novel: "[W]hen Olive flings herself onstage after Verena's defection, her desperate appearance suggests that of the archetypal mousy understudy who becomes a star"—so that what James has prepared us for is "a surprising triumph on Olive's part," an "irrevocable emergence" (*Communities of Women*, 134, 138).

39. Compare Susan Mizruchi's suggestion that "despite his insight into Olive . . . the narrator seems to share her fears" (*The Power of Historical Knowledge*, 161); or note especially Claire Kahane's observation: "The character who will never marry, whose most passionate relationships are with her own sex, Olive ultimately figures James's own problematic sexuality most closely. Like Freud with Dora, James had to identify with his subject to constitute her in language, and the identification proved extremely disturbing" ("Hysteria, Feminism, and the Case of *The Bostonians,*" 296). In arguing for a connection between Olive

222 Notes to Pages 89–93

and James's ambitions in *The Bostonians*, I do not mean to argue that she neces-sarily functions as a self-portrait, but she certainly has much more in common with James than Basil Ransom does, and there are some intriguing parallels be-tween her situation and her author's. For instance, as my colleague John Limon points out in an unpublished essay ("Missing in Action: Realism and the Civil War"), the fact that Olive lost two brothers in the Civil War recalls the fact that two of James's brothers served in the war; moreover, one of these brothers, Wilky, died in November 1883, while Henry was in the early stages of work on *The Bostonians*. Also, the most important event in James's life between *The Por-trait of a Lady* and *The Bostonians* was the death of both of his parents in 1882; the aftermath of their loss is the reason he was still in Boston in 1883, when he started work on *The Bostonians*. Olive Chancellor's parents are of course no longer living; she is, like her author, on her own.

40. "Hysteria, Feminism, and the Case of *The Bostonians*," 288.

41. The best and fullest account of this instability that I know is Alfred Ha-begger's in *Henry James and the Woman Business*, esp. 182–89. "The haughty author of *The Bostonians*," he writes, "clearly wants us to accept this myth [that James is totally in charge]. In many respects, however, his novel is absolutely out of control" (189). Oddly enough, though, Habegger then proceeds to argue that James, haunted by the ghost of his father's conservative opinions on mar-riage, sides with Basil, that "the reality James fabricates says that Basil is right" (191), that "the book would vindicate the father by showing that Basil's slavery is freedom and Olive's freedom, slavery" (204). One does not need to find this reading *wrong* to wonder whether Habegger proves it to be so *exclusively* right, and while most readers of *The Bostonians* will surely consider Habegger's analysis brilliant, few will be likely to agree that the novel supports his interpretive cer-tainty.

42. *French Writers*, 1086, 1100–1102.

43. See particularly in this connection W. H. Tilley, *The Background of The Princess Casamassima* (Gainesville: University of Florida Press, 1960). On the novel's relation to the literature of the London "spy mania," see Mark Seltzer, "*The Princess Casamassima*: Realism and the Fantasy of Surveillance" (originally published, in slightly different form, in 1981), in *Henry James & the Art of Power*, 25–58.

44. See Daniel Lerner, "The Influence of Turgenev on Henry James," *The Slavonic and East European Review* 20 (1941), 46–51 (although Lerner is in fact somewhat inaccurate in his account of the similarities between the two novels); Irving Howe, *Politics and the Novel* [1957] (New York: Avon, 1967), 136–37; Tilley, *The Background of The Princess Casamassima*, esp. 3, 11–13, 34; and Pow-ers, *Henry James and the Naturalist Movement*, 90–93. James's 1877 review, which appeared in the *Nation*, is reprinted in *French Writers*, 1000–6. James's private opinion of *Virgin Soil* was more negative than the opinion he expressed in this review. "The book will disappoint you," he wrote to Thomas Sergeant Perry in April 1877, "as it did me; it has fine things, but I think it the weakest of his long stories (quite)" (Edel, ed., *Letters*, 2:108). For one last take on all of this we

should recall that James's 1909 preface traces the inspiration for *The Princess Casamassima* to walks "during the first year of a long residence in London"—which, in James's case, means 1876–77. It was of course during this same year that he first read, and reviewed, Turgenev's *Virgin Soil.*

45. *Virgin Soil,* trans Rochelle S. Townsend (London: J. M. Dent [Everyman's Library], 1963), 6, 27–28, 100, 240.

46. *French Writers,* 1005.

47. All parenthetical page references to *The Princess Casamassima* are to the Penguin Classics edition, ed. Derek Brewer (London: Penguin, 1987), which follows the text of the original 1886 edition rather than the revised New York edition of 1909. While one might object to this choice on objective editorial grounds, the 1886 text is presumably the better indicator of James's thinking when he was in the midst of his realist phase.

48. *Essays on Literature,* 53.

49. Compare William W. Stowe's observation that Hyacinth's "precarious position between anarchism and aristocracy parallels James's own wavering between Naturalism and the more subjective psychological impressionism he was eventually to adopt" (*Balzac, James, and the Realistic Novel* [Princeton: Princeton University Press, 1983], 82–83). On connections between Hyacinth and "The Art of Fiction," see too Michael Anesko, *"Friction with the Market": Henry James and the Profession of Authorship* (New York: Oxford University Press, 1986), 110.

50. See, for instance, Powers, *Henry James and the Naturalist Movement,* 110, and Brodhead, *The School of Hawthorne,* 158–59. It should be noted, however, that only in Hyacinth's case (understandably, perhaps, since he never actually knew his parents) is the notion of influence based so heavily upon *genetic* determinism, on the force of "blood"; for other characters, such as Millicent Henning and Paul Muniment, family background constitutes primarily an *environmental* force—a force which, moreover, these characters seek to escape.

51. *"The Princess Casamassima"* (1948), in *The Liberal Imagination: Essays on Literature and Society* (New York: Scribner's, 1950), 87.

52. *Essays on Literature,* 46.

53. *The Theoretical Dimensions of Henry James* (Madison: University of Wisconsin Press, 1984), 181–82.

54. *French Writers,* 1100, 1102.

55. In hazarding this interpretation of Hyacinth's status as perpetual observer, I do not necessarily mean to imply a direct relationship between Hyacinth Robinson and Henry James, but speculation on this subject is certainly tempting. One might note, for instance, Lionel Trilling's discussion of the "familial situation" in *The Princess Casamassima,* his observations that "this child-man lives in a novel full of parental figures" and that "so much manipulation of the theme of parent and child, so much interest in lost protective love, suggests that the connection of Hyacinth and his author may be more intense than at first appears" (*The Liberal Imagination,* 75, 77). Trilling then works out speculative correspondences between Hyacinth and Henry James, Paul Muniment and

William James, and the Princess and Alice James (pp. 78–79). One might respond to the last of these by suggesting that the invalid Alice had much more
in common with Paul's bedridden sister, Rosy. And Hyacinth's prospective fascination with touching the "mutilated hand" and of "the sublime Hoffendahl"
(291) might remind us that Henry James, Sr., had lost a leg in a childhood accident. See too, on the subject of such connections, Edel, *The Middle Years:
1882–1895*, 190–92.

    56. *The Middle Years*, 282.

Part Two

    1. While this generalization is so widespread as to defy citation, a list of
classic examples would include Vernon Louis Parrington, *Main Currents in
American Thought, Vol. III: The Beginnings of Critical Realism in America* (New York:
Harcourt, Brace, 1930), 323–34; Charles Child Walcutt, *American Literary Naturalism: A Divided Stream* (Minneapolis: University of Minnesota Press, 1956);
Lars Åhnebrink, *The Beginnings of Naturalism in American Fiction, 1891–1903*
(New York: Russell & Russell, 1961); and Donald Pizer, *Realism and Naturalism
in Nineteenth-Century American Literature* (Carbondale: Southern Illinois University Press, 1966). For more recent examples, some of which depart significantly
from the classic definitions of American naturalism, see John J. Conder, *Naturalism in American Fiction: The Classic Phase* (Lexington: University Press of Kentucky, 1984); June Howard, *Form and History in American Literary Naturalism*
(Chapel Hill: University of North Carolina Press, 1985); Walter Benn Michaels,
*The Gold Standard and the Logic of Naturalism: American Literature at the Turn of
the Century* (Berkeley: University of California Press, 1987); and Lee Clark
Mitchell's chapter, "Naturalism and the Languages of Determinism," in *Colum-
bia Literary History of the United States*, ed. Emory Elliott (New York: Columbia
University Press, 1988), 525–45; and his book, *Determined Fictions: American
Literary Naturalism* (New York: Columbia University Press, 1989).

    2. John Condor (in *Naturalism in American Fiction*) and Lee Mitchell (in
his essay in the *Columbia Literary History of the United States* and in *Determined Fictions*) still insist on a belief in determinism as the defining quality of
literary realism.

    3. *The Complete Works of Frank Norris* (Garden City, N.Y.: Doubleday,
1928), 7:167–68.

    4. "A Case in Point" (*Literature* [March 24, 1899]), reprinted in *Criticism
and Fiction and Other Essays by W. D. Howells*, ed. Clara Marburg Kirk and
Rudolf Kirk (New York: New York University Press, 1959), 282.

    5. *Form and History in American Literary Naturalism* (Chapel Hill: Uni-
versity of North Carolina Press, 1985). "The paralysis of the observer,"
Howard writes, "like the apparition of the brute, recurs repeatedly in naturalism; it inheres . . . in the form itself. The tensions between determinism
and reformism, between quotidian realism and the exotic setting inhabited
by the Other, reveal the structure of the genre" (125).

6. See, for instance, in addition to Howard's *Form and History*, Michaels's *The Gold Standard and the Logic of Naturalism*, and Mark Seltzer, "The Naturalist Machine," in *Sex, Politics, and Science in the Nineteenth-Century Novel*, ed. Ruth Bernard Yeazell (Baltimore: The Johns Hopkins University Press, 1986), 116–47.

7. "The Naturalist Machine," 5. Seltzer is typical of the 1980s new historicism in his assumption (accurate, in my view) of a fundamental *continuity* between realist and naturalist practice. "The realist novel," he writes, "through techniques of narrative surveillance, organic continuity, and deterministic progress, secures the intelligibility and supervision of individuals in an evolutionary and genetic narration. . . . Far from resisting the realist premises of genesis and generation, the naturalist aesthetic doctrines of determinism and degeneration systematically render explicit and reinforce these premises and the power-effects inscribed in them" (140).

8. *Complete Works*, 7:26.

9. "The Experimental Novel," trans. George J. Becker in *Documents of Modern Literary Realism*, ed. Becker (Princeton: Princeton University Press, 1963), 191.

Chapter Four

1. "The Naturalist Machine," in *Sex, Politics, and Science in the Nineteenth-Century Novel*, ed. Ruth Bernard Yeazell (Baltimore: Johns Hopkins University Press, 1986), 116. Norris also looms large, for example, in Walter Michaels's *The Gold Standard and the Logic of American Naturalism* (Berkeley: University of California Press, 1987), particularly in the title essay, and he is one of the three principal subjects (the other two being Jack London and Theodore Dreiser) of June Howard's *Form and History in American Literary Naturalism* (Chapel Hill: University of North Carolina Press, 1985). For a recent dissent from the connection of Norris with naturalism, see chap. 1, "Norris's Dubious Naturalism," in Barbara Hochman, *The Art of Frank Norris, Storyteller* (Columbia: University of Missouri Press, 1988), 1–19.

2. The principal source of biographical information remains Franklin Walker, *Frank Norris: A Biography* (Garden City, N.Y.: Doubleday, 1932). Valuable briefer accounts of Norris's career include Maxwell Geismar, *Rebels and Ancestors: The American Novel, 1890–1915* (Boston: Houghton Mifflin, 1953), 1–66; Kenneth Lynn, *The Dream of Success: A Study of the Modern American Imagination* (Boston: Little, Brown, 1955), 158–207; and Larzer Ziff, *The American 1890s: Life and Times of a Lost Generation* (New York: Viking, 1966), 250–74.

3. Parenthetical volume and page references to Norris are to *The Complete Works of Frank Norris*, 10 vols. (Garden City, N.Y.: Doubleday, 1928).

4. *The Letters of Frank Norris*, ed. Franklin Walker (San Francisco: Book Club of California, 1956), 30–31.

5. *The Literary Criticism of Frank Norris*, ed. Donald Pizer (Austin: University of Texas Press, 1964), 72.

6. Ibid., 71–72.

7. There would of course also appear to be a fair amount of sexual anxiety lurking in Norris's concern with "big things" and "little things." For instance, in *Moran of the Lady Letty*, when Wilbur kills a Chinese beachcomber, we are told that "all that was strong and virile and brutal in him seemed to harden and stiffen in the moment after he had seen the beach comber collapse limply on the sand under that last strong knife-blow" (3:290). What matters most here, of course (as is also true of the comments on Zola), is that masculine force is equated with aggressive violence. Compare Mark Seltzer's observation that "a capitalizing on force as a counter to female generativity in particular and to anxieties about generation and production in general may help to explain, at least in part, the appeals to highly abstract conceptions of force in the emphatically 'male' genre of naturalism" ("The Naturalist Machine," 121).

8. *Realism and Naturalism in American Fiction*, 98.

9. On this aspect of Norris's thought, see especially Maxwell Geismar's *Rebels and Ancestors*, 1–66.

10. *The Letters of Frank Norris*, 23, 48.

11. Ziff, *The American 1890s*, 270; Berryman, *Stephen Crane* (New York: Meridian, 1962), 288.

12. Particularly intriguing in this passage is its jarring introduction of literal liquid ("from ocean to ocean") into the metaphorical cascade of "maelstrom," "vortex," and "ebb and flow." And the suggestion that "the great Result" would "refuse to come" without the intervening grip of "a master hand" might recall Mark Seltzer's observation that "creation, in Norris's final explanation, is the work of an inexhaustible masturbator, spilling his seed on the ground, the product of a mechanistic and miraculous onanism"—placing "power back into the hands of the immortal and autonomous male technology of generation" ("The Naturalist Machine," 124).

13. According to Maxwell Geismar, for instance, *Vandover* is a "key novel" because it deals with "that young western aristocracy—the sons of the rich—which was Norris's natural medium" (*Rebels and Ancestors*, 52–53).

14. "Reality in America," in *The Liberal Imagination* (New York: Scribner's. 1976), 10.

Chapter Five

1. For biographical information on Crane I have relied on R. W. Stallman's *Stephen Crane: A Biography* (New York: Braziller, 1968), and on the biographical portions of Edwin H. Cady's excellent *Stephen Crane* (Boston: Twayne, 1980; rev. ed.). I am indebted as well, even though they are often unreliable on matters of fact, to Thomas Beer, *Stephen Crane* (New York: Alfred A. Knopf, 1923) and John Berryman, *Stephen Crane* (Cleveland: Meridian, 1962; rev. ed.).

2. *William Dean Howells: Representative Selections*, ed. Clara Marburg Kirk and Rudolf Kirk (New York: Hill and Wang, 1961), 393, 386, 393, 385.

3. *The Correspondence of Stephen Crane*, ed. Stanley Wertheim and Paul Sorrentino (New York: Columbia University Press, 1988). 677.

4. John J. Conder overlooks this point when he argues that "the lessons [the correspondent] learns are central to Crane's naturalistic vision" (*Naturalism in American Fiction: The Classic Phase* [Lexington: University Press of Kentucky, 1984], 22). Charles Child Walcutt finds in Crane an "obvious interest in scientific or deterministic accounting for events" (*American Literary Naturalism: A Divided Stream* [Minneapolis: University of Minnesota Press, 1956], 67), but far more accurate, in my view, is Edwin Cady's insistence that Crane "had nothing at all of that smug confidence about summing up the universe in neat formulae . . . which characterized the popular scientism— and some of the serious science and philosophy—of [his] day"; quite absent from *The Red Badge of Courage*, according to Cady, "is the tremendous procession of natural and social 'forces' characteristic of naturalism—of Frank Norris or Dreiser trying to be Zola" (*Stephen Crane*, 98, 123).

5. Reprinted in Richard M. Weatherford, ed., *Stephen Crane: The Critical Heritage* (London: Routledge & Kegan Paul, 1973), 122, 141, 90.

6. For example, Charles Child Walcutt sees *Maggie*, Crane's slum novel, as a work of naturalism because in it "what [Crane] says and what he renders are one," but he protests, when the narrator engages in apparent verbal irony, that his terms "come from a world of reference beyond this grisly slum"—that, for instance, "to call a grubby child's screams infantile orations is to deflect the impact of the scene and make us aware of the writer" (*American Literary Naturalism*, 69–71). For an account of Crane's supposed naturalism that seems totally untroubled by his verbal irony, see Lars Åhnebrink, *The Beginnings of Naturalism in American Fiction, 1891–1903* (New York: Russell & Russell, 1961), 89–104, 150–55.

7. Crane inscribed a copy of *The Red Badge* to Howells "as a token of the veneration and gratitude of Stephen Crane for many things he has learned of the common man and, above all, for a certain re-adjustment of his point of view victoriously concluded some time in 1892." Crane described this "re-adjustment" more fully in a letter to Lilly Brandon Munroe: "I developed all alone a little creed of art which I thought was a good one. Later I discovered that my creed was identical with the one of Howells and Garland" (*Correspondence*, 247, 63). Crane remained grateful for Howells's example as an opponent of literary fakery and for his early support, but his sense that his creed and Howells's were "identical" cannot have lasted very long. In 1894, for example, Howells returned a manuscript of the "lines" later published as *The Black Riders*, commenting: "It is a pity for you to do them, for you can do things solid and real, so superbly" (ibid., 40), and Crane could not have been unaware of Howells's disappointment with *The Red Badge*.

8. Crane first published *Maggie* in 1893, at his own expense and under a pseudonym. The book did not sell, but it did bring Crane to the attention of Howells and Hamlin Garland, to whom he presented gift copies. In 1896, in

order to capitalize on the popularity achieved by *The Red Badge of Courage*, Crane produced a rather sloppily expurgated new version of *Maggie*. For a discussion of the process of *Maggie*'s revision, see Hershel Parker and Brian Higgins, "Maggie's 'Last Night': Authorial Design and Editorial Patching," *Studies in the Novel* 10 (1978): 64–75.

9. For an extreme development of this view, arguing that "the Naturalism of *Maggie* [can] be identified as a rigorous, Darwinistic determinism," see David Fitelson, "Stephen Crane's *Maggie* and Darwinism," *American Quarterly* 16 (1964): 182–94.

10. *Correspondence*, 53. Crane sent copies, with more or less identical inscriptions, to several influential or potentially sympathetic critics and writers; this version is from the copy he sent to Hamlin Garland.

11. "Maggie herself," Donald Pizer writes, "is strangely untouched by her physical environment. She functions as an almost expressionistic symbol of inner purity uncorrupted by external foulness" (*Realism and Naturalism in American Literature* [Carbondale: Southern Illinois University Press, 1966], 121).

12. Parenthetical page references to *Maggie* are to the Norton Critical Edition, ed. Thomas A. Gullason (New York: Norton, 1979), based on the first (1893) edition of the novel.

13. The description of little Jimmy's body as "writhing" might recall Michael Fried's reading of "writhing" (and "rioting"), in a crucial passage in Crane's *The Monster*, as "rhyming, audially and visually," however unconsciously, with "*writing*" (*Realism, Writing, Disfiguration: on Thomas Eakins and Stephen Crane* [Chicago: The University of Chicago Press, 1987], 96). Such evocations and thematizations of writing, Fried argues, "call into question the very basis of writing as communication—the tendency of the written word at least partly to 'efface' itself in favor of its meaning in the acts of writing and reading" (120). I'm not sure I believe all of Fried's examples of the evocation of writing in Crane's fiction, and I am certainly not arguing for such a reading of "writhing" in the second paragraph of *Maggie*, but Fried's more general sense of the way Crane's fiction calls into question the effacement of language in communication is in many respects similar to my own argument that Crane sabotages one of the central ambitions of Howells's realism and Norris's naturalism—that style might become a transparent conveyer of meaning.

14. Norris, *The Literary Criticism of Frank Norris*, ed. Donald Pizer (Austin: University of Texas Press, 1964), 165–66; Howard, *Form and History in American Literary Naturalism* (Chapel Hill: University of North Carolina Press, 1985), 104–5.

15. *Stephen Crane*, 58.

16. I am indebted here to Alan Trachtenberg's excellent discussion of the technique of Crane's newspaper sketches, "Experiments in Another Country: Stephen Crane's City Sketches," *Southern Review* 10 (1974): 265–85 (reprinted in Eric Sundquist, ed., *American Realism: New Essays* [Baltimore: Johns Hopkins University Press, 1982], 138–54). While Trachtenberg's account of "limiting perspective" and Crane's manipulation of "the structured

passages of his point of view" is concerned only with transformations of the specific conventions of the newspaper sketch of urban life, it seems to me that the implications of his argument apply as well to the operation of irony in all of Crane's best fiction, and certainly in *Maggie*.

17. See, for instance, Eric Solomon, *Stephen Crane: From Parody to Realism* (Cambridge, Mass.: Harvard University Press, 1966).

18. Larzer Ziff writes that "events were a test of [Crane's] consciousness, not its instructor," and he seems to see this as a fault. "In *Maggie*," he writes, "Crane was attempting to impose his personality on imagined material rather than to organize documentary material into a fiction," so that in the book "there is no literal level of social reality" (*The American 1890s: Life and Times of a Lost Generation* [New York: Viking, 1966], 186, 190, 191). I am inclined to agree, except that what Ziff sees as Crane's problem I would see, rather, as his point.

19. *Criticism and Fiction and Other Essays by W. D. Howells*, ed. Clara Marburg Kirk and Rudolf Kirk (New York: New York University Press, 1959), 13.

20. *Correspondence*, 671.

21. *The Performing Self: Compositions and Decompositions in the Languages of Contemporary Life* (New York: Oxford University Press, 1971), 12.

22. *Form and History in American Literary Naturalism*, 105.

23. "The Novel with a 'Purpose'" (1902), *The Complete Works of Frank Norris* (Garden City, N.Y.: Doubleday, 1928), 7:26; "Zola as a Romantic Writer" (1896), Pizer, ed., *The Literary Criticism of Frank Norris*, 71.

24. Parenthetical page references to *The Red Badge of Courage* are to the Norton Critical Edition, ed. Sculley Bradley, Richmond Croom Beatty, E. Hudson Long, and Donald Pizer (New York: Norton, 1982; rev. ed.).

25. On the rise of "virile" imperial "realism" in England, in reaction against the aestheticism of the Decadents, see, for instance, Jerome Hamilton Buckley, *The Victorian Temper: A Study in Literary Culture* (Cambridge, Mass.: Harvard University Press, 1951), 226–28, 238–46. Donald Pizer discusses the importance to the development of Frank Norris's thinking about literature of the battle in England "between the school of Wilde, Beardsley, and the *Yellow Book* and that of Henley, Kipling, and Stevenson": "Just as Norris's description of 'literature' often seems an epitome of the popular conception of Wilde," he observes, "so his idea of 'life' is intimately related both to the fiction and the aesthetic theory of Kipling" (*Realism and Naturalism in American Fiction*, 100–102).

26. Reprinted in *Stephen Crane: The Critical Heritage*, 140–41.

27. Ibid., 141.

28. "Frank Norris," in *William Dean Howells: Representative Selections*, 385–86. When *The Red Badge* first came out Howells was able to praise Crane's "skill . . . in evolving from the youth's crude expectations and ambitions a quiet honesty and self-possession manlier and nobler than any heroism he had imagined" (*Harper's Weekly* [October 26, 1895], reprinted in *Stephen Crane: The Critical Heritage*, 91–92), but even in 1895 Howells thought *The Red Badge* significantly inferior to *Maggie*.

29. Kirk and Kirk, eds., *William Dean Howells: Representative Selections,* 393, 385, 393.

30. For Norris's account of meeting Crane—to whom he refers only as "The Young Personage" and whose refusal to act and dress the part of Famous War Correspondent Norris clearly resents—see "News Gathering at Key West," in *The Letters of Frank Norris,* ed. Franklin Walker (San Francisco: Book Club of California, 1956), 10–18.

31. Edwin Cady takes a balanced view of this subject: Crane, he writes, "was torn between loyalties . . . to the emotions and modes of the [antiheroic] realists and those of the Rooseveltian, 'strenuous life,' neo-romanticists"; but he "was no Wister, Remington, nor Roosevelt. His vision was not only darker but deeper. Where they saw pain, struggle, and victory he saw agony and despair—at best tragedy"; "he went beyond them in the depth of his forceful compassion for losers" (*Stephen Crane,* 87, 103, 104). See, too, Cady's "Stephen Crane and the Strenuous Life," *ELH* 28 (1961): 376–82.

32. Lee Mitchell is far more inclined than I am to find in *The Red Badge* a "narrative voice . . . which slides back and forth between the free indirect discourse of Henry's atomized perspective and an omniscient third person" (*Determined Fictions: American Literary Naturalism,* 113). Our disagreement stems, I think, from Mitchell's willingness to read as "omniscient" intrusions passages in which "diction and perspective . . . exceed Henry's modest capacities" (ibid., 114).

33. Compare Donald Pease's observation that "in *The Red Badge of Courage,* narratives do not follow battles and provide needed explanation; instead they precede and indeed demand battles as elaborations and justifications of already narrated events" ("Fear, Rage, and the Mistrials of Representation in *The Red Badge of Courage,*" in Sundquist, ed., *American Realism: New Essays,* 160).

34. For an argument that the final chapter is to be read straight, see, for instance, Marston LaFrance, *A Reading of Stephen Crane* (Oxford : Oxford University Press, 1971), 120–24. "I am unable to find much irony in the closing paragraphs of the novel," he writes. "Certainly Henry is not fooling himself. . . . And the final image seems to me merely an emblem of what has just happened to [him]" (ibid., 123). The contrary position is taken, for example, by Frederick Crews, who insists that "Crane's ironic handling of Henry's ego becomes not less but more pronounced in the closing sentences of the novel. The tone there becomes idyllic—much too idyllic to be taken seriously" (Crews, ed., *The Red Badge of Courage* [New York: Bobbs Merrill, 1964], xxii).

35. *The Complete Works of Frank Norris,* 3:309; Pizer, ed., *The Literary Criticism of Frank Norris,* 71–2.

Chapter Six

1. For biographical information I am especially indebted to W. A. Swanberg, *Dreiser* (New York: Scribner's, 1965); and Ellen Moers, *Two Dreisers* (New York: Viking, 1969).

2. Dreiser, *A Book about Myself* (New York: Liveright, 1922). 1; Dreiser, Interview in *New York Times Saturday Review of Books*, June 15, 1907 (reprinted in Donald Pizer, ed., *Sister Carrie* [New York: Norton, 1970], 475); Mencken, "Theodore Dreiser," in *A Book of Prefaces* (New York: Knopf, 1917), 115; Lewis, "Nobel Prize Address," reprinted in George Perkins, ed., *The Theory of the American Novel* (New York: Rinehart, 1970), 302.

3. The best-known contemporary attack is Stuart P. Sherman's "The Barbaric Naturalism of Theodore Dreiser" (1915), reprinted in *On Contemporary Literature* (New York: Peter Smith, 1917), 85–101. Although Sherman admired *An American Tragedy* when it appeared in 1925, he did not revise his opinion of the earlier work (See "Mr. Dreiser in Tragic Realism," *The Main Stream* [New York: Scribner's, 1927], 134–44). That Dreiser's supposed immorality continued to be a problem long after the debate of the mid-teens had subsided is indicated, for instance, by Randall Stewart's "neo-orthodox" attack on his work in the 1950s, "Dreiser and the Naturalistic Heresy," *Virginia Quarterly Review* 34 (1958): 100–16.

4. *The Liberal Imagination: Essays on Literature and Society* (New York: Scribner's, 1950), 15–16.

5. For Moers's account of the scientific backgrounds of *Sister Carrie*, see *Two Dreisers*, 133–52; on his later scientific interests, see pp. 159–69, 256–70. For an excellent recent discussion of Dreiser and science, and of the importance (or unimportance) of "scientific" ideas in *Sister Carrie*, see John Limon, *The Place of Fiction in the Time of Science: A Disciplinary History of American Writing* (Cambridge: Cambridge University Press, 1990), 160–69.

6. Dreiser, *A Book about Myself*, 33; Mencken, *A Book of Prefaces*, 95; Dreiser, *A Book about Myself*, 107–8.

7. *A Book about Myself*, 25, 120, 129–30. Compare Kenneth Lynn's observation that "definitely [for Dreiser], 'art' was the open sesame to success" (*The Dream of Success: A Study of the Modern American Imagination* [Boston: Little, Brown, 1955], 21).

8. *It Was the Nightingale* (London: William Heineman, 1934), 15–16. For guiding me to this story I am grateful to my colleague Don Gifford, to whom I also am more generally indebted for his many wise and provocative comments about Dreiser.

9. "Dreiser," in *Portraits from Life* (Boston: Houghton Mifflin, 1937), 178.

10. Mencken, for instance, wrote in 1917 that "one feels him at last to be no more than a helpless instrument (or victim) of that inchoate flow of forces which he himself is so fond of depicting" (*A Book of Prefaces*, 68). One might compare Alfred Kazin's assertion that Dreiser "stumbled into the naturalist novel as he . . . stumbled through life. . . . Naturalism was Dreiser's instinctive response to life" (*On Native Grounds: An Interpretation of Modern American Literature* [Garden City, N.Y.: Doubleday, 1956], 66).

11. *Portraits from Life*, 176.

12. Parenthetical page references to *Sister Carrie* are to the Norton Critical Edition, ed. Donald Pizer (New York: Norton, 1970).

232 Notes to Pages 156–161

13. Amy Kaplan writes that "it is well known that *Sister Carrie* opens on two discordant narrative registers: the documentary description of a young girl's journey to the city, and the sentimental commentary on the moral ramifications of her venture" (*The Social Construction of American Realism* [Chicago: University of Chicago Press, 1988], 140). I would not want, however, to use these terms to describe the novel's discordant narrative voices since, among other things, the voice that documents seems to me to be the same as the voice that moralizes, and what I call the "immediate" voice engages in *neither* "documentary description" *nor* "sentimental description."

14. *Form and History in American Literary Naturalism* (Chapel Hill: University of North Carolina Press, 1985), 106, 47.

15. *Theodore Dreiser* (New York: Delta, 1951), 65.

16. *The Gold Standard and the Logic of Naturalism* (Berkeley: University of California Press, 1987), 45. The original version of Michaels's influential chapter on Dreiser's novel, "*Sister Carrie*'s Popular Economy," first appeared in 1980, in *Critical Inquiry*.

17. "The Language of Realism, the Language of False Consciousness: A Reading of *Sister Carrie*," *Novel* 10 (1977): 102, 104, 109. This essay elicited a rejoinder from Ellen Moers; for her debate with Petrey, see *Novel* 11 (1977): 63–69.

18. Compare Amy Kaplan's recuperation of Dreiser's sentimental style in *The Social Construction of American Realism*, as in her insistence that "rather than choose one narrative stance as more realistic than the other, we might see them constructing competing versions of the real" (151).

19. *Maggie: A Girl of the Streets*, ed. Thomas A. Gullason (New York: Norton, 1979), 34.

20. Ibid., 27.

21. *Hard Facts: Setting and Form in the American Novel* (New York: Oxford University Press, 1987), 160, 167. (Fisher's discussion of *Sister Carrie* originally appeared in *American Realism: New Essays*, ed. Eric Sundquist [Baltimore: Johns Hopkins University Press, 1982], 259–77.) Compare Rachel Bowlby's observation that in *Sister Carrie* "the theatre . . . is not the site of a radical contrast with the world outside it. . . . The Broadway scene, with 'fashion's throng, on parade in a showplace,' is as much a place of illusion and costume as the literal stage" (*Just Looking: Consumer Culture in Dreiser, Gissing and Zola* [New York: Methuen, 1985], 64–65).

22. Larzer Ziff, comparing Dreiser and Crane, writes that "Crane, characteristically, contrasts . . . misty notions with the harsh realities of Maggie's life in order to make an ironic comment on the human condition. But Dreiser was a partaker of Maggie's dream himself. Though he eventually saw its hopelessness, he never lost his sensitivity to its attractive power, and his deluded characters become objects of compassion rather than irony" (*The American 1890s: Life and Times of a Lost Generation* [New York: Viking, 1966], 336).

23. As Rachel Bowlby writes of Carrie's imitative propensities: "To be

'something' means, paradoxically, to imitate passively and minutely gestures which are not her own" (*Just Looking*, 62).

24. *Sister Carrie*, ed. John C. Berkey, Alice M. Winters, James L. West III, and Neda M. Westlake (Philadelphia: University of Pennsylvania Press, 1981). The editors justify their reliance on the typescript by arguing that Dreiser was not really or intentionally responsible for the revised ending of the version published by Doubleday in 1900 (see 583–85), but this argument, like those offered for quite a few of their editorial decisions, seems based mainly on taste, and what I am arguing here is that Dreiser's taste may have been better and surer (or maybe just luckier) than they recognize. We should note, in any case, that their argument directly contradicts Dreiser's own account (in a 1907 interview in the *New York Herald*) of adding the present ending, that Dreiser as author clearly approved the new ending, and that he in fact wrote it in what he described as a moment of inspiration.

25. Matthiessen, *Theodore Dreiser*, 73; Michaels, *The Gold Standard and the Logic of Naturalism*, 41; Fisher, *Hard Facts*, 167.

26. *Native Son* (New York: Harper & Row, 1966), xxxi.

27. Dreiser reported Howells's supposed comment to Dorothy Dudley (see her *Forgotten Frontiers: Dreiser and the Land of the Free* [New York: Smith and Haas, 1932], 197).

28. *My Literary Passions* (New York: Harper and Brothers, 1895), 258.

Prologue, Part Three

1. *Harper's Bazar* 16, no. 3 (August 1883): 534. The story was reprinted in Wilkins's first collection, *A Humble Romance and Other Stories* (New York: Harper and Brothers, 1887), 37–48. Parenthetical page references are to this collection.

2. At the beginning of 1887, as plans for her first collection were going forward, Wilkins suggested that "A Symphony in Lavender" and another previously published tale ("The Bar Light-House") might be omitted, a suggestion that was ultimately not carried out (see Brent L. Kendrick, ed., *The Infant Sphinx: Collected Letters of Mary E. Wilkins Freeman* [Metuchen, N.J.: The Scarecrow Press, 1985], 78).

3. Perry D. Westbrook, for instance, writes that "Caroline Munson's timidity—her failure to force herself to see the truth that she was afraid of marriage—. . . stems from her own emotional immaturity, a stunting of the will. To live with her lilacs and her Bible and her constant prayers was easier than to live with a husband" (*Mary Wilkins Freeman* [New York: Twayne, 1967], 39).

4. *A New England Nun and Other Stories* (New York: Harper and Brothers, 1891), 146, 153, 159.

5. In allowing her poem to be published, Marjorie Pryse writes, "Betsey has stepped over the line, threatening to rival the minister's own occupation" (Pryse, ed., *Selected Stories of Mary E. Wilkins Freeman* [New York: Norton,

1983], 329). This is no doubt true, although one suspects his occupation as published poet is more important, in the context of the story, than his occupation (to which Pryse is referring) as minister. It is also a bit difficult to accept Pryse's assertion that Betsey "triumphs at her death" (330).

Chapter Seven

1. James, "Mr. and Mrs. James T. Fields," reprinted in *Henry James: Literary Criticism: Essays on Literature, American Writers, English Writers* (New York: Library of America, 1984), 174; Cather, "Miss Jewett," in *Not under Forty* (New York: Alfred A. Knopf, 1936), 89; Berthoff, "The Art of Jewett's *Pointed Firs*" (originally published in 1959), reprinted in *Fictions and Events: Essays in Criticism and Literary History* (New York: E. P. Dutton, 1971), 263. Cather's 1936 essay incorporates most of the preface she wrote in 1925 for *The Best Stories of Sarah Orne Jewett*, but it drops that preface's final two paragraphs, including the claim that *The Country of the Pointed Firs*, *The Scarlet Letter*, and *Huckleberry Finn* are the "three American books which have the possibility of a long, long life" (reprinted in *The Country of the Pointed Firs and Others Stories* [Garden City, N.Y.: Doubleday, 1956], 11). For a provocative recent discussion of Jewett's supposedly "minor" status and ambitions, see Louis A. Renza, *"A White Heron" and the Question of Minor Literature* (Madison: University of Wisconsin Press, 1984).

2. For characteristic examples of this inclusion of regional and local color writing within the "larger" current of realism, see the section, "Regionalism, Local-Color Realism," in Warner Berthoff's *The Ferment of Realism: American Literature, 1884–1919* (New York: Free Press, 1965), 90–103; and Eric Sundquist's chapter, "Realism and Regionalism," in the *Columbia Literary History of the United States*, ed. Emory Elliot (New York: Columbia University Press, 1988), 501–24.

3. Jewett's father quoted in Jewett, "Looking Back on Girlhood," *Youth's Companion* 65 (January 7, 1892): 6; Jewett to Cather in *Letters of Sarah Orne Jewett*, ed. Annie Fields (Boston: Houghton Mifflin, 1911), 249.

4. *Criticism and Fiction and Other Essays by W. D. Howells*, ed. Clara Marburg Kirk and Rudolf Kirk (New York: New York University Press, 1959), 64, 194.

5. Ibid., 26; *My Literary Passions* (New York: Harper and Brothers, 1895), 14.

6. "The Literature of Impoverishment: The Women Local Colorists in America 1865–1914," *Women's Studies* 1 (1972): 2–40. Douglas contrasts what she sees as the impoverishment of local color writers with the ambitions and successful careers of the so-called sentimental women writers of the 1850s and 1860s. Most literary historians, however, contrast the supposed minor scope of local color fiction with the work of contemporaneous white, male "realists." As Eric Sundquist puts it: "Economic or political power can itself be seen to be definitive of a realist aesthetic, in that those in power (say, white urban males) have more often been judged 'realists,' while those removed from the seats of

power (say, Midwesterners, blacks, immigrants, or women) have been categorized as regionalists" (*Columbia Literary History of the United States*, 503). Also
see chap. 1, "'A White Heron' as a Maine Current," in Renza's *"A White Heron"*
and the Question of Minor Literature, 43–72.

7. Norris, *The Letters of Frank Norris*, ed. Franklin Walker (San Francisco: Book Club of California, 1956), 30–31; Matthiessen, *Sarah Orne Jewett*
(Boston: Houghton Mifflin, 1919), 148; Cather, *Not under Forty*, 95.

8. *The Complete Works of Frank Norris* (Garden City, N.Y.: Doubleday,
1928), 7:178–79, 181.

9. *The Literary Criticism of Frank Norris*, ed. Donald Pizer (Austin: University of Texas Press, 1964), 72.

10. *Life in Letters of William Dean Howells*, Mildred Howells, ed. (Garden
City, N.Y.: Doubleday, Doran, 1928), 2:15.

11. The most reliable source of biographical information is John
Eldridge Frost, *Sarah Orne Jewett* (Kittery Point, Maine: The Gundalow
Club, 1960). Still useful, if not wholly reliable on biographical matters, is F.
O. Matthiessen's *Sarah Orne Jewett*.

12. On Jewett's relationship with Fields, see especially Josephine Dono-
van, "The Unpublished Love Poems of Sarah Orne Jewett," *Frontiers: A*
Journal of Women's Studies 4, no. 3 (1979): 26–31 (reprinted in Gwen L.
Nagel, ed., *Critical Essays on Sarah Orne Jewett* [Boston: G. K. Hall, 1984],
107–17); and chap. 4 of Sarah Way Sherman, *Sarah Orne Jewett, an American*
Persephone (Hanover, N.H.: University Press of New England, 1989), 69–90.

13. Richard Cary, ed. *Sarah Orne Jewett Letters* (Waterville, Maine: Colby
College Press, 1967; rev. ed.), 94–95; Fields, ed., *Letters of Sarah Orne Jewett*,
62–63, 27–28.

14. Parenthetical page references are to *Deephaven* (Boston: Houghton
Mifflin, 1877).

15. Willa Cather, ed., *The Country at the Pointed Firs and Other Stories*
(Garden City, N.Y.: Doubleday, 1956 [a reprint of Willa Cather's 1925 collection, *The Best Stories of Sarah Orne Jewett*]), 208, 212, 214, 215, 216. "Going to Shrewsbury" was originally published in the *Atlantic* and then collected in *Strangers and Wayfarers* (1890).

16. Ibid., 292, 192, 304, 305. "Martha's Lady" first appeared in the *Atlantic*; it was collected in *The Queen's Twin and Other Stories* (1899). "The
Flight of Betsey Lane," first published in *Scribner's Magazine*, was collected
in *A Native of Winby and Other Tales* (1893). "The Hilton's Holiday," first
published in the *Century Magazine*, was collected in *The Life of Nancy* (1895).

17. A number of Jewett's less-known stories turn quite explicitly on issues
of gender identity and its artificiality. For instance, "An Autumn Holiday" (published in *Harper's Magazine* in 1880 and collected in *Country By-Ways* in 1881)
includes the interpolated story of a sea captain who decides, after a stroke, that
he is his own dead sister—and insists on wearing her clothes to church and to a
meeting of the Female Missionary Society. In "Hallowell's Pretty Sister" (published in *Good Company* in 1880 and never collected by Jewett), a Harvard society

man, visiting a college friend, falls for the friend's sister, only to discover that "she" has in fact been impersonated by the friend's younger brother. He ends up, however, marrying the real sister. Particularly interesting is "Tom's Husband" (published in the *Atlantic* in 1882 and collected in *The Mate of the Daylight and Friends Ashore* in 1883), in which a newlywed couple decides that the wife, having the talent and inclination, will revive the husband's family's business, while *he* will follow his own talent and inclination for supervising housekeeping. The experiment is a complete success, but the husband, humiliated by his experience of "woman's sphere," brings it to a close by insisting that they leave for Europe.

18. Parenthetical page references are to *A Country Doctor* (Boston: Houghton Mifflin, 1884). Jewett's closeness to her father, Dr. Theodore Jewett, may have been strengthened by the fact that she was named after him, having been christened *Theodora* Sarah Orne Jewett.

19. This passage might recall the moment in Charlotte Brontë's *Jane Eyre* when Jane climbs to the roof of Thornfield Hall to survey the surrounding countryside: "I . . . looked out afar over sequestered field and hill, and along dim skyline . . . [and] then I longed for a power of vision which might overpass that limit; which might reach the busy world, towns, regions full of life I had heard of but never seen" (*Jane Eyre* [New York: Penguin, 1966], 140). Immediately following this eruption of longing comes Jane's famous description of the silent rebellions of women: "[W]omen feel just as men feel; they need exercise for their faculties, and a field for their efforts as much as their brothers do; they suffer from too rigid a restraint, too absolute a stagnation, precisely as men would suffer" (141). Whether or not Jewett actually has Brontë in mind in her account of the opening of Nan's horizon, the similarity of these two moments, and of Nan's and Jane's longings, again suggests the inadequacy of the image of reclusive and conservative "Maine person" to encompass the full range of Jewett's values and ambitions.

20. These details also tie Dr. Leslie to Jewett's father. Theodore Jewett, educated at Bowdoin, had gone to Philadelphia for his medical degree; and although family loyalty brought him back to Berwick and a country practice, he continued to publish in national medical journals, he served as professor of obstetrics at Bowdoin, and his connections took him, with some regularity, to Boston and New York.

21. Louis Renza also discusses similarities between these works in *A White Heron and the Question of Minor Literature*, esp. 77–78.

22. Parenthetical page references to "A White Heron" are to Cather, ed., *The Country of the Pointed Firs and Other Stories*. The story was first published in the collection *A White Heron and Other Stories*.

23. In Jewett's second novel, *A Marsh Island* (published in 1885, just a year before "A White Heron"), Doris Owen makes an apparently similar decision. This daughter of a Maine coast farmer chooses her local suitor, a ship's blacksmith named Dan Lester, over a visiting New York artist named Dick Dale. The novel treats this romantic plot, however, rather perfuncto-

rily. It also tends to see things not from Doris's point of view but through the eyes and thoughts of the visiting artist, and in this respect it may have less in common with *A Country Doctor* or "A White Heron" than with *Deephaven* and, especially, *The Country of the Pointed Firs;* like the narrator of the latter book, Dick Dale has come into the country to pursue his art. In structural terms Dick might seem to play a role somewhat analogous to that of the urban intruder in "A White Heron," but he is neither aggressive nor even particularly "masculine." Following his long visit, for instance, Doris's mother comments: "There, it always seemed more like having a girl about than a man" (*A Marsh Island* [Boston: Houghton Mifflin, 1885], 285).

24. Fields, ed., *Letters,* 125.

25. Ibid., 60. This statement evolves, by an associational logic that is by no means clear, from a rare (for Jewett) comment on Howells's campaign for realism: "Mr. Howells thinks that this age frowns upon the romantic, that it is no use to write romance any more; but dear me, how much of it there is left in every-day life after all. It must be the fault of the writers that such writing is dull, but what shall I do with my 'White Heron' now she is written?" (59–60).

26. Compare Louis Renza's description of Jewett's "'minor' project" in "A White Heron"—which is, he argues, "to write as if she *were* a minor shielded from adulthood by the protective father" (*"A White Heron" and the Question of Minor Literature,* 103).

27. Parenthetical page references to *The Country of the Pointed Firs* are to Mary Ellen Chase, ed., *The Country of the Pointed Firs and Other Stories* (New York: Norton, 1981). Unlike Willa Cather's 1925 collection (now reprinted under the same title), which incorporates into the text of *Pointed Firs* three Dunnet Landing stories written later ("A Dunnet Shepherdess," "The Queen's Twin," and "William's Wedding"), Chase's edition reproduces the text of the book as Jewett published it in 1896.

28. This position puts its proponents in direct opposition not only to a long line of male critics but also, for instance, to Ann Douglas's argument in "The Literature of Impoverishment." The local colorists' "theme," Douglas insists, is not "that of female superiority. It is not that their women are not superior to their men: more often than not, they are. But the important and painful fact which their literature underscores is that women, whether superior or inferior, are superfluous as individuals, and strangely superannuated as a sex." The local colorists, Douglas writes, "valued . . . the conventional feminine virtues, but they had lost faith in their potency" ("The Literature of Impoverishment," 17, 16).

29. Pryse, "Introduction to the Norton Edition," in Chase, ed., *The Country of the Pointed Firs and Other Stories,* xiii, xix; Ammons, "Going in Circles: The Female Geography of Jewett's *Country of the Pointed Firs,*" *Studies in the Literary Imagination* 16, no. 2 (Fall 1983): 83–84.

30. See, too, Julia Bader, "The Dissolving Vision: Realism in Jewett, Freeman, and Gilman," in *American Realism: New Essays,* ed. Eric J. Sundquist (Baltimore: Johns Hopkins University Press, 1982), 176–98; and

Sarah Way Sherman, *Sarah Orne Jewett, an American Persephone* (Hanover, N.H.: University Press of New England, 1989), esp. 196–235.

31. *Fictions and Events*, 250.

32. Elizabeth Ammons glosses a particularly resonant image evoked in chap. 10, "Where Pennyroyal Grew." Here the narrator helps gather that herb on Green Island—where it grows, Mrs. Todd says, as it grows nowhere else in the world. Pennyroyal, Ammons explains, "is used in childbirth to promote the expulsion of the placenta; it is also . . . an agent used to induce or increase menstrual flow. Thus . . . pennyroyal suggests maternal power itself: the central awesome power of women, like the Earth, to give or not to give life" ("Going in Circles," 91).

33. As Sarah Way Sherman writes of *A Country Doctor,* "Significantly, the novel resolutely avoids Nan's bonds with other women. They have no common cause." Nan "has won her freedom by asserting her difference from other women. She has sacrificed not only marriage and family but also her place within the community of women" (*Sarah Orne Jewett, an American Persephone*, 184, 186).

34. *Fictions and Events*, 254.

35. "Going in Circles," 84.

36. "Introduction to the Norton Edition," xix.

37. Fields, ed., *Letters*, 47.

38. Cather, *Not under Forty*, 95. Henry James, acknowledging a gift copy of *The Tory Lover* in 1901, was quite explicit in telling Jewett "how little I am in sympathy with the experiments of its general (to my sense) misguided stamp," and his letter goes on to urge Jewett to "a *re*-dedication to altars but briefly, I trust, forsaken." "Go back to the dear country of the *Pointed Firs*," he writes, "*come* back to the palpable present-*intimate* that throbs responsive, and that wants, misses, needs you, God knows, and that suffers woefully in your absence" (Leon Edel, ed., *Henry James Letters*, vol. 4 [Cambridge, Mass.: Harvard University Press, 1984], 208–9).

39. Cary, ed. *Letters*, 130, 138.

40. These are: "The Queen's Twin" and "A Dunnet Shepherdess" (both published in the *Atlantic* in 1899 and collected in *The Queen's Twin and Other Stories* in the same year), "The Foreigner" (published in the *Atlantic* in 1900 and never collected by Jewett), and "William's Wedding" (first published in the *Atlantic*, posthumously, in 1910).

41. Cather, ed., *The Country of the Pointed Firs and Other Stories*, 293.

INDEX

Aaron, Daniel, 217n.46
Aestheticism: realism as reaction to, in
  England, 143, 229–30n.24
Åhnebrink, Lars, 227n.6
Alcott, Louisa May, 75–76
Aldrich, Thomas Bailey, 36
Allen, Woody, 94
Ammons, Elizabeth, 196, 198, 238n.32
Anesko, Michael, 223n.49
Auerbach, Erich, 5
Auerbach, Nina, 221n.32, 221–22n.38
Augustine, Saint, 38
Austen, Jane, 13, 45, 238n.30

Bader, Julia, 238n.30
Balzac, Honoré de, 77, 78, 83, 103
Baym, Nina, 219n.19
Beard, Dan, 67
Beer, Thomas, 227n.1
Bernhardt, Sarah, 67
Berryman, John, 122, 137, 139, 227n.1
Berthoff, Warner, 1, 2, 3, 5, 21, 175,
  197, 198, 202, 206n.4, 218n.2, 234n.2
Borus, Daniel, 206n.5, 211n.37
Boston compromise: as model for How-
  ells's idea of realism, 28, 30, 36; as re-
  fusal of Romantic alienation, 35;
  James's response to, 74, 78–79
Bowlby, Rachel, 233n.21, 233n.23
Brodhead, Richard, 14, 71, 83, 86,
  220n.30

Brontë, Charlotte, 236–37 n.19
Brooks, Van Wyck, 39–41, 46, 47
Buckley, Jerome H., 229–30n.24
Bunyan, John, 43–44
Burroughs, John, 211n.38

Cady, Edwin H., 24, 27, 208n.1,
  211n.30, 227 nn.1, 4, 230n.30
Carter, Everett, 214n.12
Cather, Willa, 7, 173, 175, 176, 202; on
  Jewett, 234n.1
Chandler, Raymond, 217n.44
Charvat, William, 28, 31, 212n.42,
  212n.44
Chase, Richard, 214n.12
Cherbuliez, Victor, 76
Chopin, Kate, 7, 173
Clemens, Jane, 51
Clemens, Orion, 51, 215n.19
Clemens, Samuel L. See Twain, Mark
Columbia Literary History of the United
  States, 208n.2
Common sense "realism," 34
Condor, John, 225n.2, 227n.4
Conrad, Joseph, 152, 163
Cooke, Rose Terry, 176
Cooper, James Fenimore, 42
Cotton, John, 38
Cox, James, 50–51, 52, 54, 60, 61, 213n.1
Crane, Cora, 144
Crane, Stephen: and Darwinism, 134,

Crane, Stephen (continued)
135–36; and determinism, 135; and
Howells, 139, 142, 147; and Norris,
139, 142, 144, 148; and science, 132;
Howells on, 131–32, 143–44, 144,
228n.7, 230n.27; Norris on, 136,
230n.29; on cowardice of slum dwellers, 141; on realism, 228n.7; parodic
effect of verbal irony in, 139–41, 145–
48; reputation of, and cult of masculinity, 132, 133; response to cult of masculinity, 144, 146–48; response to
naturalism, 134; style compared to
Dreiser's, 149, 152, 160–62; style
compared to Norris's, 132, 145.
Works: The Black Riders, 228n.7;
George's Mother, 141; Maggie: A Girl of
the Streets, 133, 134–41, 141–42, 144,
146, 147, 148, 160–61, 228n.8; "The
Open Boat," 141; The Red Badge of
Courage, 111, 132–33, 138, 141, 142–
48, 228n.7
Crews, Frederick, 231n.33
Crowley, John W., 208n.1, 210n.22,
211n.35, 217n.46

Darwinism: and Crane, 134, 135–36; and
Dreiser, 158; and naturalism, 109
Determinism: and naturalism, 109
DeVoto, Bernard, 39–41, 213n.5
Dickens, Charles, 93
Donovan, Josephine, 235n.12
Douglas, Ann, 177, 235n.6, 238n.28
Dreiser, Theodore: and Howells, 159,
164, 165; class bias in discussions of
his style, 158; defends style of Sister
Carrie, 150; early literary vocation,
153–54; literature/life distinction and
defenses of his style, 154; on litera-
ture/life distinction, 152, 153, 165;
on romance of the real, 150; on
Twain, 41; response to cult of masculinity, 152–53; science in, 151–52, 158;
style compared to Crane's, 149, 152,
160–62; style compared to Norris's,
149, 151, 152, 162. Works: A Book
about Myself, 150, 152, 153; The Financier, 152; The "Genius", 150; Sister Carrie, 111, 134, 149–50, 151, 153, 155,

155–65; Sister Carrie (1981 Pennsylvania edition), 163, 233n.24; The Titan,
152
Dumas, Alexandre, 76

Edel, Leon, 71, 74, 105, 218n.1
Edwards, Herbert, 209n.3
Eliot, George, 13, 43–44, 45, 76
Eliot, T. S., 213n.1
Emerson, Ralph Waldo, 82

Fetterley, Judith, 221n.32
Fields, Annie, 179–80, 191, 197, 235n.12
Fields, James T., 179
Fisher, Philip, 161, 164, 207n.8
Fitelson, David, 228n.9
Flaubert, Gustave, 20, 71, 77, 104
Ford, Ford Madox, 154–55, 163
Freeman, Mary Wilkins, 7, 169–72, 196;
"A Poetess," 171–72; "A Symphony in
Lavender," 169–71
Fried, Michael, 206n.6, 228–29n.12
Frost, John Eldridge, 235n.11

Garland, Hamlin, 228n.8
Gates, Lewis E., 117
Geismar, Maxwell, 226n.2, 227n.13
Gender anxiety: and James's The Bostoni-
ans, 84; and naturalism, 111–12; and
Norris's idea of naturalism, 119–20,
129; and realism, 6; and Twain's Con-
necticut Yankee, 66–69; centrality to
Howells's idea of realism, 37–38; ef-
fects on Howells, 26, 211n.35,
217n.46; Jewett on, 236n.17
Gilligan, Carol, 196
Gombrich, E. H., 5
Grant, Ulysses S., 20, 38, 58
Green, Martin, 35, 212n.43

Habegger, Alfred, 210n.22, 211n.35,
213n.2, 215n.22, 221n.32, 222n.41
Hardy, Thomas, 78
Harte, Bret, 42
Hawthorne, Nathaniel, 24, 25, 43–44,
72, 76, 83, 86, 93, 103, 221n.35
Hayes, Rutherford B., 24
Hemingway, Ernest, 37, 38, 53, 213n.1
Hochman, Barbara, 225–26n.1

Holmes, Oliver Wendell, 17, 28–29, 30, 82

Howard, June, 3–4, 110–11, 114, 136, 142, 156–57, 207n.9, 225n.5

Howe, Irving, 223n.44

Howells, William Dean: and Crane, 139, 142, 147; and Dreiser, 159, 164, 165; and James, 2; and Norris, 112, 121; and Whitman, 211n.38; and Zola, 112; as "minor" writer, 14; as central figure of "Age of Realism," 14; attack on style by, 177; Boston compromise as model for his idea of realism, 28, 30, 36; childhood, 25–26; childhood compared to James's, 73; criticisms of his campaign for realism, 18–19; declares "Realism War" in 1880s, 1; distinguishes literature from life, 20–22, 27; early literary vocation, 23–25, 26–27; effects of gender anxiety on, 26; equates realism and democracy, 32; idea of realism, and Twain, 40, 47, 49, 56–57, 58, 60, 65–66, 69; idea of realism compared to James's, 71, 79–83, 94–95; James on, 20–21, 74–75; Jewett on, 237n.25; masculine bias of realism in, 22; moral responsibility as central to his idea of realism, 47–48; move to Boston, 27–28, 36; move to New York, 29–31, 36, 211n.30; on Crane, 131–32, 143–44, 144, 228n.7, 230n.27; on James, 36, 79; on Jane Austen, 214n.14; on Jewett, 178; on New York as literary community, 211n.29; on Norris, 110, 131–32, 144; on painting, 209n.8; on realism and psychological analysis, 214n.11; on Tolstoy, 19, 20, 34; on Twain, 19–20, 34, 44–45, 58; on Zola, 19, 32; opinion of Zola compared to James's, 77; realism and gender anxiety in, 37–38; relationship with Jewett, 172, 176, 180; role in launching James's early career, 74; Twain on, 42, 43. Works: "Editor's Study" column (*Harper's*), 18, 20, 37, 44–45, 58, 69, 71, 75, 87, 105; "Henry James, Jr.," 79; *A Boy's Town*, 25–26; *Criticism and Fiction*, 6, 14, 18, 19, 20, 22, 26, 28, 30, 31–35, 37, 38, 40, 41,

48, 56, 58, 79, 80, 111, 113, 209n.4, 214n.4; *A Hazard of New Fortunes*, 29, 54, 75; *The Landlord at Lion's Head*, 23; *Letters Home*, 26; *Literary Friends and Acquaintance*, 19, 25, 27–29, 30, 32; *Lives and Speeches of Abraham Lincoln and Hannibal Hamlin*, 17; *A Modern Instance*, 18; *My Literary Passions*, 19, 20, 25, 26–27, 34, 73, 165; *My Mark Twain*, 20, 34; *The Rise of Silas Lapham*, 18, 26, 36; *Years of my Youth*, 25

Irving, Washington, 24, 25, 26, 29, 72

James, Henry: and continental realism, 71; and Howells, 2; and Howellsian realism, 71–72, 79–83, 87–88, 94–95; and literary modernism, 80–81; and naturalism, 98; and the New Criticism, 80–81; and Twain, 13–14, 71, 89, 90, 91, 220n.26; childhood of, compared to Howells's, 73; Howells's role in launching early career of, 74; Howells on, 36, 39; literary criticism of, and realism, 75–83; naturalism and determinism in, 96–97; naturalism and science in, 96–97, 102; on Alexandre Dumas, 76; on Balzac, 78; on conditions of American literary vocation, 23; on Flaubert, 77; on George Eliot, 76; on Hardy, 78; on Hawthorne, 76; on Howells, 20–21, 74–75; on Jewett, 175, 238–39n.38; on Louisa May Alcott, 75–76; on romance and chivalry, 85; on Trollope, 76, 78, 82, 83; on Turgenev, 77, 78–79, 223n.44; on Victor Cherbuliez, 76; on Zola, 77, 110; opinion of Zola compared to Howells's, 77; realism and reform in, 86, 90; realism in his career, in the 1880s, 71; response to Boston compromise, 74, 78–79; Twain on, 43–44, 45. Works: "The Art of Fiction," 41, 71, 78, 79–83, 94, 95, 99, 100, 101, 103, 104; *The Bostonians*, 43–44, 71, 83–84, 84–92, 93, 94, 97, 98, 103, 105, 129, 135; *Hawthorne*, 76; *The Middle Years*, 72; *Notes of a Son and Brother*, 72, 73; *The Portrait of a Lady*, 70; Preface to

242   Index

James, Henry *(continued)*
  The Portrait of a Lady, 80; Preface to
    The Princess Casamassima, 92, 100–101;
    The Princess Casamassima, 71, 83–84,
    92–105, 182; *A Small Boy and Others,*
    72, 73
James, William, 72, 75, 81, 103, 219n.7
Jefferson, Thomas, 34–35, 38, 68
Jewett, Sarah Orne: ambivalence toward
  "local color" values, 184, 189, 191;
  and Charlotte Brontë, 236n.19; and literary vocation, 191, 192; and Mary
  Wilkins Freeman, 170; feminist interpretations of, 196–99; Howells on,
  178; James on, 175, 238–39n.38; on
  cult of masculinity, 193–94; on female
  ambition, 186–87, 187–88, 192, 200,
  203–4; on Flaubert, 20, 209–10n.11;
  on Howellsian realism, 237n.25; relationship with Annie Fields, 179–80,
  197, 235n.12; relationship with Howells, 172, 176, 180; reputation, 175–76;
  response to masculine bias of realism,
  179, 184–85, 187–88, 195, 204; rural
  vs. professional identities of, 180, 187–
  88, 190; sex distinguished from nature
  by, 187, 190, 192, 197; Willa Cather
  on, 175. Works: "An Autumn Holiday," 236n.17; *A Country Doctor,* 179,
  184–88, 190, 192, 193, 198, 199, 200,
  203–4; *The Country of the Pointed Firs,*
  175, 177, 179, 184, 192–202, 203–4;
  Deephaven, 170, 179, 180–83, 184, 192–
  93, 193; "A Dunnet Shepherdess,"
  239n.40; "The Flight of Betsey Lane,"
  183–84, 184; "The Foreigner,"
  239n.40; "Going to Shrewsbury," 183;
  "Hallowell's Pretty Sister," 236n.17;
  "The Hiltons' Holiday," 183–84, 184,
  203; *A Marsh Island,* 179, 237n.23;
  "Martha's Lady," 183; "The Queen's
  Twin," 239n.40; "Tom's Husband,"
  236n.17; *The Tory Lover,* 179, 202–3,
  238n.38; "A White Heron," 188–92,
  198, 200, 203; *A White Heron and
  Other Stories,* 184
Jewett, Theodore, 176, 185, 237n.20
Joyce, James, 88

Kahane, Claire, 89, 221n.32, 222n.39
Kaplan, Amy, 3–4, 205–6n.3, 208n.12,
  232n.13, 232n.18
Kazin, Alfred, 206n.5
Kipling, Rudyard, 143
Kolb, Harold H., 206, 213–14n.5

LaFrance, Marston, 231n.33
Lerner, Daniel, 223n.44
Levin, Harry, 21
Lewis, Sinclair, 18, 21, 37, 150
Limon, John, 217n.46, 222n.39, 231n.5
Lincoln, Abraham, 17
Literature and life: distinction of, and
  Crane's reputation, 133; distinction of,
  in defenses of Dreiser's style, 154; dis-
  tinguished by Howells, 20–22, 27; dis-
  tinguished by Norris, 117, 120, 129,
  150; Dreiser on distinction, 152, 153,
  165
Local color fiction: and realism, 171, 176
London, Jack, 37, 152
Longfellow, Henry Wadsworth, 28, 30,
  74, 82
Lowell, James Russell, 17, 29, 30, 74
Lukács, Georg, 5
Lynn, Kenneth, 25–26, 29, 208n.1,
  215n.25, 226n.2, 232n.7

Malory, Sir Thomas, 42, 62
Marcosson, Isaac F., 117, 121
Martin, Jay, 206n.5
Martin, Terence, 212n.42
Marx, Leo, 213n.1
Masculinity, cult of: and Crane's reputa-
  tion, 132; and debate over Crane's *Red
  Badge of Courage,* 142–43; and Norris's
  idea of naturalism, 119–20, 129; and
  Norris's reputation, 132; Crane's rela-
  tion to, 230n.30; Crane's response to,
  144, 146–48, 142–43; Dreiser's re-
  sponse to, 152–53; in England, 143,
  229–30n.24; Jewett on, 193–94
Mather, Cotton, 38
Matthews, Brander, 18–19, 42
Matthiessen, F. O., 158, 164, 177, 218n.5
McClurg, General A. C., 133, 143, 146,
  147

Melville, Herman, 52, 59, 126, 217n.39
Mencken, H. L., 150, 152, 154, 155, 232n.10
Michaels, Walter, 3–4, 6, 159, 164, 207n.9, 225n.1
Mitchell, Lee Clark, 225n.2, 230n.31
Mizruchi, Susan L., 221n.32, 222n.39
Moers, Ellen, 151, 231n.1, 231n.5

Nabokov, Vladimir, 1, 2
Narrative aloofness: as mark of naturalism, 110–11, 136, 156, 164
Naturalism: and Darwinism, 109; and gender anxiety, 111–12; and James, 98; as departure from realism, 109, 111; continuities with realism, 18, 111–14, 121; Crane's response to, 134; defined by new subject matter, 109, 110; described by Norris, 117–19; linked with romance by Norris, 118; narrative aloofness as mark of, 110–11, 136, 156, 164; new historicist accounts of, 3–4, 111, 115–16; Norris on, in own fiction, 121; opposed to style, 112, 133, 164
Naturalism and determinism, 109; in James, 96–97; in Norris, 122; irrelevance to Crane, 135
Naturalism and science, 109; and Crane, 132; and Dreiser, 151–52, 158; and James, 96–97, 102; and Norris, 122, 125–26
Norris, Frank: and Crane, 139, 142, 144, 148; and Howells, 112, 121; attack on realism by, 110, 118–19; attack on style by, 177; centrality to new historicist account of naturalism, 115–16; cult of masculinity and idea of naturalism of, 119–20, 129; description of naturalism, 117–19; discovers Dreiser's *Sister Carrie*, 149; distinguishes literature from life, 120, 129, 150; gender anxiety and idea of naturalism of, 119–20, 129; Howells on, 110, 131–32, 144; irony in early writing, 126–28; naturalism and determinism in, 122; naturalism and science in, 122, 125–26; naturalism linked with romance by, 118; natural-

ism opposed to style by, 164; on Crane, 136, 230n.29; on naturalism in own fiction, 121; on romance of the real, 150; on Zola, 117–18; reputation of, and cult of masculinity, 132; style compared to Crane's, 132, 145; style compared to Dreiser's, 151, 152, 162; stylistic inflation of, 120, 122–23; stylistic shift in later work, 128–30. Works: *Blix*, 117, 121; "Émile Zola," 178; *A Man's Woman*, 117, 121; *McTeague*, 110, 111, 117, 121, 123, 125, 127, 129, 132, 134, 148, 151, 216n.32; *Moran of the Lady Letty*, 117, 118, 216n.32, 226n.7; "The Novel with a 'Purpose,'" 112, 120; "A Plea for Romantic Fiction," 117–18; *The Octopus*, 117, 121–22, 123–24, 128–29, 148, 151, 216n.32; *The Pit*, 117, 123, 125, 127, 128, 129, 151; *Vandover and the Brute*, 117, 126–27, 128, 216n.32; "Why Women Should Write the Best Fiction—And Why They Don't," 177; "Zola as Romantic Writer," 118–19
Norton, Charles Eliot, 74
Norton, Grace, 75

Paine, Albert Bigelow, 46, 51, 215n.15
Parker, Gail, 26
Pease, Donald, 230n.32
Petrey, Sandy, 159
Pizer, Donald, 119, 228n.11, 230n.24
Plato, 38
Poe, Edgar Allan, 19, 27, 72, 104, 151, 195
Poirier, Richard, 141
Powers, Lyall H., 218n.2
Pryse, Marjorie, 196, 197, 200, 234n.5
Pynchon, Thomas, 126

Realism: and female authorship, 171–72; and gender assumptions, 177–79; and humor, in Twain, 50–52; and Twain's career in 1880s, 71; and James's literary criticism, 75–83; and psychological analysis, Howells on, 214n.11; and reform, in James, 86, 90; and Twain's critical writings, 41–45; and vernacu-

Realism, *(continued)*
lar, in Twain, 53; as reaction to aestheticism, in England, 143, 229–30n.2;
attacked by Norris, 110, 118–19; continuities with naturalism, 18, 111–14,
121; Crane on, 228n.7; equated with
democracy, by Howells, 32; Jewett on,
237n.25; moral responsibility as central to Howells's idea of, 47–48; naturalism as departure from, 109, 111;
new historicist accounts of, 3–4; problems in definition of, 1–4, 13; responsive or reflective model of, 2; supposed
rise of following Civil War, 1; Twain's
avoidance of term, 44–45; and local
color fiction, 171, 176
Realism and gender anxiety, 6; in Howells, 37–38, 211n.35, 217n.46; in
Twain, 66–69
Realism and photography: Howells on,
110; James on, 219n.15; Twain on, 42
Realism, masculine bias of, 6; Crane's response to, 146–48; Dreiser's response
to, 152–53; in Howells's critical writings, 22, 37–38; Jewett's response to,
179, 184–85, 187–88, 195, 200–202,
204; Twain's response to, 66–69
Renza, Louis, 234n.1, 237n.21, 237n.26
Rich, Adrienne, 196
Romance and chivalry: in James, 85; in
Twain, 59–62
Roosevelt, Theodore, 112, 152, 191
Rowe, John Carlos, 99–100

Scott, Sir Walter, 42, 59, 61
Scudder, Horace, 18–19, 30, 188, 203
Sedgwick, Eve Kosofsky, 212n.46
Seltzer, Mark, 111, 115, 220n.29, 222–
23n.43, 226n.12, 227n.7
Sherman, Sarah Way, 235n.12, 238n.30,
238n.33
Sherman, Stuart P., 231n.3
Simpson, Lewis P., 29
Smith, Henry Nash, 58, 215–16n.25
Solomon, Eric, 229n.16
Spencer, Herbert, 151, 158
Stallman, R. W., 227n.1
Stevenson, Robert Louis, 143
Stewart, Randall, 231n.3

Stowe, Harriet Beecher, 62, 172, 202
Stowe, William W., 223n.49
Sundquist, Eric, 206–7n.7, 234–35n.2,
235n.6
Swanberg, W. A., 231n.1

Tarkington, Booth, 158
Thoreau, Henry David, 126
Tilley, W. H., 222n.43
Tolstoy, Leo, 19, 20, 34, 132, 165
Trachtenberg, Alan, 229n.15
Trilling, Lionel, 129–30, 206n.4; on
Dreiser, 150–51, 155, 157, 159, 163;
on Howells, 23–24, 30; on James, 85,
98, 220–21n.32, 224n.55; on Twain,
213n.1
Trollope, Anthony, 76, 78, 82, 83
Turgenev, Ivan, 71, 77, 78–79, 104,
223n.44; his *Virgin Soil* as source for
James's *Princess Casamassima*, 92–94
Twain, Mark (Samuel L. Clemens): and
Howellsian realism, 40, 47, 49–50, 56–
57, 59, 60, 65–66, 69; and James, 13–
14, 71, 89, 90, 220n.26; and Norris,
126; avoidance of term, "realism," by,
44–45; childhood, 45–47; critical disagreement over achievement of, 39–
41; critical writings of, and realism, 41–
45; Dreiser on, 41; early literary
vocation of, 46–47, 215n.22; Howells
on, 19–20, 34, 44–45, 58; on Howells,
42, 43–44; on James, 43–44, 45; on
Jane Austen, 214n.14; on realism and
photography, 42; realism and gender
anxiety in, 66–69; realism and humor
in, 50–52; realism and vernacular in,
53; response to masculine bias of realism, 66–69; romantic literature attacked by, 42, 48–49, 59; sentiment
and humor in, 62–66. Works: *Adventures of Huckleberry Finn*, 40, 42, 48–58,
58, 63–64, 68, 69, 172; *A Connecticut
Yankee in King Arthur's Court*, 42, 58–
70, 89, 90, 91; "Fenimore Cooper's Literary Offenses," 41–42, 43, 214n.12;
"How to Tell a Story," 41; *The Innocents Abroad*, 42, 52; *Life on the Mississippi*, 59; "The Notorious Jumping
Frog of Calaveras County," 52; "A Pri-

vate History of a Campaign that
Failed," 217n.46; "What Paul Bourget
Thinks of Us," 41; "Whittier Dinner
Speech," 82, 220n.26; "William Dean
Howells," 42, 45

Walcutt, Charles, Child, 227n.4, 227n.6
Walker, Franklin, 226n.2
Wardley, Lynn, 221n.32
Warner, Charles Dudley, 203
Warner, Susan, 7, 172
Wellek, René, 209n.6
Wells, H. G., 80
West, Nathanael, 126
Westbrook, Perry D., 234n.3
Wharton, Edith, 7, 173

Whitman, Walt, 32, 120
Wilde, Oscar, 37
Wilkins, Mary E. *See* Freeman, Mary
  Wilkins
Wilson, Christopher P., 206n.5
Wilt, Judith, 221n.32
Wolfe, Tom, 97
Wordsworth, William, 120
Wright, Richard, 164–65

Ziff, Larzer, 122, 226n.2, 229n.17,
  233n.22
Zola, Émile, 92, 94, 104, 109, 122; "The
  Experimental Novel," 112–13; How-
  ells on, 19, 32; James on, 77, 103, 110;
  Norris on, 117–18